GLOBALISATION,
MULTINATIONAL CORPORATION
AND ECONOMICS

CO-ARR-811

DISCARDED

GLOBALISATION, MULTINATIONAL CORPORATION AND ECONOMICS

JÁNOS HOÓS

Professor of Economics
Budapest University of Economic Sciences
and Public Administration

AKADÉMIAI KIADÓ, BUDAPEST

ISBN 963 05 7706 2

© J. Hoós, 2000

Published by Akadémiai Kiadó
H-1117 Budapest
Prielle Kornélia u. 4.
www.akkrt.hu

All rights reserved. No part of this book may be reproduced
by any means, or transmitted, or translated into machine language
without the written permission of the publisher

Printed in Hungary

CONTENTS

INTRODUCTION

"Paraphrasing" – in a special way – of the famous first sentence of K. Marx and F. Engels introducing the Manifesto of the Communist Party: *A spectre is haunting Europe and the World*, however, it is not the *spectre of Communism*, but *the spectre of globalisation* and *the prime force behind it* is not the *proletarians*, but *the multinational corporations (MNCs).*[1] In a paradox way, however, it is not absolute impossible, at least theoretically, that the final result of this globalisation will be the very same as it was predicted by the Manifesto of the Communist Party: "In place of the old bourgeois society, with class antagonisms we shall have an association, in which the free development of the condition for the free development of all".[2] This globalisation is so overall, comprehensive and it – mainly through and by the huge innovative capability of MNCs – causes such an enormous increase in the power of the production forces expending both the production and consumption for extremely high level that this possibility cannot be excluded as one of the scenarios for the future. Of course, there can be other scenarios as well and we cannot predict which one of them will come true. *What we can rationally do is to make an evaluation of this globalisation, of its driving forces and of its impacts on the economy and economics and to draw those conclusions that can help us to understand better this globalisation process and to make some modifications and corrections in teaching and judgement of the economics due to this globalisation.* Exactly this is the main aim of this book. Here we try to summarise the main findings of the book hoping that the reader will be convinced by the reading of the book that these findings have rational content and it is worthwhile to think them over again.

Especially the following can deserve a distinguished attention:

1. After the Second World War the long historical process of the globalisation has become irreversible and it has got basically new characteristics relating mainly to the latest trends of technological and organisational transformation, the growing importance of service, especially the financial services and trade. The emergence of a fully integrated, global capitalist economy has become a potentially achievable goal.

---

[1] Karl Marx, Frederich Engels, *Manifesto of the Communist Party*. In: Karl Marx, Frederich Engels, *Collective Works*. Volume 6 (Lawrence and Wishard, London, 1976) p. 1
[2] Karl Marx, Frederich Engels, *Manifesto of the Communist Party*, p. 506

2. The main driving forces and the prime mover of globalisation and its accompanying developments are the MNCs. These corporations are the most important actors and dominant forces in the world economy. The emergence of the MNCs as powerful agents of global social and economic change has been a signal development of the post-Second World War era. There are specific attributes that distinguish MNCs from non-MNCs; they represent differences of kind – that is, they are distinguished aspects of MNCs.

3. The MNCs have profound positive impact on the economy mainly through technology transfer, promotion of structural adjustment, reducing burden of debt, redressing debt-equity imbalance. But they are responsible for some very essential unfavourable impacts too, from which the followings deserve distinguished attention: they gave rise to fresh concerns about the vulnerability of economies, to disturbances in financial markets and about the world-wide growth of speculative activity; their impact on social and cultural values in host countries and their political influence.

4. Globalisation and the MNCs have profoundly changed the economy what is the subject of economics as a science and due to changes it is unquestionable that they have fundamental impact on economics as on a science including its three main branches, that is, on micro-, macro- and public economics.

4.1. As regards microeconomics, it is time to modify its assumptions about the firm's objectives, especially the profit maximizig and about the ownership, the pricing strategies, the competition.

4.2. As regards the macroeconomics, the assumptions of it have to be placed into globalised framework, it means that: globalisation and the integration of national economies in one world economy means that Keynesian counter-cyclical intervention has to be global and systematic, collectively agreed, co-ordinated, and financed.

4.3. As regards the public choice theory, its assumptions have to take into consideration that globalisation and the MNCs have a major and substantial impact on both the market and government failures and also on the way and direction of government policies and measures aimed to correct and/or eliminate the markets and government failures. It means:

- the market has been gaining influence against the government mainly due to the fact that the MNCs have became the major and the most influential actors of the globalised market;
- the MNCs have a very influential lobby power;
- the growing estrangement of the elected representative;
- in the cases of social policy deregulation, liberalisation and privatisation in many instances while they intend to correct the government failures they go so far that the final results are increasing market failures, decreasing efficiency of

the government policies in terms of growing income inequality and occurring waste of economic resources;

- there is a need for global governance, for global polity, and in this connection there is a need to re-examine and change the Washington consensus and for creating a new one, a new doctrine, which is better suited to meet the requirement of the globalised world today.

5. By analysing and investigating the globalisation, the MNCs and their impacts useful lessons can be drawn

- for better understanding of the economics as science by redefining its paradigm according to the new reality having been created by the impact of them;
- for the policies which could and/or should be elaborated and implemented by the respective governments and MNCs in order

to exploit the huge potentialities for economic development provided by the globalisation and MNCs and

to eliminate and/or decrease the negative effects, problems and tensions caused by the process of globalisation and the activities of the MNCs.

THE SUMMARY AND THE MAIN FINDINGS
OF THE BOOK

We are witnessing the accelerated speed of globalisation of the world – growing activities and influence of multinational corporations (MNCs), demonstration effects of consumption, spreading regional integration and deepening interdependency in fields of economy, technology, environment –; the world economy has been unstoppably going to this direction. The end of the Cold War in Europe marked the beginning of a period in history in which the emergence of a fully integrated, global capitalist economy has become a potentially achievable goal. The rapid spread across much of Eastern and Central Europe, the former Soviet Union of political regimes committed to the establishment of market economies, together with the economic liberalisation in China means that the two principle geopolitical blocks which have remained largely outside the sphere of international business, economic globalisation during the post-war period – and indeed throughout most of the twentieth century – have now become areas of fresh opportunity for international investment and economic activities. However, Russia and China should be considered as a special category in this respect. Due to their sizes, huge markets, rich natural resources, real and potential military and economic powers they have their own substantial impact on the globalisation process of the world as well, it means that while they have to adjust their economies (and policies) to the objective requirements of the globalisation their economies (and policies) have a well articulated feedback on the world economy and policy as well. Though Russia and China do not belong to the most influential forces of the globalisation, they have to be reckoned as major economic and political powers in the globalisation process, the speed and the modes of how they become organic part of the globalised world can determine the concrete characteristics and state of world economy and policy as a whole.

The globalisation of the world economy is not a new and recent phenomenon. What are new and recent phenomena are the technical, the technological conditions in which the globalisation has been unfolding, its scope and its changed characteristics, its impact on economic and political life and on economics as a science as well. A fundamental prerequisite of the globalisation, the evolution of the transnational corporations is the development of technologies in which the frictions of space and time are overcome. The most important of such enabling technologies – and the most obvious ones – are the technologies of transport and communications. In terms of the time it takes to get one part of the world to another there is no doubt that the world has "shrunk" dramatically. Both the time and relative cost of transporting materials, products and people have fallen dramatically as the result of technological innovation in the transport media. However, such a development has depended, to a considerable degree, on parallel developments in communications technology. Communications technologies should now be regarded as the key technology transforming relationships on a global scale. The world-wide spread of the electronic media has, in McLuhan's famous metaphor, created a global village in which certain images are shared and in which events take on the immediacy of participation. Electric circuitry has overthrown the regime of "time" and "space" and pours upon us instantly and continuously the concerns of all other men. It has reconstituted dialogue on a global scale. Its message is Total Change, ending psychic, social, economic, and political parochialism. The old civic, state, and national groupings have become unworkable. Nothing can be farther from the spirit of the new technology than a place for everything and everything in its place. You cannot go home again.

The globalisation today refers to the emergence and spread of a supranational dimension of social relations. In institutional terms, the process has unfolded through the proliferation and growth of MNCs, popular associations and regulatory agencies, sometimes termed global companies, global civil society and global regimes respectively.

Globalisation has variously been defined, and no consensus exists on the cause of this phenomenon. For our discussion we use McGrew's general definition. He claims that globalisation is the multiplicity of linkages and interconnections that transcend the nation-state (and by implication the societies), which make up the modern world system. It defines a process through events, decisions, and activities in one part of the world can have significant consequences for individuals and communities in quite distant parts of the globe.

Globalisation is traced through three arenas of social life. They are: economy, polity and culture. The principle characteristics of economic globalisation consist of the following:

- the globalisation of financial markets;
- the internationalisation of corporate strategies, in particular their commitment to competition as a source of wealth creation;
- the diffusion of technology and related R & D and knowledge world-wide ;
- the transformation of consumption patterns into cultural products with world-wide consumer markets;
- the internationalisation of the regulatory capabilities of national societies into a global political economic system;
- the diminished role of national governments in designing the rules for global governance.

If we look at the recent changes in the general globalisation motives and drivers we can see the intensification of this globalisation process. Out of these motives and drivers the technological and organisational transformation, and those which are related to the services, have especially distinguished importance.

The 1980s have witnessed great technological change and organisational innovation:

- information technology has been a dominant force that has affected all dimensions of production, shifting industrial innovation toward electronically integrated manufacturing processes;
- at the same time, the standard logic and principles of mass production have been challenged by organisational innovations in the management of materials and people, which stress flexibility, quality and co-operation over a strict division of labour and rigid production patterns.

These two sets of innovation have led to substantial cost reductions and improvements in efficiency.

The other major change during the last two decades was the internationalisation of services, the increasing trans-nationalisation of service corporations and especially the internationalisation of finance markets.

The internalisation of financial markets has been one of the most dramatic economic developments of the 1980s. Three specific changes of technical or institutional character have been at work altering the scale and character of international financial market. These are the advances in computer and telecommunications technology, the trend towards abandonment of many financial regulations and the introduction of a wide range of new financial instruments on the securities markets.

The main driving forces and the prime mover of globalisation and its accompanying developments are the MNCs. These corporations are perhaps the most important actors in the world economy. They are certainly the dominant forces in the world economy.

Different schools have used different attributes to characterise the MNCs. Such attributions include the geographic scope of the firm's value chain (that is, the sequence of value-adding activities or functions within the firms), management styles, ownership of productive assets, commonality of strategy formulation and worldwide implementation, and organisation structure.

MNCs can be defined as:

- MNCs are those type of corporations, which own and manage business in two or more countries, which are agencies of direct, as opposed to portfolio, investment in foreign countries, holding and managing the underlying physical assets rather than securities based upon those assets; these types of enterprises confront the problems of designing, producing, marketing, and financing their products and services within foreign nations, and make a substantial direct investment in foreign countries' assets, entail a responsibility for managing organisations of people in alien societies.

There are two specific attributes that distinguish MNCs from non-MNCs. They can be called:
- "multiple sources of external authority" and
- "multiple denominations of firm's value".

The overriding principle underlying cross-border relationships is that of sovereignty. The sovereignty of a nation-state is embodied in its authority to influence events within its legal territory and its choice to be relatively immune to outside influences. This authority generally manifests itself in terms of laws and regulatory institutions, political institutions, official language(s), norms of behaviour, culture, and so forth. Consequently, the MNC has exposure to multiple (and often conflicting) sources of external authority. The second distinguishing aspect of MNCs results from the fact that there are multiple denominations, or numeraires, of firm value. That is, the firm's cash flows are denominated in different exchange rates.

MNCs have a long history in the capitalist market economy, but they have drawn a really exceptionally distinguished attention to themselves after the Second World War. It is not accidental: the emergence of the MNC as a powerful agent of world social and economic change has been a signal development of the post-Second World War era.

Cross-border business has been driven forward by three main things: falling regulatory barriers to overseas investment; tumbling telecommunications and transportation costs; and freer domestic and international capital markets in which companies can be bought, currency and other risks can be controlled.

But the emergence and the growing role of the MNCs based upon
in the one hand:
- on the very essential and specific features of modern capitalist market economy, that is:

  a) Market in this economy – among other things – is also an institution that includes not only the introduction of a new process or product, entry a new market, access to new supplies of input, but certain type of a new organisation. It has created a factory system and efficient industrial, commercial and service enterprise firms. This organisation arrangement permits greater utilisation of productive resources; business firms of the capitalism undertake investment strategies in response to new market and technological opportunities and that then put in place organisational structures to ensure economic success;

  b) Today market means first and foremost world market; and
on the other hand:
- under the contradiction between these market features, especially the market as a world market and the other basic characteristics of the Modern Western World, namely, is based upon Modern Democracy covering an English type sovereign national state with elected Parliament, sovereign lawmaking body elected by territorial constituencies and by virtually universal suffrage. These

16

political forms of citizens, unlike the economic, are always nationally coloured. Economic freedoms relate to global space: they are universal, cosmopolitan. Economics and politics – along with their constitutive principles, the market and the democratic process – therefore constitute distinctive realms. National states dispose of differential power within the world system and make barriers for the free functioning and expanding of the market by creating special "market failures", efficiency losses in international arena of the world market.

Emergence of MNC has created an efficient institution to overcome or to decrease these failures originated by the contradiction between the international, global character of the market and the national character of the modern democratic process of national states.

The forces behind corporate multinationals are so potent that there is high probability that multinational business will continue to expand relative to domestic business well into the future.

This development has been intensified by the most widespread trends in international business in the recent years: the strategic alliance of the MNCs. The three reasons most commonly cited for alliances were to gain access to a market, to exploit complementary technology, and to reduce the time taken for innovation. That alliance is generally used to help a firm leapfrog its competitors (or catch up with them) or plug a technological or product gap that would otherwise be too costly to fill. Spanning countries and continents, strategic alliances could significantly modify the character of trans-nationalisation. Although mainly among MNCs of equivalent size and market power, they also take the form of corporate galaxies in which a large MNC is linked via joint ventures, sub-contracts, marketing agreements and the like.

The MNCs have profound positive impact on the economy mainly through technology transfer, promotion of structural adjustment, reducing burden of debt, redressing debt-equity imbalance, but they influence employment practice and the environment in many favourable ways, too.

The MNCs have not only favourable impact on the economy and the society but they are responsible for some very essential unfavourable impacts too, from which the followings deserve distinguished attention:
- they gave rise to fresh concerns about the vulnerability of economies to disturbances in financial markets and about the world-wide growth of speculative activity;
- unintended impact on the environments;
- an impact on social and cultural values in host countries;
- political influence.

Having seen and experienced all of these tendencies presented in this book, it is not accidental, that there are such forecasts that: in the future business would be dominated by vast-company alliances coming together to handle big complicated projects, and industry will be dominated by a few giant firms, world-wide. Even if these predictions can be considered as exaggerations, it is unquestionable that the emergence of MNCs – in a close relationship with the globalisation – has fundamental impact not only on the society and economy, but on economics as a science, too, including its three main branches, that is, on micro-, macro- and public economics.

As we have known the basic model of the microeconomics
- consists of rational, self-interested individuals and profit-maximising firms, interacting in competitive markets; and according to this model
- the profit motive and private property provide incentives for rational individuals and firms to work hard and efficiently.

That is, this traditional or "neo-classical" approach assumes that
- decisions are made under condition of perfect knowledge, and
- the objective of the firms is to maximise profits.

In practice, however, these theoretical assumptions are rarely to be found and this is due to MNCs in a great respect that have intensified those reasons which can be offered as justification for abandoning these assumptions. These relate to the followings.

1. The Growth in Oligopoly

Oligopoly is the most common form of the market structure in reality and, yet, it is the structure to which the traditional assumptions fit least well. There are two reasons why the traditional theory of the firm, based on the assumptions of perfect knowledge and profit maximisation behaviour, fails to provide a satisfactory explanation of market behaviour under oligopoly. These relate to:
- the extent to which firms are interdependent, and
- the degree of uncertainty that exists in oligopoly market.

2. The Growth of Managerial Capitalism

The traditional assumption of profit maximisation implies that the "firm" somehow has a mind of its own, capable of arriving at independent, rational decisions. In reality, of course, firms do not make any decisions – it is entrepreneurs and managers (i.e. individuals) who make business decisions. A "firm" is nothing more than an abstract concept covering owners, managers and employees.

Once we acknowledge that managers in the private and perhaps more particularly in the public sector are able, to some degree, to pursue their own goals rather than that of profit maximisation, the question arises as to what are these goals and what is the effect on prices and outputs. We shall consider the following three possible goals:

- sales revenue maximisation;
- managerial utility maximisation;
- corporate growth maximisation.

There appears, therefore, to be a potential division between the goal of shareholders and the goals of management in the real world. This issue has been approached through the agency theory. In the private sector, the principals are those who ultimately have the right to the assets or who "own" the firm. In joint-stock companies these are the shareholders and they appoint directors as agents to manage these assets in the interest of the principals but in practice this cannot be guaranteed. Some economists question the significance of shareholder power, arguing instead that shareholders are fairly inert to management performance. Most shareholders rarely attend annual general meetings and the existence of transactional costs and capital gains taxation may reinforce a tendency to hold onto share hoping that things will get better. If things do get better those who have held on to their shares benefit and this produces a "free rider" problem. Shareholders may be reluctant to sell, hoping, however, other shareholders do sell. Further, it is not obvious that it is necessary for the less profitable firms which succumb to be taken over. Sometimes what appear to be profitable, well-managed firms face hostile take-over bids.

3. The Organisational Complexity of Firms

As with growth of managerial capitalism and as globalisation has been gaining place, these reflect the fact that as firms have increased in size, so too they have become much more complex in terms of their organisation structure. This structure will reflect the often conflicting views of owners, managers, workers and consumers. Within each grouping there will be still more complex structures: perhaps different categories of shareholders with different share holdings who are interested in different objectives (short-term versus long-term profits perhaps); different managers at different levels with different aims and aspirations; blue-collar workers and white-collar workers with different career expectations and reward packages, perhaps represented by different unions; finally, there will be different groups of consumers to be satisfied (such as the one-off consumer versus the long-term, loyal consumer).

Given the degree of complexity of organisational structures today, some economists argue that it is unlikely that a useful theory of business decisions can be based on a single objective and that instead the subject should be approached through a study of the behaviour of individuals or groups within the firm. Such an approach should start from the position that people in firms, including mangers, do not aim to maximise anything – they simply aim to "satisfy" a range of objectives.

Some of the goals could be related to the following:

- production: a goal that output must lie within a certain satisfactory range;
- sales: a goal that there must be a satisfactory level of sales;
- market share: a goal indicating a satisfactory size of market share as a measure of competitive success as well as growth;
- profit: still an important goal, but one amongst many rather than necessarily of overriding importance.

Consequently, there is no single objective of the firm; instead, there are multiple goals that emerge from the potential for conflict amongst interest groups within the firm.

4. The Change of the Ownership

The content, characteristics of the ownership have undergone major changes as well, especially with regard to private ownership of corporation. It was already realised in the 1930s that the modern corporation is characterised by the separation between shareholders, owners of the company, and the managers who control the assets and activities of the firm. Since then, very complex corporate governance has developed: the corporate governance can be defined as the outcome of the relationships and interaction between the different economic agents that operate within a corporate, limited-liability institution. Corporate governance determines both the long-term strategy of this institution and the use of its income. Typically, shareholders, management, employees, creditors, and suppliers/customers are the main actors and, to varying degrees, exert influence on the corporation within a framework given by existing laws, regulations and institutions, as well as firm-specific governance structures. In this respect it is necessary to make a distinction between "stakeholder" and "shareholder". There is a growing perception that managers have become insufficiently accountable to shareholders and other individuals or institutions that have stakes in companies (i.e. the stakeholders).

As a consequence of the dispersion of ownership rights that characterised the modern corporation, shareholders' control over managers is relaxed, and managers are free to pursue their own interests, which often are in contrast with those of the shareholders. Dispersed ownership rights have thus been associated with managerial discretion and with divergence from profit maximisation.

Ownership structures vary considerably from country to country. But enterprises in almost all countries have mixed ownership in the sense that there are everywhere examples of companies owned by the government, by banks and other financial institutions, by institutional investors, by non-financial companies, by personal investors and by foreign companies and investors. It seems, in fact, to be difficult to find a country, in which one single type of owner completely dominates the company ownership structure. Traditional company legislation generally gives owners/shareholders (including individuals who have major influence on implement-

20

ing and exercising of the property right) mastery of the firm. However, in practice, other agents have staked to claims to exercise some control and the individuals have a minor role.

In a market economy the manager, the bank, the institutional investors and personal investors share the responsibility for the functioning and efficiency of the governance system. It is a common feature that the big institutional shareholders are called upon to remember their responsibilities pertaining to corporate performance. It is reinforced by the fact that institutional share ownership has been rising all over the world. The growth of the institutional sector (pension funds, insurance companies, investment companies) has been a driving force behind structural changes in both the process of corporate governance and the structure of world capital markets.

5. The Change of the Pricing Strategies

The pricing has become a very complicated process in the MNCs dominated economy. While choosing the appropriate price to charge for good or service remains one of the most important challenges facing management of the firms. The assumptions made by the basic model of microeconomics that decisions are being made with full or perfect information available to managers about demand, competitors' reactions, supply costs, etc. are even more highly unrealistic in today's globalised world economy than they were in the less globalised one.

Pricing is driven by managerial objectives. The precise objectives pursued by management ultimately determine the kind of pricing strategy that is adopted.

The pricing strategies applied by firm have changed. Usually four pricing strategies can be distinguished:
- marginal cost pricing;
- incremental pricing;
- break-even pricing and
- mark-up pricing.

Marginal cost pricing involves setting prices, and therefore determining the amount produced, according to the marginal costs of production, and is normally associated with a profit-maximising objective. This strategy is mostly applied in highly competitive market and because in the MNCs dominated economy the market is rather oligopolistic, the emphasis has shifted towards other strategies, especially towards the incremental and mark-up pricing.

The markets have become more and more monopolistically competitive and less and less perfectly competitive in a large extent due to the growing influence of the MNCs. As markets become less competitive – i.e. as the degree of monopoly power of the firm increases suppliers will have more discretion when setting the prices.

21

Pricing strategies require a strong integration of pricing into a wider marketing mix, which takes into account other factors than price, which determine demand. Some firms may be reluctant to change price because of the uncertain effects on rivals' actions so the other marketing variables take on added importance. At the same time, consumers may only have a vague idea of the price of products they buy, which appears to relegate the importance of price in demand, though it does not remove it altogether. At the very least pricing should complement the other factors in the marketing mix. The most important elements of the marketing mix are: product, place, promotion and price. These four market mix elements determine what is called the "offer" to the consumer.

The impact of the product life cycle on pricing policy has changed, too. Because of the shortening of the product life cycle due to the accelerating technological development pushed up by the MNCs, there is a need for a more rapid diffusion of the product in the market and to achieve that there is a very intensive incentive for the firms. Especially for the MNCs to use their monopolistic position (which exists at least for short period) to exploit as much as possible the promotional and skimming price policy for their special advantages.

6. The Possibility of Applying of Price Discrimination Has Increased Due to the High Rate of Monopolisation

The majority of large corporate enterprises are multi-business, multi-market, transnational firms; the scope of their operations is by no means limited to selling a single, well-defined item in a small, mostly local market. When producing and pricing a product, the multi-product firm has to take into consideration not only the impact on the demand for that product of the price change (its own price elasticity of demand), but the impact on the demand for the other products in the firms' range (the relevant cross-price elasticity). In other words, pricing now involves obtaining the desired rate of return from the full product range rather than individual products. Such a full-range pricing means that the firm may be content to earn little or no profit on certain products, preferring to use them as "loss leader" to attract consumers who then, (hopefully), buy the higher-profit items.

Pricing in multi-plant and multi-product firms has two other important features, which need to be mentioned: transfer pricing and the internalisation of market transactions. By setting the transfer price artificially low in country A, the profits could be realised in country B. It should be noted, however, that under fiscal regulations such arrangements are usually illegal – though they are also difficult to police. Internalisation means the bypassing of the market, the firm performs the function of the market itself by internalising market transactions. If we take into consideration the decisive role of the MNCs, this internalisation is taking place in global scale. As their foreign affiliates located in different countries tend to be specialised and flows among them are internalised to reduce the transactional costs, they substitute the market in global scale.

In addition to all of these summarised above, the role of the government in pricing has changed moving from taxation and subsidies to regulation. All market economies have some state intervention in pricing in the form of taxation and subsidies, and direct controls, such as regulations and licensing. Also, in many countries state-owned industries, in many cases with MNCs, exist at central and local government levels and some decision must be taken on the pricing of their output. Therefore, the fact that the price is as likely to reflect political considerations as true marginal social costs is a major weakness of state intervention in pricing. This is likely to be an even more acute problem for government services such as social security, education, health and defence. In such services, usually no price is charged, or it is a nominal charge and all or most funding comes from taxation.

MNCs can have substantial impact on the externalities and public goods. They can intensify both the negative and positive externalities A lot of inventions made by them in fact have good public character. That MNCs play greater and greater role in the basic research: the result of which is almost pure public goods.

It seems there is a contradiction between the growing monopolistic power of MNC, which by its nature should create a lot of inefficiency and the ever expanding material wealth, improving efficiency in the globalising word economy as a whole and in the vast majority of national economies. This seemingly paradoxical situation can be explained rather convincingly by using Schumpeter's theory about the monopolistic competition. These advantages of the monopoly can outweigh the inefficiencies accompanied by the monopoly position, especially if we take dynamic approach, which is overlooked by the traditional economic theory taking usually a static approach. This cannot be said about the theory of Schumpeter, his concept of "creative destruction" is a strong and interesting dissent from the prevailing neo-classic view. So in Schumpeter's view, the disadvantages of monopoly would be more than offset by advantages of rapid innovation the monopoly profit funded. The growing role of the MNCs together with the very fact of the economic development has strengthened the rationality of the argument of Schumpeter.

Economists have always recognised that it is the unique and critical task of governments to engage in responsible and efficient macroeconomic management, even though there has been much controversy over how this task can be done. The theoretical basis for this is provided by the macroeconomics, the macroeconomic theory. The logic of macroeconomics presupposes that sovereign national states and their governments implement their economic policies under great autonomy and scale of freedom of decisions. However, this is not the case due to the globalisation of the world economy and to the influence of the MNCs on the economy. It has major impact on the macroeconomics. It poses the question: Does it make sense to keep the same macroeconomic paradigm for economic policy decision at the national and multinational levels despite the changing behavioural patterns of firms and states? Today, most governments are facing several economic policy dilemmas. To a large extent, the current confusion reflects the inadequacy of the traditional paradigm as a framework for economic policy at the macroeconomic and microeconomic levels. Monetary and fiscal policy, trade policy, labour policy and industrial policy are deeply affected by the new rules of the game in today's world economy.

In today's world economy, there are many instances in which domestic economic policies appear to be working badly. The impact of monetary policy and fiscal policy on growth, investment, employment, trade and capital movements is often uncertain. Industrial policy has lost a good deal of its *raison d'être*, following the growing difficulty in answering the question "who is us". The bottom line of economic policy dilemma is found in the widening dichotomy that exists between the globalisation process and the national interest.

Macroeconomic theory, which is used as a framework for government intervention, refers to national aggregates based on national accounting techniques that ignore the role of the game of the new world economy. Industry-policy objectives are determined by a nationalistic approach that no longer corresponds to the strategy and structures of MNCs, whatever their country of origin. The old paradigm impedes governments from realising the political frontiers of a country no longer coinciding with the economic borders. The widening dichotomy between a nation and a State is not only the result of a greater openness of the economy – with openness defined in term of trade flows – but also, and above all, the result of the multidimensional nature of its integration into the world economy. This has an important implication: MNCs are the most significant economic players in the world economy, although this is not yet recognised by the existing official economic data, national administrations and international institutions.

Monetary and fiscal policies, the two traditional main instruments of economic policy, have become less effective under the rules of the game that characterise the new world economy. With capital mobility, the targets of monetary and fiscal policies can no longer be reached with certainty. In certain cases, changes in interest rates or taxation may trigger unexpected and counterproductive effects. Governments are no longer in a position to use monetary and fiscal measures without considering their domestic impact from a world-wide perspective.

Globalisation and the integration of national economies in one world economy means that Keynesian counter- cyclical intervention has to be global and systematic, collectively agreed, co-ordinated, and financed.

Globalisation and the MNCs have a major and substantial impact on both the market and government failures, and also on the way and direction of government policies and measures aimed to correct and/or eliminate the markets and government failures.

One of the most noticeable developments is that the market has been gaining influence against the government mainly due to the fact that the MNCs have become the major and the most influential actors of the globalised market. It can be witnessed during the last three decades.

The MNCs have a very influential lobby power, there is no question about that, owing to the huge wealth they possess and control. And as we know, wealth can easily translate into power and power into privilege. Those who have power are recognisable, because they are able to effect the range of option within which others can choose what to do. It might seem that others choose freely, but the risks and penalties of going outside that range of options are so punitive that they are not seriously considered. Power and privilege can gain position in politics as well.

As a result of the globalisation, a special form of estrangement of elected representatives from their electorate has developed, it can be called "democracy illusion". As we know: democracy is based upon the sovereign national state whose parliament and government are democratically elected by the voters. This state at minimum is responsible for the voters for any number of critical functions: for the welfare of their citizens, for basic social and physical infrastructure, and for ensuring economic viability.

It used to be taken granted that nations should be considered as communities of people, which share responsibility for mutual well-being. Yet, this is becoming less and less so. What define the so called post-national nation state are two characteristics: first, weak national economy since the country's well-being is externally determined by its export and trade bloc performance; second, a substantial reduction in the ability of the state to engage in day-to-day internal economic management. Due to globalisation, countries have less democratic control over the formation of their economic policies. Decisions that used to be determined by democratically elected legislature would now be forced by non-elected commissions to set up under the terms of some kinds of free-trade agreements. By the same token, the power of central banks to operate independently of elected popular bodies effectively places the control of money, credit and interest rates outside of democratic accountability. The mobility of financial capital limits viable difference among national interest rates and thus severely restricts the ability of central banks and governments to pursue monetary and fiscal policies appropriate to their internal economies. As nation-states factually lose and formally relinquish control over their economies, electorates become liable to fall victim to a "democracy illusion": comparable to Keynes's "money illusion": that by exercising their political rights of citizenship they can purchase on their political fate. Thus the gap between formal and effective sovereignty widen and the purchasing power of national citizenship deteriorates.

The globalisation and the MNCs have a determining impact on the government policies aimed to correct government failure. It can be seen in the cases of social policy, deregulation, liberalisation and privatisation where in many instances while these policies intend to correct the government failures they go so far that the final results are increasing market failures, decreasing efficiency of the government policies in terms of growing income inequality and occurring waste of economic resources.

There is no doubt that globalisation has created such tasks and problems that require some kind of global governance, global polity. In economic field globalisation has eroded the power of the national states, and therefore it demands a globalised management of economic, financial and monetary systems. However, no economy exists without politics and without a state. Therefore, economic globalisation logically requires the construction of a world political system able to respond to the challenge, a power system capable of managing social compromise at world-wide level, just as national states manage them at their level. However, sufficient maturity does not exist in the area, not even among the group of dominant capitalist countries – OECD or within the Europe of the EU. The asymmetry between territorially based and geographically organised international political system comprised of national states and an emerging world economy, where national markets are becoming less relevant, still exists.

The world is still far away from the existence of global governance, global polity. At the same time, there are many serious problems, concerns and tasks transcending national borders, which would need or at least require strong and effective international co-operation. Among them the followings deserve distinctive attention:
- managing regional crisis;
- promoting global economic stability;
- protecting the environment;
- fostering basic research and production knowledge;
- making international development assistance more effective.

It is much easier to list these concerns and tasks than to manage them efficiently in the practice. The progress has been slow, however, increasing the worry that it will take many crises to get through and to force the respective international organisations and countries into concerted action.

In this respect the G7, the IMF and the World Bank have great responsibility in selecting and pursuing proper economic policies dealing with the world economy as a whole and with the economy of each country relating to the IMF and the World Bank. It seems that it is time to make a paradigmatic change in their economic policies. The IMF and the World Bank are the leading advocates of the neo-classic economic theory and the neo-liberal economic policies having been implemented during the last three decades all over the world. However, due to the growing political and economic problems, crisis contradicting the principles of these institutions, more and more critics and challenges of these policies can be heard around the world. Their practical policies are still based upon the so-called Washington consensus. The Washington consensus policies were based on a rejection of the state's active role and the promotion of a minimalist, non-interventionist state. The unspoken premise is that governments are worse than markets. Therefore the smaller the state the better it is. It seems now is a good time to re-examine and change the Washington consensus. The current crisis in East Asian, Latin-American countries and Russia are just underlining the doubts about this policy.

The direction of these policy changes could be the broadening of the goals and instruments (means) of the policies intending to promote economic development, and in addition to these, there is a need for a better timing, sequencing during the policy implementation.

As regarding to the goals, they should include not just term economic growth, especially short term economic growth but long-run, sustainable economic growth accompanied by increases in living standards – including equitable income distribution, improved health and education, – and by preserved natural resources, and protected healthy environment.

As to the policy instruments, it means

- on the one hand, they should include building up efficient financial systems, promotion of the competition, appropriate regulation and more effective and efficient state not only in dealing with macroeconomic stability, inflation, appropriate deregulation, liberalisation and privatisation, but in the field of social protection, welfare, building of human capital, technological development and transfer, and
- on the other hand, better use of the main instruments of the Washington consensus, (that is, of the macroeconomic stabilisation policies, fiscal and monetary policies, anti-inflation policies, deregulation, liberalisation and privatisation).

It would be important to provide such an increase in living standard, which ensure that all groups in society, not just at the top, enjoy the fruits of development. In that case it would be possible to reach two important goals at the same time: to enlarge the aggregate demand and to strengthen the social peace, as it was the case after the Second World War due to the creation of the welfare state, establishing a certain kind of social safety net. The recent development of the globalisation has increased the inequality of income and wealth distribution and has not provided favourable condition for the growth of aggregate demand. Some kind of so-called rentier's regime has been developed, a governing system by and for the rentiers, wealth holders who drive their incomes from returns on capital.

There is another unfavourable impact on the living standard and on the aggregate demand; it is the pressure for the wages to keep them low or/and their increase less than the increase of productivity. The unhinging of wages from productivity was driven by a fundamental structural change: the mass production system that for many years had guaranteed a happy convergence of interests between workers and owners was itself being dismantled – smashed by the technological revolutions and by the global dispersal of production. In the post-war decades, a "vicious circle" had operated in the core manufacturing sectors, a self-reinforcing prosperity that, in effect, shared the gains of rising productivity among owners, workers and consumers, distributed the form of profits, wages and prices. The "vicious circle" did not vanish entirely, but it was gravely destabilised by the industrial revolution and globalisation.

The overproduction, excess supply over demand, excess capacity has always been the immanent characteristic of the capitalist market economy having caused unbalanced, cyclical economic growth with repeated crises. The "vicious circle" has done a lot to ease this problem. However, the globalisation and MNCs have made harder the realisation of the less cyclical growth by having done two things:
- damaging the "vicious circle" that has slowed down the growth rate of the demand and
- having created huge potentialities for expansion of the production, they have speeded up the growth rate of supply.

The result of this is such a contradiction between the aggregate demand and supply that can undermine the basic foundation of the capitalist market economy if some mechanism, like the "vicious circle" was, will not be established to deal with it.

The restriction of social expenditures of budget and the pressure on the wages – are pushing downward the aggregate demand damaging the "vicious circle" of self-reinforcing prosperity. From this, however, we can learn another lesson as well: there is a need for caution about the so-called budget discipline: reducing the size of budget deficit (and the current account deficit) as an important component of macroeconomic stability of the Washington consensus. Cutting of the budget deficit does not always promise a genuine solution to a larger economic problem. If the deficit only dues to annual interest payment paid for the bondholders its reduction by other expenditures of the budget can harm the sustainable economic growth.

There is also a need for a more balanced evaluation of the inflation, which is different from the judgement of the Washington consensus. Controlling high and medium-rate inflation should be fundamental policy priority but pushing low inflation even lower is not likely to significantly improve the functioning of the markets and the economy. What is more, the so-called rentiers, the finance capital, have a major interest to push down inflation as low as possible.

The globalisation resulted in a relatively high real interest rate expressing the strong bargaining power of the rentiers, the capital owners. The effect of such high interest rates is likewise, slowly squeezing more out of the economic system, requiring it to run faster just to keep up with its old obligations. The condition can become pathological when the interest-rate cost persistently grows faster than economic activity expands a malignant relationship present in nearly all of the spectacular collapses of debt.

The basic idea of the Washington consensus is to correct financial imbalances first and deal with real economy later, restoring reliable national currency so that foreign capital may safely return to lend and invest. In focusing on trade liberalisation, deregulation, and privatisation, policymakers have ignored other important ingredients, especially improvement in human capital, R&D, transferring technology, regulation together with the competition, that are required, to make an effective market economy with sustainable, long-term economic growth.

The experiences have shown that a lot of countries following the Washington consensus have not achieved the expected result, even some of them had serious failure during the reform process. There is a need to change the Washington consensus and for creating a new one, a new doctrine, which is better, suited to meet the requirement of the globalised world today. The new doctrine should rely less on financial accounting and more upon economic reality and social equity. The globalised world, its globalised policy making and globalised economy, lack the institutions and mechanisms necessary for this change, but there is no political will to bring them into existence. It does not mean that it is totally out of reality to start such a process and development, which can result in a new doctrine with institution and mechanism capable to manage and to govern efficiently – or better than it is done at present – the globalised world, at least its globalised economy. The possibility of this development will be increased by economic and political crises especially if they occur with more frequency and with more damaging effects creating intensive social and political pressure of the citizens toward the policy makers for change. History has taught us that the major, paradigmic changes have never occurred without such pressure. But such a change would definitely be needed by the new reality of today's globalised world.

THE GLOBALISATION OF THE WORLD ECONOMY

THE CHARACTERISTICS AND NEW TENDENCIES OF GLOBALISATION

The world economy has become more integrated. We are far-away from the full integration when there is free movement of goods, services, capital and labour and where governments treat firms equally, regardless of their nationality; but witnessing, especially in the last decades, the accelerated speed of globalisation of the world – including trans-nationalisation – growing activities and influence of multinational corporations (MNCs), demonstration effects of consumption, spreading regional integration and deepening interdependency in fields of economy, technology, environment – the world economy has been unstoppably going to this direction.

This tendency becomes rather evident if we briefly overview the history of the globalisation process. To do this it might be rational to refer to the post Second World War era under which globalisation has got a qualitatively new character and dimension. This post-war era of full employment and high growth rate has been dubbed the "Golden Age of Capitalism"; it is a description which appears increasingly appropriate with the continued failures of the advanced capitalist economies to return to the levels of economic growth and employment witnessed from 1948 to 1973 (see Table 1). The demise of that era around 1973 has now been followed by more than twenty years of global instability and varying degrees of mass unemployment. The end of the Cold War has been marked by regional conflicts and open wars. The "freeing of the market" in the former Soviet Union and Eastern Europe has destroyed many existing structures without – at least for the time being – developing alternatives, resulting in economic regression and falling national income.[1]

Increased global competition from the Newly Industrialising Countries has been blamed for aggravating unemployment in Western Europe and North America. It has led to call for the abandonment of the welfare state and the associated social security and other provisions, which are alleged to make Western Europe, in particular, uncompetitive, and to policy proposals for "managed trade" or similar meas-

---

[1] *Managing the Global Economy*. J. Michie and J. G. Smith, ed. (Oxford University Press, New York, 1995) p. 7

TABLE 1. Growth of world output and world trade, 1870–1990
(annual percent growth rates, calculated peak to peak)

		Output	Trade
Pre-WW 1:	1870–1913	2.7	3.5
Interwar:	1913–1937	1.8	1.3
	1913–1929	2.3	2.2
	1929–1937	0.8	–0.4
Postwar:	1950–1990	3.9	5.8
	1950–1973	4.7	7.2
	1973–1990	2.8	3.9

Sources: Authors' calculations from the following:
> World Trade-Based on volume of world exports from:
> 1870–1913 – Lewis (1981), Appendix III. Table 4
> 1913–1950 – Maddison (1962), Table 25
> 1950–1991 – Wells (1993), Appendix.
World Output—based on constant price GDP series from:
> 1870–1950 – Maddison (1991). Table 4.7 (Computed from annual growth rates of sixteen
> countries.)
> 1950–1990 – Wells (1993), Appendix.

ures. What was seen by some as an alternative economic system of "social corporatism", explaining a relative escape from mass unemployment by the Scandinavian economies, has also crumbled in the face of domestic political developments and global economic pressures. The Third World debt crises may have slipped out of the news, but it is hardly resolved. And the world economy seems set to enter the twenty-first century with the industrialised world divided into three main trading blocs: the European Union, the North American Trade area and the Pacific Rim countries. This tri-polar division could either form the basis for negotiation and co-operation, or else for sort of unstable economic and political developments only before witnessed in the preludes to the two world wars.[2]

As for relative output levels, it is hard to envisage any of the world's countries or blocs emerging as an economically dominating power within the next generation or so, certainly not to the degree that Britain was prior to World War One and the USA was post World War Two. It might be supposed that Japan and the Newly Industrialising Economies will continue their rise, at the expense of the USA's continued relative decline. But even if Japan does become increasingly dominant, it would be a long time before Japan's economy alone could match NAFTA's or the EU's, and the possibility of Japan achieving the military dominance that went along with America's economic leadership – and Britain's before that – appears even more remote. Within the tri-polar impasse with which the global economy will be enter-

---

[2] *Ibid.*, p. 2

ing the twenty-first century, relative shifts in economic and political power will no doubt continue.[3] China and Russia can influence these shifts in a great extent and by doing so they can increase the uncertainly in these shifts as well. All of these can pose threat to world peace and economic stability, but, at same time, can create new opportunities for further economic development and improving of social wellbeing all over the world. But the outcome of these future possible alternative paths cannot be forecasted which in itself create an uncertainty in the world's economic and political life.

It has also seen the continuation and, in important respects, the acceleration of a trend towards greater international specialisation and economic integration that already began during the Golden Age. National states and labour movements, both important pillars of the Golden Age, have found it difficult to adapt to these changed circumstances. *Their weakness – together with the uncertainty of future economic and political paths of the world – contrasts, markedly, with the unambiguous rising influence of MNCs. This rise of the MNCs, on many accounts, marks a transition from the Golden Age to a "globalising age".* In these accounts, the role of MNCs as long-standing organisers of a broad range of cross-border economic assets and activities has been transformed by new technologies and the relaxation of regulatory controls; free from their national setting and with a fully internationalised governance structure these firms can now pursue global strategies of production, marketing, and profit seeking.[4]

Although there is disagreement over the extent to which the global age has already arrived, the basic philosophy – and the corresponding policy advice – underlying much of this analysis is that what is good for MNCs is also good for national and regional economies and ultimately for the world economy. With the pursuit of the corporate goals unhindered by discontinuous political boundaries and organised national interests, *MNCs emerge as the most efficient allocates of global resources* and the implicit – and sometimes explicit – assumption that geography and history are increasingly irrelevant as determinants of economic performance reinforces a belief that the national state is at best of marginal importance in today's world economy, more likely an obstacle to renewed growth and prosperity.[5]

So *we now live in a brave new globalised world which might be characterised along the following lines:*

> "All old-established national industries have been destroyed or are daily being destroyed. They are dislodged by new industries, whose introduction becomes life and death question for all nations, by industries that no longer work on indigenous raw material,

[3] *Ibid.*, p. 33
[4] *Ibid.*, p. 134
[5] *Ibid.*, p. 136

but raw material drawn from the remotest zones; industries whose products are consumed, not only at home, but in every quarter of the globe. In place of the old wants, satisfied by the productions of the country, we find new wants, requiring for their satisfaction the products of distant lands. We have universal inter-dependence of the nations. And as in material, so also in intellectual production."[6]

True, of course. But new? This characterisation of globalisation was actually written almost 150 years ago in 1847 (published 1848) by K. Marx and F. Engels in The Communist Manifesto. Globalisation caused an enormous increase in the power of the capitalist class because it opened up new markets for it. Indeed the discovery of America and the opening of navigation routes to Asia established a "world-market" for modern industry.[7] The bourgeoisie rushed into this opportunity with alacrity: "The need of a constantly expanding market for its products, chases the bourgeoisie the whole surface of the globe. It must nestle everywhere, settle everywhere, establish connections everywhere."[8] But this development is cultural as well as economic, Marx argues, because it gives a cosmopolitan character not only to production but to consumption :

> "The intellectual creations of individual nations become common property. National one-sidedness and narrow-mindedness become more and more impossible, and from the numerous national and local literatures, there arises a world literature."[9]

Nor is this process restricted to Western Europe. The bourgeoisie draws even "barbarian" nations into its "civilisation" using the "heavy artillery" of cheap commodities to batter down "all Chinese wall". The bourgeoisie is, for Marx, recreating the world in its own image.[10]

That is, *the globalisation of the world economy is not a new and recent phenomenon. What are new and recent phenomena are the technical, the technological conditions in which the globalisation has been unfolding, its scope and its changed characteristics, its impact on economic and political life and the economics as a science as well.*

A fundamental prerequisite of the globalisation, the evolution of international production and of the transitional corporations is the development of technologies in which the frictions of space and time are overcome. The most important items of such enabling technologies – and the most obvious ones – are *the technologies of transport and communications*. Neither of these technologies can be regarded as the cause of the globalisation, of international production or of the MNCs; rather, they

---

[6] Karl Marx, Frederich Engels, *Manifesto of the Communist Party*. In: K. Marx, Fr. Engels, *Collective Works*. Volume 6 (Lawrence and Wishard, London, 1976) p. 502

[7] Malcolm Waters, *Globalisation* (Routledge, London, 1995) p. 6

[8] Karl Marx, *Manifesto of the Communist Party*, p. 504

[9] Karl Marx, *Manifesto of the Communist Party*, p. 506

[10] Malcolm Waters, p. 6

make such phenomena feasible. But without them, today's complex global economic system simply could not exist.[11]

In terms of time it takes to get to one part of the world to another there is no doubt that the world has "shrunk" dramatically (Figure 1). The twentieth century, and especially the past few decades, has seen an acceleration of this process of global shrinkage. In global terms, the most important developments have been the introduction of commercial jet, the development of much larger ocean-going vessels (superfreighters) and the introduction of containerisation, which greatly simplifies trans-shipment from one mode of transport to another and increases the security of shipments. Of these, it is the jet aircraft which has the most pervasive influence. As a consequence, in terms of time, New York is now closer to Tokyo than it was Philadelphia in the days of the thirteen colonies. Figure 2 gives some indication of the effect of the introduction of large commercial jets on international air traffic from and to London. From the late 1950s the growth curve was virtually a straight line with a steep upward slope.[12]

Both the time and relative cost of transporting materials, products and people have fallen dramatically as the result of technological innovation in the transport media. However, such developments have depended, to a considerable degree, on parallel developments in *communications technology*.[13] Communications technologies should now be regarded as the key technology transforming relationships at the global scale. The telecommunications technologies can be considered as the electronic highway of the information age, equivalent to the role played by the railway system in the process of industrialisation. The communications technologies are significant for all economic activities but they are especially vital to those economic sectors and activities whose primary function is to collect, transform and transit information; that is, burgeoning business services, including finance. Global communications systems have been transformed radically during the past twenty or thirty years through a whole cluster of significant innovation in information technology. Probably the most important catalyst to enhanced global communications has been the development of satellite technology.[14] Satellite technology, together with a whole host of other communications technologies, is making possible quite remarkable levels of global communication of conventional messages and also transmission of data. In this respect, the key element is the linking together of computer technologies with information-transmission technologies over vast distances. It has become possible for a message to be transmitted in one location and received in another on the other side of the world virtually simultaneously.[15]

---

[11] Peter Dicken, *Global Shift* (Paul Chapman Publishing Ltd., 1982) p. 103
[12] *Ibid.*, p. 105
[13] *Ibid.*, p. 105
[14] *Ibid.*, p. 106
[15] *Ibid.*, p. 106

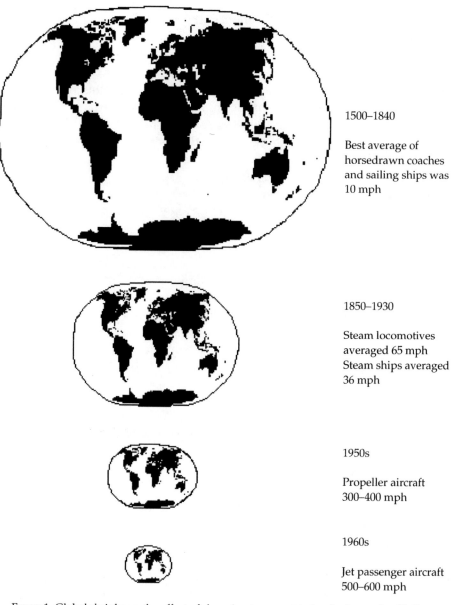

1500–1840

Best average of
horsedrawn coaches
and sailing ships was
10 mph

1850–1930

Steam locomotives
averaged 65 mph
Steam ships averaged
36 mph

1950s

Propeller aircraft
300–400 mph

1960s

Jet passenger aircraft
500–600 mph

FIGURE 1. Global shrinkage: the effect of changing transport technologies on "real" distance
(Source: based on McHale, 1969, Fig. 1)

Developments in the communication media have revolutionised the potential
for large organisations to operate over vast geographical distances and, as such,
have played a key role in facilitating the development of the MNCs. But there is
another sphere – that of *the mass media* – in which innovations have transformed the

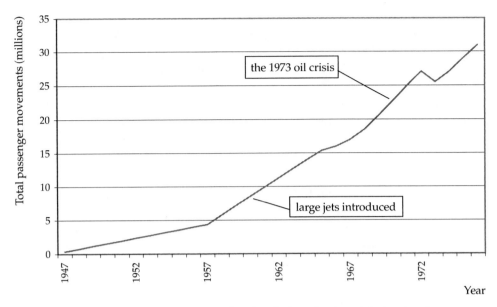

FIGURE 2. The "take-off" of air traffic after the introduction of the jet aircraft
(*Source:* based on Cherry, 1978, Fig. 3.16)

global economy and are facilitating the globalisation of markets. Large business firms require large markets to sustain them; global firms need global markets. The existence of such markets obviously depends on income levels, but it depends, too, on potential customers becoming aware of the firm's offering and being persuaded to purchase them. Even when consumer incomes are low, the ground may be prepared for possible future ability to purchase by creating a desirable image. The mass media are particularly powerful means both of spreading information and of persuasion, hence their vital importance to the advertising industry. On the global scale, it is the electronic media – particularly radio and television – which are the most significant. In part, this is because of their vividness and sense of immediacy and involvement. But an important characteristic of the electronic media is that they make no demands on literacy, a demand which even the most primitive news-sheet makes.[16] Perhaps more than any other innovation in the mass media it has development of the transistor radio receiver which has had the most revolutionary effects, especially in developing countries. Not only is it portable but it is also relatively cheap.

The electronic media transmit messages of all kinds. The most important point is that a very large proportion of these messages are commercial messages aimed at

---

[16] *Ibid.*, p. 104

the consumer. The communication media, in effect, open the doors of national markets to the heavily advertised products of the transitional producers.

The world-wide spread of the electronic media has, in McLuhan's famous metaphor, created a global village in which certain images are shared and in which events take on the immediacy of participation.[17]

For McLuhan the determining principle of culture is the medium by which it is transmitted rather than its content. Media include any means of extending the senses and therefore include technologies of both transportation and communication. He makes a periodisation of history into two principle epochs. The first might be called the tribal epoch, which is based on the technologies of the spoken world and the wheel. In this oral culture human experience is necessarily instant, immediate and collective as well as subtle, sensitive and complete. The second is the industrial epoch based on technologies of the written world and of mechanisation. In this literate culture, human experience is fragmented and privatised. Writing or reading a book is isolated and individualised, even lonely. Moreover, it emphasised the sense of sight at the expense of sound, touch and smell, which leaves the viewer distant and unengaged. Print also constructs thought into connecting linear sequences that allow society to rationalise and thereby to industrialise.[18]

This transformation also had globalised effects. The use of paper, wheels and roads allowed the first moves in direction of what is called time-space distanciation. In their capacity to speed up communication, they started to connect distant localities, to reduce the consciousness of tribe or village. They also allowed power centres to extend their control over geographic margins. McLuhan shows that this reorganisation of space through time is accompanied by the development of two other important universalising devices. First, the mechanical clock disrupted recursive and seasonal conceptions of time and replaced them by durational conception where time is measured in precise divisions. Measured, universal time become an organising principle for a modern world divorced from the immediacy of human experience. As McLuhan says, the division of labour begins with the division of time by using the mechanical clock. The second device is money which increases the speed and volume relationships.

Current circumstances constitute a further epochal shift. The predominant industrial and individualising media of print, the clock and money are being displaced by electronic media that restore the collective culture of tribalism but on an expansive global scale. Its key characteristic is speed. Since electronic communication is virtually instantaneous, it drags events and locations together and renders them totally interdependent. Electricity establishes a global network of communication that is analogous to the human central nervous system. It enables us to ap-

---

[17] *Ibid.*, p. 110
[18] Malcolm Waters, *Globalisation*, p. 34

prehend and experience the world as a whole: with electricity we extend our central nervous system globally, instantly interrelating every human experience.

The accelerating effects of communication and rapid transportation create a structural effect that McLuhan calls "implosion". By this he means that they, as it were, bring together in one place all the aspects of experiences – one can simultaneously sense and touch events and objects that are great distances apart. The centre-margin structure of industrial civilisation disappears in the face of synchrony, simultaneity and instantaneousness. As McLuhan calls it: "This is the new world of the global village." Just as members of tribal society had been aware of their total interdependence with other members, so members of the global village cannot avoid a consciousness of human society in its entirety. But global space is not at all similar to a tribal neighbourhood.

Electric circuitry has overthrown the regime of "time" and "space" and pours upon us instantly and continuously the concerns of all other man. *It has reconstituted dialogue on a global scale. Its message is Total Change, ending psychic, social, economic, and political parochialism. The old civic, state, and national groupings have become unworkable. Nothing can be further from the spirit of the new technology than "a place for everything and everything in its place". You cannot go home again.*[19]

The globalisation today refers to the emergence and spread of a supranational dimension of social relations. In institutional terms, the process has unfolded through the proliferation and growth of MNCs, popular associations and regulatory agencies (sometimes termed global companies, global civil society and global regimes respectively). Ecologically, globalisation has taken place in the shape of planetary climate change, atmospheric ozone depletion, world-wide epidemic and decline of Earth's bio-diversity, among other things. Economically, in what Karl Marx anticipated as capital's "annihilation of space by time", globality has been realised *inter align* in twenty-four-hour round-the-world financial markets, whole-world production lines and a host of global consumption articles. Normatively, globalisation has occurred through the expansion of world-wide standards (e.g., common scales of measurement and so-called universal human rights) as well as through non-territorial networks of collective solidarity (e.g., among women, the disabled or indigenous peoples). Psychologically, globalisation has developed through growing consciousness of the world as a single place, an awareness reinforced by everyday experiences of diet, music and dress, as well as by photographs from outer space showing planet Earth as one location. In this way, *the rise of supra-territoriality has been comprehensive, in some form and to some degree spanning all aspects of social relations.*[20]

The origin of the modern globalised world economy lies in the eighteen century transition to an industrial world. This transition finally broke the predictable and

[19] *Ibid.*, p. 36

[20] *Globalisation: Theory and Practice.* Eleonore Kofman and Gillian Young, ed. (Pinter, New York, 1996) p. 46

essentially static relation common to agricultural production and introduced deep-seated changes in the organisation of economic activities. The rise of the industrial enterprise provoked a continuous search for more effective ways of producing goods and services through the application of capital-intensive techniques and scientific knowledge, the novel use of natural resources, and the organisation of longer production runs resulting in a steady increased scale of economic activity. Of equal importance, the simplification and standardisation of industries gave rise to an increasingly specialised division of labour and more complex linkages in the chain of production transforming raw materials into finished goods and services. These advantages of scale and specialisation depend upon the size of the available market. But the process is cumulative and interdependent; expending production, by enlarging the potential market, further reinforces the opportunities for specialisation through a continual subdivision of industrial activities. The structures and strategies of capitalist firms have continuously been shaped by these dynamic internal and external economies.[21]

Although the earliest stages of industrialisation were confined to products manufactured, finished, and sold within national economies, the combined pressure to enlarge production, specialise activities, and seek markets quickly outgrew local conditions and larger domestic firms soon faced the choice of whether to compete internationally by extending production activities abroad through foreign direct investment (FDI) or to export from their domestic base. At the industry level, historical accident and cultural influences certainly appear to have a far from marginal role in influencing this choice. Trial and error, routine and inertia, and above all the creation of industrial and technological heritage have shaped particular patters of expansion abroad. However, it is the constant pressure on firms to grow in size and remain industry leaders, to extend economic activity abroad through foreign production facilities, jumping natural and artificial barriers to compete directly with domestic production in the expectation that larger rents from firm-level advantage will offset the additional costs accompanying production in an unfamiliar environment.[22]

DEFINITION OF GLOBALISATION

This globalisation is a continuous process of extending interdependent cross-border linkages in production and exchange, pursued by firms, many of which by definition are multinational, transnational, with the aim of advancing their particular interests, and regulated by states and other institutions with the aim of ensuring the potential benefits are obtained by wider communities.

---

[21] *Managing the Global Economy.* J. Michie and J. G. Smith, ed., p. 137
[22] *Ibid.*, p. 137

Globalisation is traced through three arenas of social life. They are:

- the *economy*: social arrangements for the production, exchange, distribution and consumption of goods and tangible services;
- the *polity*: social arrangements for the concentration and application of power, especially insofar as it involves the organised exchange of coercion and surveillance (military, police etc.), as well as such institutionalised transformations of these practices as authority and diplomacy, that can establish over populations and territories;
- *culture*: social arrangements for the production, exchange and expression of symbols that represent facts, affects, meanings, beliefs, preferences, tastes and values.[23]

The principle characteristics of economic globalisation consist of the followings:

- the globalisation of financial markets;
- the internationalisation of corporate strategies, in particular their commitment to competition as a source of wealth creation;
- the diffusion of technology and related R & D and knowledge world-wide;
- the transformation of consumption patterns into cultural products with world-wide consumer markets;
- the internationalisation of the regulatory capabilities of national societies into global political economic systems;
- the diminished role of national governments in designing the rules for global governance.

A summary of the concepts and actual processes of globalisation is presented in Table 2.[24]

Globalisation has been variously defined, and no consensus exists on the cause of this phenomenon. For our discussion we can use McGrew's general definition. He claims that globalisation is the multiplicity of linkages and interconnections that transcend the nation-state (and by implication the societies) which make up the modern world system. It defines a process through events, decisions, and activities in one part of the world can come to have significant consequences for individuals and communities in quite distant parts of the globe.[25]

Globalisation as concept refers both the compression of the world and the intensification of the consciousness of the world. This compression is normally accounted for through the rapid advances in technology and the increased intensification of economic activities. It is this interpretation of national societies which subverts the competence of national authorities and erodes their autonomy. Moreover, the

---

[23] Malcolm Waters, *Globalisation*, p. 7

[24] *States against Markets*. S. Robert Boyer and Daniel Drache, ed. (Routledge, London, 1996) p. 64.

[25] *Globalisation: Theory and Practice*. Eleonore Kofman and Gillian Young, ed., p. 116

TABLE 2. Concepts of globalisation

Category	Main elements/processes
1. Globalisation of finances and capital ownership	Deregulation of financial markets, international mobility of capital, rise of mergers and acquisitions. The globalisation of shareholding is at its initial stage.
2. Globalisation of markets and strategies, in particular competition	Integration of business activities on a world-wide scale, establishment of integrated operations abroad (including R&D and financing), global searching of components, strategic alliances.
3. Globalisation of technology and linked R&D and knowledge	Technology is the primary catalyst: the rise of information technology and telecom enables the rise of global networks within the same firm, and between different firms. Globalisation as the process of universalisation of Toyotism/lean production.
4. Globalisation of modes of life and consumption patterns; globalisation of culture	Transfer and transplantation of predominant modes of life. Equalisation of consumption patterns. The role of the media. Transformation of culture in 'cultural food', 'cultural products'. GATT rules applied to cultural flows.
5. Globalisation of regulatory capabilities and governance	The diminished role of national governments and parliaments. Attempts to design a new generation of rules and institutions for global governance.
6. Globalisation as the political unification of the world	State-centred analysis of the integration of world societies into a global political and economic system led by a core power.
7. Globalisation of perception and consciousness	Socio-cultural processes as centred on 'One Earth'. The 'globalist' movement. Planetary citizens.

Source: A broadened and revised table based upon W. Ruigrok and R. van Tulder, 'The Ideology of Interdependence'. Doctoral dissertation, University of Amsterdam, June 1993.

development of transnational networks and global authority structures dislocates and fractures national decision-making. Accompanying this physical shrinking of the world, as it were, and the idea of a global village, is a changing conception of time and space. Globalisation increases the processes whereby network of communication and system of production link the local and global levels so that social relations can no longer be conceived solely in local terms. Our everyday life is structured in such a way that social interactions are embedded in global networks. In this formulation, globalisation is defined as the intensification of world-wide social relations which link distant localities in such a way that local happenings are shaped by events accounting many miles away and vice versa.[26]

The new phenomenon of globalisation makes possible the design, development, production, distribution and consumption of process, products and services on a world scale, using instruments such as patents, databases, new information, communication and transport technologies and infrastructures. Many of the new products are geared to satisfy increasingly diversified and customised global markets regulated by "quasi-universal" norms and standards. As well, the modern corporation has changed its organisational structure dramatically. More then ever, successful firms are looking to form networks with other private-sector actors capable of operating on a world basis. Finally, capital, too, is increasingly owned by a multiplicity of shareholders from different countries; business culture is said to obey a world strategy even if it is difficult to identify the specific territorial and legal basis of these organisations.

We can take a few examples of the kinds of intensive forms of interrelationships and integration that lead to the production, distribution and consumption of global kinds of goods and services.

Credit cards are a typical illustration of a global services devised for a specialised, high-value-added world market, based on the integration of whole clusters of new technologies (data processing, materials, telecommunication, etc.), and managed by globalised organisations with a growing world expertise. *The car* is also a typical example of a global product. The car is no longer "Made in USA", "Made in France", "Made in Japan", but is more and more "Made in the world". This applies not only to the production side, but, more importantly, to the whole system which facilitates the production of about 40 million cars per year. Of even greater significance is the explosion of *inter-firms strategic alliances* that have, in the last fifteen years, deeply modified the international structures of the car sectors, and even more, other sectors of the economy. An increasing number of products are jointly designed by several firms requiring their engineers to work together on the same idea over a long period of time. Similarly, the complexity of the elements on the production process requires firms from different countries to collaborate. Different firms have to share their strategies with others.[27]

This globalisation process has different developing stages.

---

[26] *Ibid.*, p. 117
[27] *States against Markets.* S. Robert Boyer and Daniel Drache, ed., p. 73

DIFFERENT DEVELOPING STAGES OF GLOBALISATION

The Period 1870–1913

The period 1870–1913 is often presented as an exemplary episode of rapid economic progress and unprecedented international integration. An open regulatory framework prevailed: short-term and long-term capital movements were unsupervised; the transfer of profits was unhampered; the gold standard was at its height and encompassed almost all the major industrial countries by the period's ending and most smaller agrarian nations; citizenship was freely granted to emigrants; and direct political influence over the allocation of resources was limited. Technological progress reinforces openness and Britain's undisputed leadership role underpinned the international gold standard, upheld the virtues of free trade (both through access to its owned domestic market and enforced openness accompanying colonial rule), and provided the complementary financial and commercial services in part at the expense of its own manufacturing base.[28]

Under these conditions, markets linked a growing share of world resources and output; exports outgrew domestic output in the core capitalist countries, and export per capita rose not only in these countries but in a number of developing countries and the migration of labour was unprecedented.[29] (Between 1870 and 1915, 36 million people left Europe, two-thirds for the USA, for example). But the full extent and impact of international economic integration and globalisation cannot be gauged independently of changes in production and the ability of states before the First World War to foster structural changes in economic activities. The capital intensity of new industrial techniques simultaneously pushed the industrial take-off beyond the domestic resources of most countries and added impetus to the search for a reliable supply of inputs and guaranteed markets. Correspondingly, long-term capital flows were the single most important element of this increased international economic integration; the growth in long-term foreign investment exceeded both trade and output and according to one estimate, total stock of long-term foreign investment had, by 1914, reached $44 billion,[30] no less than one third taking the form of direct investment.

Two very different development paths emerged from the interdependence of cross-border market and production linkages in the period prior to the First World War. On the one hand, for a large group of countries and territories, international integration was the result of primary exports. This was facilitated and reinforced by

---

[28] *Managing the Global Economy.* J. Michie and J. G. Smith, ed., p. 140
[29] *Ibid.*, p. 140
[30] *Ibid.*, p. 141

44

foreign direct investment (FDI), labour flows, and liberal commercial policies. International primary production was extensive – accounting for 55 percent of total stock of FDI in 1913 – integrated through strong vertical linkages at the firm level, and complemented by FDI in transportation and trade. The gain from integration accrued to the capital-exporting (commodity-importing) countries but also to the small elite clustered around these capital-intensive growth poles. These conditions were usually reinforced by the absence of a strong development state. During this period, some of the largest recipients of FDI, such as China and India, experienced a period of "de-industrialisation" and other countries such as Russia, Austro-Hungary, and Latin America which were industrialising, in part through FDI, continued to fall behind the core economies. In many cases, this path was reinforced by colonial governance structures but even normally independent states were weakened by these international forces.[31]

On the other hand, the preconditions for rapid industrialisation were being successfully established – with the help of strong states – in a few core countries and behind rising tariff barriers. Close complementarities between capital exporters (in search of profitable opportunities) and the capital-scarce countries supported this industrialisation drive through long-term capital and labour flows. These were concentrated in a small group of newly industrialised countries in North America and Europe; in a number of these countries foreign investment represented a very high share of gross domestic fixed investment (for example, between 1880–1890 this share was 50.0 percent in Australia, 47 percent in Sweden). These investments were mainly in the form of bonds with very long maturities and went predominantly to public projects – such as railways – where they were often matched by large amount of government assistance. Foreign direct investment in manufacturing – although small – by adding technological and managerial flows, reinforced the advantages of the late industrialisators. However, these international production linkages were not strongly integrated and, even as technological progress was breaking down the spatial constraints on shallow integration in financial and labour markets, the expansion of production activities abroad was strongly influenced by geographical proximity.[32]

The Period from the First World War

Between the beginning of the First World War and the end of the Second, many of the linkages established across the world economy over the preceding forty years were severed. Wartime control persisted after 1918 and, although economic growth

---

[31] *Ibid.*, p. 142
[32] *Ibid.*, p. 142

accelerated in the 1920s, the international financial system was marked by increased instability, the export of long-term capital from industrial countries slowed dramatically, and world trade failed to recover to its pre-war levels. The international economic order crumbled in 1929 with world recession and a retreat into national autarkic recovery strategies.[33]

The renewal of international market linkages – shallow integration – began in the 1950s under new international institutional frameworks and United States leadership. The United States assumed the mantle of free trade at the end of the war, but it was flexible on the timetable adopted by other advanced countries; under the General Agreement on Trade and Tariffs, the tariff on manufactured export has steadily fallen from an average of around 40 percent at end of the war to under 4 percent with the conclusion of the Uruguay Round. The United States was less flexible on the construction of an international monetary framework. However, the Bretton Woods institutions were nurtured through their infancy with the help of extensive foreign aid and overseas military expenditures and domestic macroeconomic regimes maintained firm control of national economic management. For most of the Golden Age, international financial integration was subordinate to the successful adaptation and implementation of national recovery and growth strategies. Under these conditions, and particularly because rapid economic growth, full employment, structural convergence, and equalisation of incomes and demand patterns within and between industrial countries provided a particularly favourable economic environment, the process of shallow integration appears to have gone further, lasted longer, and involved more countries than before the First World War. The process was led by trade; trade integration surpassed the previous peak of 1913 sometime in the late 1960s and only in the 1980s have rates of export growth dropped below those registered before the First World War (see Table 3). The internationalisation of financial markets began later and had to overcome tighter control on the movement of capital. For much of this period, financial integration was tied to integration through trade and, only with the end of the Golden Age and the return to fixed exchange rates, were the constraints on financial flows more fully relaxed. Since the early 1970s, international banking has grown at about 20 percent per year, considerably faster than world output, trade and FDI.[34]

However, this globalisation process that began during the Golden Age did not simply repeat the shallow market integration of the 1870–1913 period. In contrast to the earlier period, international labour flows have been less significant and the geographical patterns of shallow integration have been changed significantly. In particular, colonial trade linkages have been replaced by closer regional ties. These regional influences have been strongest between industrial nations at a similar level of development, led by Western Europe.

---

[33] *Ibid.*, p. 143
[34] *Ibid.*, p. 143

TABLE 3. Growth of world trade and output, 1870–1990. Average annual percentage change

Item	1870–1913[a]	1913–1950[a]	1950–1960	1960–1970	1970–1980	1980–1990
World trade	3.9	2.0	6.5	8.3	5.2	3.7
World GDP	2.5	1.0	4.2	5.3	3.6	2.8
Difference	1.4	1.0	2.3	3.0	1.6	0.9

Source: Maddison, 1989; World Bank, 1991; UNCTAD, Trade and Development Report, 1993.
Note: [a] Includes Australia, Austria, Belgium, Canada, Denmark, France, Finland, Germany, Japan, Italy, Netherlands, Norway, Sweden, Switzerland, United Kingdom, United States.

But the greatest changes in globalisation during the Golden Age were in international production. Foreign direct investment was, in fact, a robust component of the international economy during the inter-war period; between 1914 and 1938 the stock of outward FDI almost doubled, most of the increase occurred during the 1920s. But, most significantly, it was the rise of the United States towards becoming the leading home country. Although the United Kingdom was still dominant in 1938, its share of the world FDI stock had fallen to under 40 percent, whilst that of the United States was approaching 30 percent. Much of this expansion was in manufacturing affiliates in Europe.

This process accelerated after the war as FDI by large United States manufacturing corporations extended domestic oligopolistic rivalry overseas in search for market share. Scale advantages – an important determinant of overseas production – combined with a clear lead in the financial, technological, and organisational assets that underpin international competitiveness to give the initial impetus for the formation of foreign affiliates. Only a small number of firms from traditionally internationalised economies – such as the United Kingdom, the Netherlands, and Switzerland – could match the operations of United States MNCs.

The international diffusion of mass production systems began informally soon after the war ended – with numerous productivity "missions" to the United States – and, more formally, from the late 1950s, through FDI itself. But by creating an environment favouring larger manufacturing firms, the national structures of the Golden Age themselves provided an important stimulus to international production. From the late 1960s, the cumulative impact of economic convergence, regional consolidation, industrial policies, mergers and acquisitions, and the growth and increasing sophistication of domestic markets in Europe and Japan laid the basis for the intensification of international competition through FDI. This challenge, and the intensification of international rivalry, were already apparent by the late 1960s.[35]

Macroeconomic constraints on the world trading system and rising wage pressures in Europe and Japan reinforced the trend to meet the challenge from U.S.

---

[35] Ibid., p 145

MNCs through FDI and an increasingly liberal environment allowed U.S. corporations to respond in kind, giving a further impulse to international production.

Under these pressures, FDI flows have increased steadily throughout the post-war period and more rapidly with the ending of the Golden Age. The stock of FDI rose from $67.7 billion in 1960 to $1,949 billion in 1992, a compound annual growth rate of over 11 percent. Much of this increase occurred during the 1980s – and coincided with a shift to FDI flows in services – with a corresponding increase in the relative importance of FDI flows vis-à-vis other international flows, particularly trade, and as well in relation to domestic economic activities – including domestic investment.[36]

For much of the Golden Age, globalisation pressures through renewed international market and production linkages were a reflection of growth and convergence among the developed capitalist economies under the leadership of the United States with new ways of managing economic activities. Declining trade barriers and technological revolutions supported this trend, which has evolved furthest at the regional level.

Beginning in the 1980s, many developing countries have adopted a more open stance, including on FDI. In nominal terms, the stock of FDI in the developing world, rose threefold and FDI inflows have been more rapid during the 1990s. The experience of some of countries in East Asia and Latin America suggests the FDI can finance a significant share of domestic capital formation. However, the transition to fuller participation in the international division of labour has proved difficult for many developing countries. Only a small number of developing countries have been able to integrate FDI with successful domestic industrialisation strategies, notably Singapore and Hong Kong. But in others – South Korea and Taiwan – the graduation from import substitution to export-led growth owed less to FDI. Particularly in the latter case, successful industrialisation has also begun to give rise to a growing number of MNCs. Despite these different channels of reintegration in the globalisation process, a new dynamic regional with strong interdependent economic links is now clearly visible. Coinciding with the slow-down in productivity growth in the developed market economies, these developments have added new pressures to the globalisation of economic activity in the post Golden Age period. Whilst international integration has also been pursued by many developing countries as a necessary condition for renewed growth, by contrast to the so-called "miracle" economies of East Asia, the trends overcoming countries – rapid liberalisation, renewed FDI, and weakening states – share uncomfortable similarities with the last decades of the late nineteenth and early twentieth centuries.[37]

---

[36] *Ibid.*, p. 146
[37] *Ibid.*, p. 149

Recent Changes

If we look at the recent changes in the general globalisation motives and drivers we can see the intensification of this globalisation process. Some of these widespread changes include the following:[38]

There are some very important *market drivers* for globalisation, such as

- per capita income converging among industrialised nations (e.g. , Japan overtaking the United States, Hong Kong overtaking New Zealand);
- convergence of lifestyles and tastes (e.g., McDonalds's in Paris and Perrier in America);
- increasing travel creating global consumers;
- organisations beginning to behave as global customers;
- growth of global and regional channels (e.g., agreement in 1989 by three of Europe's largest supermarket chains to co-operate in purchasing and marketing, namely, Casino of France, Ahold of the Netherlands, and Argyll Group of Britain);
- establishing of world brands (e.g., Coca-Cola, Levi's, Louis Vuitton);
- push to develop global advertising (e.g., Saatchi & Saatchi's commercials for British Airways).

There are *cost drivers* of globalisation such as

- continuing push for economics of scale (but offset by flexible manufacturing);
- accelerating technological innovation;
- advances in transportation (e.g., use of Federal Express to deliver urgent supplies from one continent to another);
- emergence of newly industrialising countries with productive capability and low costs (e.g., Taiwan, Thailand, and China);
- increasing cost of product development relative to market life.

The government has created important drivers too such as

- reduction of tariff barriers (e.g., Canada-United States Free Trade Agreement of 1987; the North American Free Trade Agreement);
- creating of trading blocs (e.g., Europe 1992);
- decline in role of governments as producers and customers (e.g., denationalisation of many industries in Europe);
- privatisation in previously state-dominated economies in Latin America;
- shift to open market economies from closed communist systems in Eastern Europe;
- increasing participation of China and India in the global economy.

The *competition drive* also the economy toward to the globalisation, such drivers are:

---

[38] G. S. Yip, *Total Global Strategy* (Prentice-Hall, Inc., New Jersey, 1995) p. 9

- continuing increasing in level of world trade;
- more countries becoming key competitive battlegrounds;
- rise of new competitors intending to become global competitors (e.g., Japanese companies in automotive and electronics industries);
- growth of global networks making countries interdependent in particular industries (electronics);
- more companies becoming globally centred rather than nationally centred (e.g., Stanley Works, a traditional U.S. company moving its production offshore; Uniden, a Japanese telecommunications equipment producer that has never manufactured in Japan);
- increased formation of global strategic alliances.

However there are other important globalisation drivers as well, such as
- revolution in information and communications (e.g., personal computers and facsimile machines);
- globalisation of financial markets (e.g., listing of corporations on multiple exchanges, global market collapse on Black Monday in 1997);
- improvements in business travel (e.g., Concorde and rise of international hotel chains).[39]

Out of these motives and drivers the *technological and organisational transformation* and *those which are related to the services* have especially distinguished importance.

THE LATEST TRENDS OF THE TECHNOLOGICAL AND ORGANISATIONAL TRANSFORMATION

The 1980s have witnessed great technological change and organisation innovation:
- information technology has been a dominant force which has affected all dimensions of production, shifting industrial innovation toward electronically integrated manufacturing processes;
- at the same time, the standard logic and principles of mass production have been challenged by organisation innovations in the management of materials and people which stress flexibility, quality and co-operation over a strict division of labour and rigid production patterns.

These two sets of innovation have led to substantial cost reductions and improvements in efficiency.[40]

The rapid spread of micro-electronic-based information technologies into production processes for goods and services has been one of the outstanding features

---

[39] *Ibid.*, p. 10

[40] *Transitional Corporations in World Development. Trends and Prospects* (United Nations, New York, 1988) p. 41

of world development in the 1980s. The use of these technologies in flexible manufacturing systems and in the processing and transfer of information in service sectors has come to define a new mode of "best practice" or "least cost" production. At the same time, emerging trends in biotechnology, with its applications in agriculture, energy, health and chemical, and new materials, associated with the development of superconductors, ceramics, super-adhesives, composite materials and new plastics, which are expected to have a growing impact on production in the 1990s, are adding to the growing sense that the world economy has entered a new industrial era.

This process of transition is being driven by the emergence of two forces for change. *The first is technological in nature and stems from the development and diffusion of a family of technologies with the capacity to transform both the products and processes of production throughout the economic system.* The development of information technology (IT) and its widespread application to the electronics complex, manufacturing and services, are the dominant technical forces in the current period and have already had a profound and well-publicised impact on all dimensions of production and competition.[41]

The second major force for change relates not to technological change, but to *organisational innovation.* An entirely new approach to the organisation and management of production at the intra-firm and inter-firm level has emerged, initially developed and cultivated within Japan, but now diffusing to other countries, which stresses flexibility, quality and co-operation. The nature of those organisational innovations inherently contradicts the logic and principles of the mass-production model. Much of Japan's international competitive success in the 1970s and 1980s can be attributed to the gain in quality, productivity and responsiveness that Japanese firms derived from the assiduous application of these new approaches.[42]

Innovations in Information-based Production Technology

Technological change is at the heart of the process of economic growth and economic development. As Joseph Schumpeter pointed out, the fundamental impulse that sets and keeps the capitalist engine in motion comes from the new consumers' goods, the new methods of production or transportation, the new markets, the new forces of industrial organisation that capitalist enterprise creates.

Technological change is the prime motor of capitalism, the great growing engine of change, the fundamental force in shaping the patterns of transformation of economy, the chronic distributor of comparative advantage. Although technologies, in the form of inventions and innovations, originate in specific places, they are

---

[41] *Ibid.,* p. 42
[42] *Ibid.,* p. 42

no longer confined to such places. Indeed, one of the most significant sets of innovations is in the sphere of communications, which itself facilitates such technological diffusion.

Technology is, without doubt, one of the most important contributory factors underlying the internationalisation and globalisation of economic activity:

> "It has long been understood that technological change, through its impact on the economics of production and on the flow of information, is a principal factor determining the structure of industry on national scale. This has now become true on global scale. Long-term technological trends and recent advances are reconfiguring the location, ownership, and management of various types of productive activity among countries and regions. The increasing ease with which technical and market knowledge, capital, physical artefacts, and managerial control can be extended around the globe has made possible the integration of economic activity in many widely separated locations. In doing so, technological advance has facilitated the rapid growth of the MNCs with subsidiaries in many countries but strategies determined by headquarters in a single nation."[43]

Information technology is the new techno-economic paradigm around which the next wave of technological and economic changes will cluster. Three main phases of information technology can be identified:

1. Simple pictorial representation and written language, evolving eventually into printing: its basic elements were paper, writing instrument, ink and printing presses.
2. Mechanical, electromechanical and early electronic technologies which developed during the late nineteenth and early twentieth centuries: the basic elements were the telephone, typewriter, gramophone/phonograph, camera, tabulating machine, radio and television.
3. Microelectronic technologies, which emerged only in the second half of the twentieth century: the basic elements are computers, robots and other information-handling production equipment, and office equipment (including facsimile machine).

Point 1 can be regarded as old IT and 2 and 3 together as new IT. A further term "convergent IT" can be defined to refer to the newest advances of the 1970s and 1980s, whereby computers and telecommunications are integrated into a single system of information processing and exchange. Figure 3 shows the nature of this convergence between communications technology, which is concerned with the transmission of information, and computer technology, which is concerned with the processing of information. As the diagram indicates, it is not until the early 1960s that we can clearly identify convergent information technology.[44]

---

[43] Peter Dicken, *Global Shift* (Paul Chapman Publishing Ltd., 1982) p. 97
[44] *Ibid.*, p. 103

The most prominent new developments in production technology are derived from applications of electronic miniaturisation of the processing of information. Developments in semiconductor industry have increased the power and complexity of integrated circuits, while simultaneously reducing their costs of production. As individual circuits have taken on the characteristics of complete electronic systems or sub-systems, their range of application has widened. With declining costs, those wider applications have come within the reach of greater range of production processes. Coupled with reduction in unit costs, there has been a vast improvement in technical performance of the end-user products in areas such as speed, capacity and reliability. All available evidence indicates that components will continue to become smaller, cheaper, more powerful and more reliable. These factors – declining relative prices and major performance improvements – constitute an extremely powerful set of economic incentives compelling the substitution of the new micro-electronic-based products for earlier vintages. At the same time, the increasing use of micro-electronics in all economic activities has triggered the development of a growing array of entirely new products and services and the opening up of new market opportunities for producers.[45]

The key to the generic character of micro-electronics is concerned with information processing. This means that it can be introduced into virtually every aspect of a company's operations. Because of this flexibility, by the late 1970s, a widening array of industrial applications had emerged. Computer-aided design (CAD) has become the principle automation technology for use in design activities. In manufacturing, four key technologies have emerged: computer-numerical control (CNC) for machinery control, initially machine tools, industrial robots, automated transfer systems, and process-control systems for instantaneous monitoring and control of production. Finally, many aspects of the management function have been affected by the development of office technologies.[46]

Since, like the micro-processor, those automation technologies are generic and highly flexible, they have found widespread application in practically all economic sectors. More importantly, they exhibit significant technical and economic advantages over other technologies, and they consistently yield declines in unit costs. By themselves, each of the technological breakthroughs is a major innovation in its own right, and their use at the firm level in a rapidly growing range of sectors has led to substantial gains in productivity. User and supplier firms will be preoccupied with the future development of those automation technologies as "stand-alone" installations for some time to come.[47]

The most important feature of these innovations, however, is that they are also building blocks that can be combined together to allow much higher level of inte-

---

[45] *Transitional Corporations in World Development. Trends and Prospects*, p. 45

[46] *Ibid.*, p. 41

[47] *Ibid.*, p. 43

Communication technology	Information technologies			Computer technology
		Year		
• Radio • Military mobile radio		1940–1949		• Single-function computer • General-function computers
• Tape recording • Cable TV • Microwave links • Crossbar switching • Direct distance calling • Video tape recording		1950–1959		• Commercial computers • Programming languages • Translator
• Communications satellites • Digital communications • Electronic switching	Materials planning, stock control and scheduling Electronic mail and teleconferencing Computer aided design Computer aided manufacture Computer aided diagnostic Remote sensing devices	1960–1969	On-line enquiry Professional data bases Management information systems Integrated text and data processing Transaction clearing system Professional problem-solving	• Integrated circuits • Minicomputers • Structured programming
• Facsimile transmission • Mobile radio • Packet switching • Videotext • Teletext • Optical fibre • Videodisks • Teleconferencing		1970–1979		• Database management system (dbms.) • LSI • Applications generators • Microprocessor • Relational dbms. • Spreadsheets • VLSI
• Local area networks • Cellular radio • Wide areas networks • Private satellites • Integrated service digital networks • Personal telephones		1980–1989		• Portable computers • Logic languages • Optical disk storage • Expert systems • Transputer • Voice recognition • Data-flow processors • Water scale integration

Communication technology	Information technologies			Computer technology
		Year		
• Switched wideband services • Personal mobile communications (via satellites)		1990–		• Gallium arsenide chips • Parallel processing • Learning capability • Natural language recognition • Optical chips • Bio-chips • Ultra-intelligent machines

FIGURE 3. Information technology: the convergence of the technologies of communications and computers (Source: based on Freedman, 1987, Fig. 2)

grated, system automation. In theory, individual systems can be linked together because automation technologies use a common way of processing and transmitting information. System-level integration involves not only the automation of the manufacturing sphere, but also the integration of manufacturing with design under the co-ordination of management. Studies indicate that the greatest benefits of IT in terms of higher productivity are realised when CAD and manufacturing technologies are utilised to integrate functions and divisions within a corporation, and not when it is just applied to specific tasks or within single departments. This ultimate merging of the design, manufacturing and management functions has been termed the "factory of the future".

"A good example of it is the case of General Motors (GM). After lagging behind its rivals for years in development of new cars and trucks, GM said it could now match world standards in the speed of developing new products. Central to GM's transformation is the adaptation of what the company calls 'an integrated portfolio of computer math-based tools' from the design to the factory floor. What it means is that all of the various designs and manufacturing activities use the same Unigraphics software package, which turn every aspect of a vehicle into digital and mathematical models. GM is spending about $ billion a year on this sort of computing.

Engineers and executives showed how GM uses these tools to take a vehicle design from a designer's initial computer-screen pen strokes all the way into production. This saves money by eliminating the need for physical models, cutting down engineering changes, reducing lead times 50 percent for ordering production tooling and making it possible to solve manufacturing problems in 'virtual' factories instead of real ones. (*The Wall Street Journal*, Europe, Monday, October 12, 1998.)"[48]

---

[48] *Ibid.*, p. 43

The imagery of the "factory of future" is quite dramatic though in fact, there are only very few fully integrated and automated factories in the world. The future is not here yet and, even when it does arrive, the totally unmanned factory will still be the exception rather than the rule. There is no question, however, that the broad thrust of industrial innovation in the industrialised countries has shifted toward the design and introduction of integrated manufacturing processes.[49]

Thus multi-purpose CNC machine tools and materials-handling robots are being combined into flexible manufacturing cells (FMC) capable of performing a related series of operations on entire families of parts; FMCs are being linked together via the use of automated handling and transport systems, such as automatic-guided vehicles (AGV) and automated conveyors, to form flexible manufacturing systems (FMS).

The development and diffusion of FMC/FMS is receiving the most attention now, but major advances are taking place in other areas, such as the linking of CAD with computer-directed machining operations , known as CAD/CAM; CAD links into computer-based inventory and purchasing systems; and the linking of all three via computer-integrated manufacturing (CIM). Integration, however, has not stopped there, as a variety of possibilities are being explored for on-line links in design, production scheduling, purchasing, shipping etc. between suppliers and customers. The key feature of these technological developments are integration and flexibility, which yield enormous gains in efficiency and reduce average costs.[50]

Organisational Change in Production Management

Several studies have shown that the competitive superiority of Japanese firms during the late 1970s was due not to a superior process technology alone, but also to a completely different approach to production organisation and management.

Japanese firms pioneered in the development of flexible methods of organising production. They differ in many respects from the traditional mass-production paradigm, which emphasises large production runs of a single basic design, large inventories of work in process and a strict division of labour. Flexible manufacturing, on the other hand, involves production in smaller batches, rapid changes in production lines and a continuous effort to produce to the specifications of the consumer or user. Another aspect of the Japanese approach to organising production is a pervasive commitment to quality.

The new methods of organisation have proved to be superior to old ones even in the absence of automatisation. However, they are now being integrated with computer-aided manufacturing. In conjunction with computer-aided manufacturing

---

[49] *Ibid.,* p. 43
[50] *Ibid.,* p. 43

technologies, they yield very significant increases in factory productivity and reductions in costs. The key to the new methods is organisational flexibility and closer integration of design, testing and production activities. Those characteristics often lead to shorter product-development cycles and allow companies to respond more rapidly to market changes.[51]

The new organisational methods cover three areas:

- the management of materials;
- the management of people and
- the management of relations with suppliers.

The management of materials has been the focus of just-in-time system of inventory control, developed by Toyota and utilised in varying degrees by Japanese MNCs and domestic firms. Just-in-time is an attempt to reduce waste by maximising the level of work-in-process inventories, thereby forcing managers to devote immediate attention to solving the many production problems that inhibit the attainment of the most efficient production methods. With inventory created and passed along as needed, assembly lines can be built to take advantage of flexibility inherent in the new automation technologies. Low-cost production can be achieved with shorter production runs, a feature that allowed Japanese automobile manufacturers to produce at lower cost than their United States and Western European rivals. At the same time, the minimisation of inventories requires greater quality control, which then becomes a competitive advantage in the market-place.

The management of the work-force has also altered significantly. More efficient management of materials and more flexible organisation of specific production processes require a greater decentralisation of decision-making. The new methods of organisation involve placing responsibility for actions closer to the point at which actions occur. That implies more authority and a greater variety of skills for individual workers and a shift in the role of managers becoming co-ordinators of team efforts. In addition, with greater flexibility and more rapid decision-making, managerial need for instantaneous information and analysis has increased and has placed greater demands upon information technology. Thus, just as technical developments have fostered a shift to flexible production methods, these methods have generated new requirements for information technology.[52]

The new approaches to organisation have also led to *changes in the relationship between suppliers and their customers.* Under the mass-production system, assembly-line manufacturers choose suppliers largely on the basis of price. Manufacturers frequently shift orders between suppliers or between outsourcing and in-house production largely on the basis of price and cost-related factors. Buyers frequently engage in multiple sourcing in order to keep prices low through competition. Quality

---

[51] *Ibid.*, p. 43
[52] *Ibid.*, p. 44

is seen as a second criterion, and a trade-off between quality and price is often perceived to exist.

As manufacturers switch to flexible techniques and just-in-time inventory-management systems, relations with suppliers are changing. *Quality and reliability are becoming more important determinants* in the choice of a supplier. In addition, the more widespread use of electronics and new materials has raised the technical sophistication of components and encouraged the development of modular designs. Manufacturers and suppliers need to develop close and ongoing relationships *that emphasis on long-term contractual relationships and less reliance upon price as the single determinant of the choice of supplier.*[53]

Dissemination of New Production and Organisation Methods

The technological and organisational changes described above are beginning to have significant impact in industries outside of the electronics complex. The spread of information-based automation technologies began in the late 1970s as CAD system, CNC machine tools and industrial robots began to enter the market at competitive prices. While these stand-alone technologies represent the most common form of manufacturing automation, the focus of the innovative effort of suppliers and users has shifted increasingly to achieving integration across a number of separate systems. And *the growing use of automated technologies has often gone hand-in-hand with the adaptation of the new organisational methods.*

While the potential benefits from integrated automation are real, the difficulties of achieving such benefits in practice can be quite substantial. One difficulty is that the technology is still under development and each application may involve new problems, especially in large organisations with long-established procedures. Greater decentralisation approaches require changes that are sometimes difficult for managers to make, since the new emphasis is on co-operation rather than the exercise of authority. The potential gains in productivity, however, are so significant that the new methods are spreading rapidly throughout the economies of the industrialised countries.[54]

The rapid introduction of IT and the still-to be exploited advances in biotechnology and new materials could lead to a long-term step-up of world economic growth. At present, however, the potential for economic growth that is implicit in those technological breakthroughs is not being realised. Moreover, *unless deliberate efforts are made by policy-makers at the national and international levels, the fruits of these advances could be concentrated among the developed market economies and might fail to spread*

---

[53] *Ibid.,* p. 44
[54] *Ibid.,* p. 47

58

to the developing countries. Thus the new technologies carry with them great promise, but they also pose a number of yet unresolved problems.

So far, IT has been used to reduce production costs and raise the quality and reliability of final output. Capital-output ratios and labour productivity have risen in a wide range of industries and in several countries. Unfortunately, the dissemination of IT has not yet led to a visible increase in the rate of economic growth. Many developed market economies are still following basically anti-inflationary policies, while growth in developing countries has been hampered by the debt crisis and by generally unfavourable external environment. In the world in economic context, the widespread adaptation of IT has contributed more to unemployment than growth.[55]

THE GROWING IMPORTANCE OF SERVICE

The other major change characterising the last two decades takes place in the *internationalisation of services*, the increasing trans-nationalisation of service corporations and especially *the internationalisation of finance markets.*

The globalisation and internationalisation of industrial activity through trade, production and foreign direct investment (FDI) required an increasing reliance on supporting service in trade, finance, accounting, advertising etc.,[56] a reason why many services affiliated were established by industrial corporations. While the internationalisation of service production by MNCs lagged behind that of the industrial sector until the early 1970s, it has been expanding more rapidly over the past 30 years or so. A good part of this process appears to have been the result of service MNCs following industrial MNCs abroad, as the greater part of growth in services FDI has been in intermediate rather final consumer service. In the process, service MNCs gained experience and discovered the advantages of operating internationally, which they built upon to penetrate new markets. The reasons for the growing importance of services and their globalisation are related to those factors which have resulted in the share of service in GDP's increasing over the past decade or so in virtually all developed market economies and developing countries. By the mid-1980s, the services sector accounted for more than half of the GNP of all developed market economies, and it was the single largest sector in most developing countries.[57]

---

[55] *Ibid.,* p. 47

[56] These activities include such important areas as trade, transport, communications, finance institutions, insurance, real estate, business services (including legal services, accounting and auditing; date processing, advertising, credit renting agencies, business management and consulting services), social and related services (including education services; research and scientific institutions; medical services, recreation and cultural services), public administration.

[57] *Ibid.,* p. 365

The growth of the share of services in GDP and employment reflects a combination of both demand and supply-led forces.[58] These include:

1. The increasing role of intermediate or producer services in the valueadded process. Advances in technology, in particular, have helped firms to incorporate new data-based services within their own structures and to diversify the services they are able to offer to their customers.

2. The growth of per capita output and the high income elasticity of demand for at least some discretionary consumer services (particularly in industrialised countries).

3. The increasing tendency of firms in non-service industries to externalise certain service activities (for example, accounting, transport, business consultancy).

4. The growing importance of marketing, distribution and after-sales maintenance and servicing activities in relation to the value of a physical product (for example, a copying machine, an aircraft, a power station).

5. The increasing role of the state in providing or encouraging the production of intermediate services (for example, education and telecommunication), final services directly related to governance (for example, civil service, tax collection, social security).

6. The growth of finance, banking, legal, insurance, transport and other support services necessary for the efficient functioning of modern society.

7. The emergence of new intermediate markets for services (for example, the Euromarket, reinsurance, securitisation, new forms of data transmission).[59]

The number of reasons, services play an important role in the economic development of any country:

- *Infrastructure*. Services such as transportation, communication, banking, education, health and utilities are part of a country's basic infrastructure. The possession of many of these services is a prerequisite for economic development.
- *Inter-linkages*, especially through producer services providing intermediate inputs into the production of goods or other services. Some of the services already mentioned under the heading "infrastructure" fall into this category as well. Also important are such services as insurance, trading, data services, accounting, R & D, engineering, construction, legal services and advertising, all of which provide important intermediate inputs as producer services. Their availability and sophistication affect economic competitiveness through interaction with industrial activities and other services.
- *Strategic significance* for the economy. Some services, such as banking and finance, in general, are considered by many countries as being central to eco-

---

[58] *Ibid.*, p. 365
[59] *Ibid.*, p. 365

nomic growth and development. Without controlling such an instrument of macroeconomic policies, these countries feel handicapped in the management of their economies.

- *Structural adjustment.* In a number of countries, especially those that are competitive in international transactions, service industries are considered as one of the prime source of growth and structural adjustment to replace declining industries.
- *Socio-cultural impact.* Services such as the mass media, advertising, education, publishing, and tourism have a socio-cultural dimension through which attitudes, behavioural patterns and consumption patterns are influenced.[60]

Many services belong to several of those categories, but what most of them have in common is that they serve important functions in any economy, at whatever level of development. Their efficient provision, domestically or internationally, ought to be, therefore, a matter of considerable concern.

In the process of globalisation and internationalisation of services the finance and trade-related services (banking, insurance and other financial services and wholesale and retail trade and marketing) play the leading role. The 1980s have been characterised by a significant expansion of FDI in services, accounting for about 40 percent of the world's stock of FDI and 50 percent of annual FDI flows.[61] Finance-and trade-related services have been the most dynamic and important determinants of change in the sectoral composition of FDI.

The Trans-nationalisation of Banking

The internationalisation of financial markets has been one of the most dramatic economic developments of the 1980s. It has come about largely through the deregulation of national financial markets, and, thanks partly to numerous innovations in financial instruments, and it has mainly taken place in the form of huge expansion in securities markets. Those securities markets have become the main channel through which funds flow from lenders to borrowers, overshadowing the syndicated bank lending that dominated international financial transactions in the past. Partially supplanted in their role as intermediaries, as well as being restrained by the large developing-country dept that they hold, the transnational banks have shifted the emphasis from their deposit-taking and credit-supplying functions to be fee-generating and underwriting activities more akin to those of investment banks and brokerage houses.[62]

The internationalisation of financial markets and diversification of financial instruments should, in principle, have brought net benefits to the international

---

[60] *Ibid.*, p. 367
[61] *Ibid.*, p. 367
[62] *Ibid.*, p. 93

economy by improving the availability mechanisms for the allocation of financial resources and by lowering the costs of borrowing. At the same time, however, they have given rise to fresh concerns about the vulnerability of economies to financial market disturbances and about the world-wide growth of speculative activities.

The scale of international financial activity has been increasing strongly since the 1960s. One measure of its growth is that, during the period between 1972 and 1985, the funds raised in international financial markets grew at an annual rate of some 23 percent. This far outreached the growth in the value of world trade, which rose annually over the same period by some 13 percent. Without doubt, the pace of internationalisation of financial markets acquired a powerful new momentum in the 1980s. This has been closely linked to the emergence of the international securities market as the principal medium for cross-border acquisition of financial firms in the leading industrial countries over recent years.[63]

In the years immediately after the Second World War, there was little that could be called a financial world market. Even national markets were highly segmented, each separate market being serviced by different types of financial institutions – such as banks, brokerage houses or investment specialisation. Financial regulations, which were particularly detailed for the banks, reinforced the segmentation of markets. Together with exchange controls, these regulations ensured governments a large degree of control over both domestic and foreign financial activities

It was in the 1960s, when the Eurocurrency market came into being, that the first movement toward the internationalisation of financial markets occurred. This market flourishes, it my be noted, not because of any policy decision by governments, but because MNCs have been able to earn more on their liquid assets in an unregulated international market than they could through repatriation of those assets for investment within the regulatory and fiscal framework of their home countries. In more recent years, the MNCs and other non-bank financial institutions have been similarly motivated to enlarge their foreign activities.

The internationalisation of financial markets received fresh impetus in the 1970s from two sources. First, the oil-exporting countries emerged from the price increases of 1973–1974 with huge surplus savings, which they sought to lend abroad; and much was recycled by the multinational banks (MNBs) to the deficit developing countries. Secondly, in the mid-1970s, the Federal Republic of Germany and the United States dismantled their exchange controls on capital movements, and they were followed, towards the end of the decade, by Japan and the United Kingdom.[64]

The events of the 1970s catapulted the MNBs into prominence as institutions dominating the world financial market; but with the advent of debt crises in 1982,

---

[63] *Ibid.*, p. 102
[64] *Ibid.*, p. 103

their pre-dominance as suppliers of international finance began to wane. This was partly because the flows of the private loan capital through the banks to the developing countries dropped to a trickle. But it was also the dismantling of exchange controls on capital movements and other financial deregulation that led to a large and vigorous growth in the international securities market, mainly among the developed market economies. The growth continues today, and the market now far outreaches bank inter-mediation as the principle medium for the lending and borrowing of international loan capital. The banks, however, have been active participants in the booming market, not in their former role as intermediary borrowers and lenders, but as agents facilitating direct lending and borrowing among others.[65]

Besides this broad change in economic circumstances, *three specific changes of technical or institutional characteristics have been at work altering the scale and the character of international financial market. These are the advances in computer and telecommunications technology, the trend towards abandonment of many financial regulations and the introduction of a range of new financial instruments on the securities markets.*

The New Telecommunication and Computer Technologies in the Financial Markets

The world of finance has been fundamentally changed by technology. More than in any other areas of activity, the growth of international communications, the development of the data-processing capability of the big computer and the personal desktop facility, and the arrival of the wired society have revolutionised the way in which finance is transacted. As a result, since 1994, the real cost of recording, transmitting and processing information (including financial information) has fallen by more than 95 percent. This tremendous cost reduction makes it cheaper to assess the risks and rewards of financial assets, cheaper to record and process trades, cheaper to manage portfolios and cheaper to match users with suppliers of capital.

The development of satellite communication systems has been especially important to the development of international financial markets. In the mid-1980s, 50 percent of all international financial transactions were made by satellite-linked telephone calls. Financial services firms are probably the heaviest users of telecommunications systems. The major effects of the information technologies on financial services are the following:

1. They have vastly increased productivity in financial services.
2. They have altered the patterns of relationships or linkages both within financial firms and also between financial firms and their clients.

---

[65] *Ibid.*, p. 103

3. They have greatly increased the velocity, or turnover, of investment capital. For example, the ability to transfer funds electronically – and, therefore, instantaneously – has saved billion of dollars in interest payments which were formerly incurred by the delay in making a transfer.

4. At the international scale, they have enabled financial institutions both to increase their loan activities and also to respond immediately to fluctuations in exchange rates in international currency markets.[66]

The new telecommunications and computer technologies have been transforming financial markets by making the international enlargement and integration of markets possible on a scale that was previously unthinkable. These technologies have been breaking down the barriers between geographically dispersed markets that are thrown up by time-lags in flows of information about current transactions. The "information revolution" has also been proved to be an important spur for securitisation markets. It reduces the need for a direct relationship between borrower and lender, and the systematic treatment of large amounts of data on the creditworthiness of individual firms makes it possible for more borrowers to enter the market. In addition, the new technologies have ensured the means for processing a much larger volume of financial transactions at low cost.[67]

Those developments have given rise to virtually instantaneous world-wide trading in some markets. Financial exchanges have linked themselves together electronically, and they have been cross-listing securities or contracts so that these instruments can be traded around the clock in one or another exchange. From a technological viewpoint, therefore, it is possible for financial services firms to engage in global twenty-four-hour-a-day trading, whether this be in securities, foreign exchange, financial and commodities futures or any other financial service. The ability to transmit data electronically over vast geographical distances creates the potential for continuous financial transactions world-wide, at whatever time of the day or night. Figure 4 shows the way in which the trading hours of the world's financial centres overlap. True twenty-four-hour trading is currently limited to certain kinds of transactions, partly because, although the technology is available, either the organisational structure or the national regulatory environment remains an obstacle. But there is no doubt at all that global twenty-four-hour trading will become a standard in virtually all kinds of financial services.

To the extent that such electronic transactions do not require the direct physical proximity between seller and buyer they are a form of an "invisible" international trade. In that sense, therefore, financial services are one form of service activity,

---

[66] *The Rules of the Game in the Global Economy Policy Regimes for International Business.* Lee E. Preston and Duane Windsor, ed. (Kluwer Academic Publishers, Boston 1991) p. 361

[67] *Transitional Corporations in World Development. Trends and Prospects,* p. 106

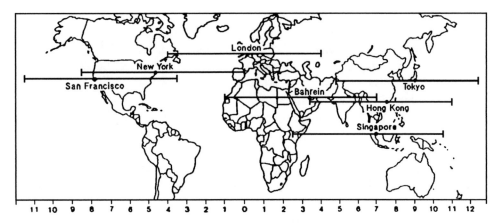

FIGURE 4. The trading hours of major world financial centres (*Source:* Walf, 1989, Fig. 5)

which is tradable. Electronic communications have also contributed greatly to the bypassing of the commercial banks and the trend towards the greater securitisation of financial transactions. Securitisation, in the broad sense, is simply the conversion of all kinds of loans and borrowings into "paper" securities which can be bought and sold on the market. Such transactions may be performed directly by buyers and sellers without necessarily going through the intermediary channels of commercial banks.[68]

However, while financial markets throughout the world are now informed almost instantaneously about changes in the prices of financial assets and other evens, this is by no means an unalloyed advantage. Recent world-wide plunges in stock market prices attest to this fact. When circumstances give rise to a fearful and panicly mood among participants in one major market, the rush to sell can spread with breathtaking rapidity to markets throughout the word. Such "globalisation of the herd" – to use a phrase of the Chancellor of the Exchequer of the United Kingdom) – is a consequence of the new technologies, which could be dangerously destabilising.[69] Shocks which occur in one geographical market now spread instantaneously around the globe. The collapse of prices on the notorious Black Monday of 19 October 1987, or the recent crises in Mexico, Asia or Russia surged immediately around all the world's stock markets. Billions of dollars blew off company stocks, and even though the world's market recovered or might recover, the incident brought home to everybody just how sensitive and volatile the global financial system can be as a consequence of the telecommunications revolution.[70]

[68] *The Rules of the Game in the Global Economy Policy Regimes for International Business*, p. 362
[69] *Transitional Corporations in World Development. Trends and Prospects*, p. 106
[70] *The Rules of the Game in the Global Economy Policy Regimes for International Business*, p. 362

The influence of telecommunications technologies on the speed and geographical extent of financial transactions between seller and buyers of financial services is one expression of the effect of technological change on the financial services industries. Another one is the effect of information technology on the internal operation of financial service firms. For example, banks and insurance companies were among the earliest adopters of computer technology to automate the internal processing of financial transactions; the so-called "back-office" functions that are otherwise highly labour-intensive. Subsequently, computerisation and related technologies were applied to the firm's "front office": to direct interface between firms and their customers. In retail banking, for example, counter clerks or tellers now invariably operate on-line computer terminals; automated teller machine and cash dispensers have become the norm, giving customers access to certain services outside normal banking hours; home banking by computer terminal has been introduced, too.

The equivalent of such services for the large corporate customers is the development of electronic cash management systems in which the corporate customer's computers are linked directly to the bank. In their most sophisticated version, these electronic cash management systems provide corporate treasurers with up-to-date account-by-account balance information and give them control over the transfer of funds among the company's accounts. This allows ... [corporate] ... treasurers to invest their cash flow into money market instruments and to optimise their use of funds in a world economy that has become characterised by greater volatility in interest, inflation and ... exchange rates.[71]

Deregulation of the Financial Markets

The internalisation of financial markets – along with the breaking down of segmented markets within national economies – owes a good deal to the progressive deregulation of financial activities. Though deregulation is consistent with the market-oriented approach of present governments in most market economies.[72]

As interest rates paid by banks on deposit or savings accounts were regulated, funds were quickly drained away into unregulated markets, threatening the liquidity of those institutions. The authorities consequently were obliged to eliminate interest ceilings.

Exchange controls intended to regulate capital movement have likewise been abandoned in most developed countries, partly because their effectiveness in the face of the growth in volume of permitted international finance transactions has been diminishing.

---

[71] *Ibid.,* p. 363
[72] *Transitional Corporations in World Development. Trends and Prospects,* p. 106

Another circumstance generating pressures for deregulation has been the inten-sification of competition among financial enterprises. The different types of finan-cial institutions have been moving outside their long established and specialised markets, diversifying the range of their financial activities. The banks, however, have often found themselves at a particular disadvantage in this competitive strug-gle, because their activities are subject to more regulatory restrictions; the conse-quent anomalies have been persuading the authorities to modify those restrictions. A case in point is the exclusive banks in the United States and Japan (though not, for example, in Germany and the United Kingdom) from the business of underwriting securities.[73] Brokerage houses, by contrast, have been free to engage in some forms of business traditionally considered to be the province of banks.

The migration of financial business abroad has long been a way for both banks and non-bank institutions to escape domestic financial and fiscal restrictions. It was a powerful stimulus to the emergence of the Eurocurrency market and it similarly lay behind the growth of the offshore banking centres. In more recent years, MNBs have been active in establishing or acquiring subsidiaries in other leading financial centres so that they can engage in activities, such as dealing in securities, from which they are excluded at home. However, as the volume of business transacted outside national borders has grown over the years, the regulatory authorities have increas-ingly sough to modify regulations in order to allow the business to be conducted at home. An important step was taken by the United States in this direction, for exam-ple, when it authorised banks to accept deposits from and make loans to foreign entities much as though they were operating as offshore branches through the me-dium of the international banking facilities. In December 1986, Japan also author-ised the opening of international banking facilities.[74]

Forces have also been at work to lower barriers to the operation of foreign enti-ties in the leading financial centres. As liberalisation has granted access to foreign entities in some countries, their establishment has generated demands for recipro-cal access in the home country of the foreign entities. The governments of Western Europe and the United States pressured Japan to improve access to its more highly regulated market. Some countries have also opened up access to previously shel-tered markets in the hope of attracting more international business and of enhanc-ing their competitiveness through their increased scale of operations. The "Big Bang" in London, for example, opened up membership of its Stock Exchange to a larger number of foreign firms, and the "Little Bang" in Paris made membership available to foreign firms and to both domestic and foreign banks.[75]

---

[73] *Ibid.*, p. 106
[74] *Ibid.*, p. 106
[75] *Ibid.*, p. 107

Innovations in Financial Instruments

Innovations in telecommunications and in process technologies have helped to transform the operations of financial services firms. But there has also been a variety of product innovations. In this sense, the number of financial markets has proliferated in the 1970s and 1980s, as "financial engineering" (the invention of new financial instruments) has become an important "art form"of the late twentieth century; markets like those in options and futures (which trade in forward contracts in commodities, money and share) and equities (which trade in stocks and shares) have taken their place alongside the Eurodollar and Eurobond markets as important global markets.

A whole new array of financial instruments has appeared on the scene which can be categorised and those which facilitate greater spreading of risk. Table 4 provides some insight of these innovations.[76]

TABLE 4. Product innovations in financial markets

Type of financial instrument	Basic characteristics
Floating-rate notes (FRNs)	Medium to long-term securities with interest rates adjusted from time to time in accordance with an agreed reference rate, e.g. the London Inter-Bank Offered Rate (LIBOR) or the New York bank's prime rate.
Note issuance facilities (NIFs)	Short- to medium-term issues of paper which allow borrowers to raise loans on a revolving basis directly on the securities market or with a group of underwriting banks.
Eurocommercial paper	Non-underwritten notes sold in London for same-day settlement in U.S. dollars in New York. More flexible than longer-term Euronotes of 1, 3 or 6 months' duration.
Loan sales	The sale of a loan to a third party with or without the knowledge of the original borrower.
Interest-rate swaps	A contract between two borrowers to exchange interest rate liabilities on a particular loan, e.g. the exchange of fixed-rate and floating-rate interest liabilities.
Currency swaps	Financial transactions in which the principal denominations are in different currencies.

Source: based on UNCTC (1988), Box VIL2; Lewis and Davis (1987), pp. 415–431.

Financial innovations have been another set of changes heightening the attractiveness of the international financial market. While aided by deregulation, these innovations have been sparked by market competition or have been devised in response to broader changes in economic and financial conditions. There have been two main

---

[76] *The Rules of the Game in the Global Economy Policy Regimes for International Business*, p. 363

kinds of new financial instruments – those offering a new way of lending and borrowing and those allowing a greater spreading of risks.[77]

The introduction of short-term notes has done much to broaden the international securities market in recent years. Note issuance facilities (NIFs) were of particular importance in launching this innovation. By use of these facilities, borrowers have been able to raise loans on a revolving basis directly on the securities market, an alternative, which has proved cheaper than syndicated bank loans. The facilities are provided by banks, which undertake the placement of note issues and accept a contingent obligation to lend to a borrower the balance of any issue not taken up by the market either initially or on refinancing. In the last years, NIFs have been overtaken in popularity by Euro-commercial paper, with which the banks restrict their obligation to making their "best efforts" to place the issue. There are several other new instruments, mostly variants on the same theme of replacing bank credit with securitised loans.

The new instruments allowing a greater spreading of risks include interest rate and currency swaps, options and futures. In the present-day world of unstable exchange rates and variable interest rates, those instruments should, in principle, contribute towards the strengthening of the international financial market. By creating additional markets in specific risks, they have made it possible for both lenders and borrowers to hedge against the risk attaching to specific loans. The greater spreading of risks among market participants has, it should be noted, been made easier by the growth in securitised loans, since it allows the "unbundling" of risks associated with the loans.[78]

The new technologies, deregulation and the new financial instruments have greatly enlarged the international financial market in recent years and the expansion has occurred through the rapid growth in the securities market. Syndicated bank loans, which had amounted to 60 to 70 percent of international financial transactions in the early 1980s, accounted for only 16 percent in 1985 and 1986. A general explanation is the shift in the pattern of net international private lending that took place from the 1970s to 1980s. Unlike the 1970s, both gross and net lending in the 1980s have been overwhelmingly dominated by financial transactions among the developed market economies. But there have also been more specific reasons why borrowing and lending through the banks has suffered such a relative decline.

The MNBs have been at a disadvantage in competing as lenders with the international securities market. With large doubtful debts in their portfolios, the banks have been less able to attract deposits cheaply, and the insistence by bank supervisors that the banks conform to more stringent conditions has also raised their costs. The relative cost of syndicated loans has, accordingly, increased. But the banks have

---

[77] *Transitional Corporations in World Development. Trends and Prospects*, p. 107
[78] *Ibid.*, p. 112

also had a positive interest in promoting securitised lending. After the onset of the debt crisis, the main concern of bank supervisors was to urge the banks to strengthen their financial positions by raising their capital-to-assets ratio. The banks have thus had an incentive to limit the growth of their balance-sheet assets and seek ways of generating income through off-balance-sheet activities. Participation instrument as note-issuance facilities or stand-by letters of credit have admirably suited this purpose; such business has generated income and not added to assets, giving rise to only a contingent obligation. The new instruments, moreover, have helped the banks to improve their balance sheets themselves. The banks have been making use of such new borrowing facilities to lengthen the maturity of their liabilities, and they have sought to improve their liquidity by designing assets which could be more ready traded on the market. Further, such hedging instruments as interest and currency swaps have extensively been exploited by the banks to spread their risk. With such changes under way, the long familiar distinction between the deposit-acceptance and loan-creation activities of the commercial bank, on the one hand, and the fee-generating and underwriting activities of the securities firms and investment banks, on the other hand, has become decidedly blurred.[79]

Lending and borrowing through securities markets now dominates international financial transactions. MNBs are important participants in those markets, they back note issues on the part of others through such devices as note-issuance facilities and stand-by letters of credit; and outside Japan and the United States, banks can also be important underwriters of securities. None the less, a large proportion of international financial business now bypasses the banks altogether. There are the non-bank financial entities that have been leading institutions servicing the growing securities markets. The operations of those entities, however, are systematically reported and they have usually been subject to less stringent regulatory surveillance. Indeed, in view of the much enlarged scale of operations of the non-bank financial entities, the enhanced international linkages among markets and institutions, and the blurring of the distinction between banking and non-banking business, many concerns have been expressed in recent years about the adequacy of current regulatory structures.

While nearly every kind of non-bank financial firm, as well as some non-financial entities, has become involved in international finance, the most important ones have been securities and financial services firms. Those are firms engaged in stock-brokerage (including research and margin lending), investment portfolio management, and investment banking (underwriting and assistance in mergers and acquisitions). A great deal of the activity is similar to traditional banking in that it earns income from the difference between rates charged and rate paid, as, for example, in margin lending, provision of money-market accountings or arbitrage. But

---

[79] *Ibid.*, p. 112

many are also involved in risk-taking like in trading positions or underwriting new issues.[80]

A key activity of securities firms is their ability to reduce the cost to clients of raising funds on the market. This requires size, a large sales force, a diversified client base and relative freedom from regulations, all of which reduce the risk of not being able to distribute an issue. The dominance of U.S. firms can be explained by a large volume of securities business that normally takes place in the United States, together with the high degree of regulatory tolerance of securities industry in that country. The prominence of the Japanese firms stems from the large pool of funds available for placement abroad and an aggressive strategy of acquiring securities firms abroad as a means of escaping domestic regulations, which separate banking from securities underwriting and placement.

Most of the international financing that these firms service is in the form of Eurobonds. Those are bonds denominated in currencies other than the currency of the country in which the bonds are issued. The bulk is denominated in dollars and is transacted in London. Fifty firms account for most of the Eurobond finance world-wide, the top eight accounting for over half. Non-bank securities firms are prominent, though not dominant, in the arrangement of note issuance facilities and share the market with MNBs in placing Euro-commercial paper.

The transactional role of those firms has partly been an outcome of the difference among countries in fiscal and financial regulations relating to domestic and external transactions. Like the banks, whose main motive for trans-nationalisation in the 1960s and 1970s was to escape regulations, the securities markets have been subject to similar influences.[81]

The rapid growth of FDI in finance-related services is, first and foremost, a reflection of the world-wide expansion of transnational banking networks. That banks expanded mainly during the 1970s and had established almost 5000 offices abroad by 1980 – practically the same number as in 1985.[82] But scarcely less significant is the proliferation of finance-related affiliates established by non-financial corporations especially in the trading, manufacturing and petroleum industries. The principle task of these affiliates is to improve the efficiency of the financial management of their corporate systems by such means as facilitating the flow of funds among the various entities of corporate system; investing surplus funds as profitably as possible; raising funds locally; utilising optimally the facilities offered by tax havens. Insurance MNCs also establish finance affiliates in major finance centres.

---

[80] *Ibid.*, p. 118
[81] *Ibid.*, p. 119
[82] *Ibid.*, p. 382

Independent transnational trading corporations, firms that basically market the products of unrelated companies or purchase inputs from various sources, belong to the oldest types of MNCs. But important are also foreign trade establishments, which are affiliated with industrial companies and specialise in the marketing of the final products of their parent companies.

Among the independent transnational trading corporations, four different types, each with a specific historical background and a clear specialisation, have evolved:[83]

- *Agency houses.* Independent agency houses are the oldest type of transnational trading corporations, most of which are of Western European origin and were established before the Second World War. Their affiliates specialise in the import and distribution of final goods and services from non-principals in developed countries.

- *General trading companies.* The nine Japanese general trading companies (sogo shosha) are the prototype for this category. They are the world's largest and most diversified trading companies in terms of products, markets and functions. During the year ending March 1986, they handled approximately 8 percent of the world trade, in addition to a large share of Japan's domestic trade.

- *Commodity traders.* The market structure of international commodity trade has given rise to a type of transnational trading corporation specialising in one or more commodities. They are found in those markets which are not dominated by vertically integrated MNCs and where neither producers and nor final consumers are in a position to establish their own international marketing or procurement systems. They are particularly prominent in the international trade of agricultural commodities such as grains, sugar, coffee, cocoa and cotton.

- *Retailers and buying agents.* Retail chains undertake two types of transnational activities. One consists of the expansion of retailing units abroad, and the other of the establishment of a network of foreign buying offices or agents to supply the chains. The largest transnational retail chains are mostly of Western European and United States origin. They operate mainly in each other's territory, although they are also present in developing countries.

At the same time, buying offices of large retail chains in developed market economies have emerged over the past two decades as new, vertically integrated marketing channels for final product exported from developing countries. Retailing companies, such as Sears Roebuck & Co., May Department Stores or Quelle, maintain affiliates buying offices in numerous countries. Increasingly, such buying agents also produce goods and services for third parties. The major function of buying agents is to identify low-cost producers, to provide them with samples and to control quality. In fact, the specifications to which those agents buy are often so com-

---

[83] *Ibid.*, p. 384

prehensive that they buy production capacity rather than products. While garments continue to be the most important product group for buying offices, various other products (such as leather articles, kitchen and giftware and electronic consumer goods) have become important lines for buying agents.

The share of buying agents in the manufactured exports from developing to developed countries has been estimated at as much as 20 percent. These new trading channels play an important role in transmitting soft technology, such as product design, quality control and packaging techniques, to producers in the host countries.

Apart from those various types of independent transnational trading companies, many parent corporations have established marketing affiliates abroad, primarily to distribute their goods and services. In the case of industrial companies, these affiliates are normally mere conduits through which final products are distributed. In case of service firms, the distinction between distribution and producing affiliates is often difficult to make because the nature of service normally requires that services be produced where they are consumed. However, the increased use of trans-border dataflows is likely to lead a service-specific brand of distribution affiliates, that is, affiliates which become more and less conduits through which services produced elsewhere distributed in host countries.

Downstream integration into distribution and marketing activities has been a widely embraced strategy for large manufacturers producing differentiated and marketing-intensive products, in order to internalise transaction costs and advantages arising from the producer-specific knowledge of their products. Trade-mark and brand-name considerations, as well as the growing importance of global market strategies, have become a major investment determinant for the establishment of marketing affiliates. This trend has been fostered by the fact that trade marks and brand names are normally granted for an indefinite period – in contrast to patents and copyrights. In industries such as petroleum, chemicals, office equipment and computers, pharmaceuticals, and food and beverages, the MNCs have established their global network of marketing affiliates.[84]

---

[84] *Ibid.*, p. 386

MULTINATIONAL CORPORATION

The main driving forces and the prime mover of globalisation and its accompanying devel-opments are the MNCs. These corporations are perhaps the most important actors in the world economy. They are certainly the dominant forces in the world economy. Their activities encircle the globe and penetrate its remotest sites. The ability of these huge companies to re-deploy assets and technology on a global basis to become manufacturing, servicing capacity and to develop global markets, has become one of the most important characteristics of the contemporary international scene. They straddle national boundaries, and the biggest MNCs have sales which exceed the aggregate output of most countries.[1]

Of the 100 largest economic units in the world today, half are nation-states and the other half MNCs.[2] The foreign content of output, assets and employment in many of them is large, in some instance ranging from 50 percent to over 90 percent. All told, adding their home-country output and their production abroad, they account for a significant proportion of total world output. It is estimated, for example, that the largest 600 industrial companies account for between one-fifth and one-fourth of value added in the production of goods in the world's market economies.[3] Sales and assets of MNCs are growing faster than world GDP, exports and gross fixed capital formation. About 44,000 MNCs with 280,000 foreign affiliates are active today. (In 1970 their number was 7,000, in 1992 35,000 with 170,000 foreign affiliates.)[4] Within that number, power is indeed concentrated: the UN thinks that the largest 100 multinationals, excluding those in banking and finance, accounted for $3.1 trillion of world wide assets in 1990, of which $1.2 trillion was outside firms' respective home countries.

The top 100 multinational probably account for about 40–50 percent of all cross-border assets.[5] The growth of their international production reflects rapid changes

---

[1] *Transitional Corporations in World Development. Trends and Prospects* (United Nations, New York, 1988) p. 106

[2] Peter Dicken, *Global Shift* (Paul Chapman Publishing Ltd., 1982) p. 16

[3] *Transitional Corporations in World Development. Trends and Prospects*, p. 106

[4] *World Investment Report. 1997. Transitional Corporations, Market Structure and Competition Policy* (United Nations, New York, 1997) p. 5

[5] Multinationals. *The Economist*, March 27th 1993, p. 17

in their corporate structure and is being pursued through a wide variety of equity and non-equity link ups and investment channels.

Their importance as exporters and importers is also great. For example, between 80 and 90 percent of the exports of both the United States of America and the United Kingdom of Great Britain and Northern Ireland is associated with MNCs. MNCs also loom large in international capital flows. Multinational banks (MNBs) and other non-bank financial companies account for the bulk of international lending. Moreover, owing to transnational character of assets in several currencies and, in recent years, they have become important participants in world financial markets. And, of course, MNCs are responsible for the vast majority of foreign direct investment (FDI) abroad in addition to production and service.[6] The largest MNCs control the bulk of FDI in many major home countries: in most of the countries for which data are available, the top outward investors control a half of the outward FDI. For smaller countries the share controlled by the to MNCs may be over 70 percent.[7]

The largest 56 MNCs have sales ranging between $10 billion and $100 billion. This does not mean that the universe of multinational corporations is confined to very large corporations. In fact, most MNCs are medium-size companies, with typical sales running well below $1 billion. While the vast majority of MNCs are based in developed market economies, a new phenomenon that has received considerable attention in recent years has been growing the importance of corporations from developing countries as foreign investors. Most of these companies are relatively small, although 33 of them have sales of $1 billion or more.[8]

The United States industry abroad has become the third largest economy in the world, foreign production of American firms has grown twice as fast as domestic economies. MNCs are rapidly increasing their shares of the world's business. The number of MNCs has grown at least sixfold in the last 20 years; their control over cross-border assets has risen alongside; almost half of the world trade is now conducted by firms that can be considered as MNCs; proportion of trade that takes place within companies rather than at arms' length has risen, probably to as much as a third of all trade. Already some people are asserting that not more than 300 MNCs will control 90 percent of the world trade by the end of the century.[9]

---

[6] *Transitional Corporations in World Development. Trends and Prospects*, p. 16

[7] *World Investment Report. 1997*, p. 28

[8] *Transitional Corporations in World Development. Trends and Prospects*, p. 16

[9] *The Multinational Enterprise in Transition*. A. Kapoor and P. D. Grub, ed. (The Darwin Press, Princeton, 1972) p. 3

MULTINATIONAL CORPORATION DEFINED

The term "multinational company" applies to a variety of definitions extending from a company with production located in two or more countries, to a more restrictive definition of a management philosophy, which is "outward-looking" with international awareness. Understanding of the term has further been complicated by additional descriptions from trans-national (used by United Nations) to more loosely called international company, which may have a large part of its earnings from exports or related activities.

The OECD in its Guidelines for Multinational Enterprises also does not give a rigid definition, but it broadly describes present-day multinationals as:

- companies or entities whose ownership is private, state or mixed, established in different countries and so linked that one or more of them may be able to exercise a significant influence over the activities of others and, in particular, to share knowledge and resources with others.

Different schools also have used different attributes to characterise the MNCs. Such attributions include the geographic scope of the firms's value chain (that is, the sequence of value-adding activities or functions within the firms), management styles, ownership of productive assets, commonality of strategy formulation and implementation world-wide, and organisation structure:[10]

- A distinction is made between "global" and "multidomestic" MNCs, based on co-ordination and geographic configuration of the firms' value chain. MNCs with high co-ordination among and concentrated configuration of the different parts of the value chain are called "global", while those with low co-ordination among and dispersed configuration of the different parts of the value chain are called "multidomestic."
- A distinction is made on the basis of management styles in the MNCs – geocentric (world oriented), polycentric (host-country oriented), or ethnocentric (home-country-oriented). A firm's true degree of multinationality is measured by the extent to which its executives think geocentrically.
- The MNCs is defined as an organisation that owns productive assets in different countries, and has common strategy formulation and implementation across borders.
- The MNC is defined as any firm that "owns" outputs of goods and services originating in more than one country.
- A distinction is made based on organisation structure: "global" (tightly controlled with a centralised hub structure), "multinational" (decentralised fed-

---

[10] Anant K. Sundaram and J. Steward Black, *The International Business Environment* (Prentice-Hall, New Jersey, 1995) p. 2

eration), and "transitional" (structures that permit retaining local flexibility while simultaneously achieving global integration).

At one extreme are MNCs that are "global", which are primarily national corporations with tightly controlled foreign operations, characterised by ethnocentric management styles, high co-ordination among (and concentrated configuration of) the various elements of the firms's value chain, organisational structures like a centralised hub, and a common set of strategies world-wide. At the other extreme are MNCs that are "multidomestic". They are characterised by polycentric management styles, low co-ordination among and dispersed configuration of the various elements of the value chain, decentralised organisation structures that operate as loose federations, and a diverse and perhaps uncoordinated set of strategies worldwide.

In between are the more complex MNCs that might be called "transitional", which variously combine attributes that characterise the previous two forms. Such MNCs might be characterised as complex global or networks of subsidiaries performing different functions. Such manifestations would be consistent with a geocentric management style, and there is a growing recognition that MNC organisation forms are taking this direction. The reasons for this include decreasing costs of worldwide co-ordination, decreasing importance of the need for concentrated configuration of the firm's value chain, and the necessity of managing the imperatives of global integration, local responsiveness, and diffusion of innovations simultaneously.[11]

Regardless of the particular MNC organisation form, there are certain common themes that emerge from the various definitions:

- they are those of an entity which, viewed from the "home" (parent) perspective, sells and/or produces in at least one other sovereign "host" (subsidiary) country where the nature and extent of multinationality may be divided further to include certain specific attribute.

The crucial thing to note is that attributes of specific interest – whether it be output, sales, investment, management styles, organisational structure, co-ordination and configuration, or commonality of strategy formation and implementation – manifest themselves across sovereign boundaries. Using these insights, the MNCs can be defined as: any enterprise that carries out transactions in or between two sovereign entities, operating under a system of decision-making permitting influence over resources and capabilities, where the transactions are subject to influence by factors exogenous to the home country environment of the enterprise.[12]

This definition is not only inclusive of past definitions, but it contains features that describe both the environment in which the MNC operates (features that derive from the common attribute that transactions span sovereign boundaries) and

---

[11] *Ibid.*, p. 3
[12] *Ibid.*, p. 3

its internal organisation (features that depend on the system of decision-making) and influence over resources and capabilities. This definition is also similar to the following one that expresses the very essence of modern MNC:

- MNC is a type of corporation that owns and manages business in two or more countries, which is an agency of direct, as opposed to portfolio, investment in foreign countries, holding and managing the underlying physical assets rather than securities based upon those assets; this type of enterprise confronts the problems of designing, producing, marketing, and financing its products and services within foreign nation and makes a substantial direct investment in foreign countries' assets, entail a responsibility for managing organisations of people in alien societies.[13]

The phrases used in the definitions above are inclusive rather than exclusive. The notion of "enterprise" is broad enough to include all organisational forms from unitary organisations to the more fluid network relationships. "Transactions" is broad enough to encompass the exchange across borders of people, products, capital, technology, and so forth. The notion of "sovereign" is inherent to the etymology of the word "multinational". The fundamental element of the MNC is the obvious idea that relevant transactions taking place both within and outside the firm are conducted across national boundaries. "System of decision-making permitting influence" refers to the firm's ability to co-ordinate and control organisational variables (for example, resources, subsidiaries, managers) and market variables (buyers, supplier, competitors). "Subject to influence by factors" refers to the effect of exogenous or environmental variables on transactions (for example, exchange rate, political and regulatory systems, cultures, tariff and taxation system).[14]

The pervasive feature that affects almost any transaction undertaken by the MNC is the manifestation of sovereignty, or the relative authority of the sovereign state over exchange rates, politics, culture, regulation and languages. There are two specific attributes that distinguish MNCs from non-MNCs. They can be called:

- *"multiple sources of external authority" (MA)* and
- *"multiple denominations of firm's value" (MV).*

The overriding principle underlying cross-border relationships is that of sovereignty. The sovereignty of a nation-state is embodied in its authority to influence events within its legal territory, and its choice to be relatively immune to outside influences. This authority generally manifests itself in terms of laws and regulatory institutions, political institutions, official language(s), norms of behaviour, culture, and so forth. Consequently, *the MNC has exposure to multiple (and often conflicting) sources of external authority (hereafter the phrase of MA is used).*

There are three aspects of MA that merit consideration: *a)* the number of geographic locations that the firm operates in; *b)* the variance in country environments

---

[13] *The Multinational Enterprise in Transition*, p. 22

[14] Anant K. Sundaram and J. Steward Black, *The International Business Environment*, p. 4

resulting from operating in different geographic locations; *c)* the lack of a super-structure to mediate threats or opportunities that arise at the interaction of the variances in country environments. While *a)* and *b)* represent differences of degree, although substantial degree, between MNCs and non-MNCs, aspect *c)* represents a difference of kind – that is, it is a distinguished aspect of MNC, and emerges from the environment or the context in which it operates.

Clearly, the issue of geographic dispersal and scope per se (and the related problems of communication and co-ordination) is not unique to MNCs. Many large firms face these problems even within a single sovereign country. Similarly, on the question of variances in country environments, one could argue that laws, institutions, and behavioural norms can also vary within a sovereign country. In this case, however, differences among sovereign countries are likely to be a matter of greater severity but analogous to differences among regions within countries. Consequently, such differences between countries are likely to result in a substantially greater degree of environmental complexity and uncertainty for firm, but may not raise issues that are categorically different from those in a non-MNC setting.[15]

However, even through particular manifestations of external authority (for example, laws, political institutions, or cultures) may vary from region to region within the sovereign state, the existence of overarching and commonly applicable frames of reference provide a source of resources in the event of conflicts. Firms can use such frames of reference as guides for strategy development and implementation. In the cross-sovereign setting, there are no commonly applicable legal, cultural, or political mechanisms that the firm can take resource to in designing and implementing exchanges. Even if the issue of resolving conflicts arising from variances in specific country environments is manageable, the notion of sovereignty precludes the enforcement of resolutions without common agreement of all sovereign entities involved (despite the existence of treaties or global institutions to the country).

Consequently, the distinguishing feature of MNC environment arises out of the interaction of differences in country environments. In the absence of commonly applicable and enforceable institutional mechanisms, all conflicts arising from cross-border transactions at this intersection of differences in sources of external authority create both opportunities and risks that non-MNCs do not face. The opportunities and risks arise as a consequence of the lack of any superstructure or supranational institution to mediate conflicts.[16]

The second distinguishing aspect of MNCs results from the fact that there are multiple denominations, or numeraires, of firm value (hereafter it is called MV). That is, the firm's cash flows are denominated in different exchange rates. This, in turn, results in a triple effect on the MNC: *a)* "translation exposure," which is the problem of ex-post

---

[15] *Ibid.*, p. 4.
[16] *Ibid.*, p. 5.

setting up and valuation of transactions already undertaken across multiple currencies; b) "transaction exposure," which is the problem of hedging known or anticipated cash flows against future exchange rate shifts; and c) "economic exposure," which is the problem of the impact of unanticipated changes in real exchange rates on the firm's competitive position.[17]

Translation and transaction exposures are primarily manifestations of differences in denominations of value. This is similar to the issues of geographic dispersal and differences in country environments. As in the case of differences in MA, translation and transaction exposures may result in a greater degree of environmental complexity and uncertainty but are unlikely to raise strategic management issues that are substantially different from those in a non-MNC setting. The problem of translation exposure to exchange rates (and the accounting rules to deal with it) are conceptually similar to the problem of having to hedge in, say, commodities markets by non-MNCs.

However, the distinguishing aspect of the MNCs environment is the problem of economic exposure to exchange rates. As before, this problem accures at the intersection of differences in currency values: economic exposure is the consequence of breakdowns in the mechanism that works to equilibrate differences in real currency values across countries.[18]

MNCs have a long history in the capitalist market economy, but they have drawn a really exceptionally distinguished attention to themselves after the Second World War. The rise of the MNCs is often cited as one of the most powerful forces operating in the world today and is the object of considerable scholarly research. It is not accidental, that *the emergence of the MNC as a powerful agent of world social and economic change has been a signal development of the post-Second World War era.*

THEORIES OF MULTINATIONAL CORPORATION

Just as there are great variations in definitions of what constitutes a multinational, so there are many differing theories about the existence and growth of multinationals. Theories related to MNCs seek to explain why firms based in one country control production and service activities in other countries and to identify and assess the factors influencing the ability and willingness of firms to engage in foreign production activities. Much of the literature on the subject has been dealing with transnational activity in form of FDI, that is, control through equity ownership. However, it is increasingly being recognised that firms may also be engaged in foreign

---

[17] *Ibid.*, p. 6.
[18] *Ibid.*, p. 6

production by means of wide range of non-equity arrangements (e.g. management contracts, franchising), as well as co-operative alliances with foreign firms, all of which allow the non-resident partner some control over production and the use of resources.

Literature on the theory of MNCs, which has primary (though not exclusively) addressed the phenomenon of goods-producing corporations, identifies the determinants of production undertaken by MNCs outside their national boundaries as including, first, their specific advantage of ownership, or competitive capacity to supply particular products, by trade or foreign production; second, the location specific or comparative advantages of countries as sites for value-added activities; and third, the advantages of controlling and co-ordinating these advantages within the firm rather than making use of external markets, i.e. their internalisation advantages.[19]

Some writers on the subject focus exclusively on the last factor mentioned above, namely internationalisation, as the *reason d'être* for the trans-nationalisation of firms. In their view, MNCs, which are considered as a particular form of multi-activity firms, exist because market imperfection in intermediate product markets give rise to certain transaction costs, and those costs can be reduced or eliminated by undertaking the production of the goods and services concerned by themselves rather than exchanging in the market.

The dominant explanation of international production, however, is the *eclectic paradigm*. It asserts that it is the interaction between the competitive (or ownership advantages) of MNCs or potential MNCs, and the comparative or location advantages of countries that decide the structures of the foreign activities of firms. But the way in which those activities are organised (i.e. by hierarchies or markets) will depend on the extent to which internalisation advantages exist. It is further accepted that the configuration of these three advantages varies according to industry-country, and firm-specific characteristics. The last of these has more recently been recognised to include firm-specific differences in strategic behaviour. A number of economists as well as business analysts have attempted to identify and/or evaluate the significance of different strategic variables as factors influencing decisions of firms regarding the adaptation of hierarchical structures, as well as modes of entry into, or expansion in particular markets and the development of competitive advantages.[20]

The question of the applicability of the theories of international production, and the eclectic paradigm in particular, to services as a group has received attention only relatively recently. There is a broad general agreement in the literature that the

---

[19] *Transitional Corporations and World Development* (International Thomson Business Press, London, 1996) p. 365

[20] *Ibid.*, p. 365

eclectic paradigm provides a framework which is as useful for understanding the extent, pattern and growth of international production by MNCs in services as it is for those in goods.[21]

It can be worthwhile to summarise these theories in a little bit more detail.

The Hymer–Kindleberger Tradition

The initial core of modern theory of the multinational enterprise was a deceptively simple proposition, namely, that in order to compete with indigenous firms that possess innate strengths such as knowledge of the local environment, market and business conditions, foreign entrants must have some compensating advantage. At the stroke, this proposition took foreign direct investment away from the theory of capital movements into the theory of industrial organisation, For, in a perfect market, foreign direct investment (FDI) could not exist because local firms would always be able to out-compete foreign entrants.[22]

The initial phase of the Hymer–Kindleberger approach was therefore to search for compensating "advantages", which foreign investors possessed. Kindleberger's exposition examined four main areas of internationally transferable "advantages". First, departures from perfect competition in good markets, including product differentiation, marketing skills and administered pricing; secondly, departures from perfect competition in factor markets, including access to patented or "proprietary" knowledge, discrimination in access to capital and skill differences embodied in firm (particularly its management); third, internal and external economies of scale, including those arising from vertical integration; and finally, government intervention, particularly those forms restricting output or entry. Such advantages enable the foreign entrant to overcome its lack of knowledge of local conditions innate in the local firm, which the foreign firm can only acquire at a cost, and also serve to compensate for the foreigner's cost of operating at a distance.[23]

Given the specific advantages that enable the firm to invest successfully abroad (that is, the necessary condition) it remains to be proven that direct investment is a preferred means of exploiting the advantage (that is, the sufficient condition). The basis for the decision, according to Hymer and Kinleberger, is profitability. In many cases direct investment will be preferred to either exporting or licensing the "advantage" to a host-country firm. Exporting will, in many cases, be excluded by tariff and transportation cost barriers – also a local producer may be better placed to

---

[21] *Ibid.*, p. 365

[22] Peter J. Buckley and Mark Casson, *The Theory of Multinational Enterprise* (The MacMillan Press Ltd., London, 1985) p. 2

[23] *Ibid.*, p. 3

adopt his product to local conditions and a local presence may have the effect of stimulated demand.

The arguments that firms will often prefer FDI to licensing are more subtle. Hymer argued that the advantage-possessor cannot appropriate the full return (or rent) from its utilisation because of imperfections in the market for knowledge. Such imperfections arising from "buyer uncertainty" (the buyer being unable to assess the worth of the knowledge to him util he is in possession of it), lack of an institutionalised market for knowledge and the dependence of the value of knowledge on its secrecy. The seller thus cannot induce competitive bids in order to appropriate the full returns. Further factors that favour FDI over licensing the advantage to host-country firms are the desire for control by the advantage-possessor and the danger that the advantage-seller will create a competitor if the buyer uses the advantage in "ways which have not been paid for". Licensing thus may incur heavy firm-to-firm transfer costs, including "policing" the transferred property rights – costs that do not arise in the case of transfers from parent to subsidiary.

Shortly, therefore, this approach suggests that a multinational entrant must possess an internally transferable "advantage", the possession of which gives it a quasi-monopolistic opportunity to enter host-country markets. Barriers to trade and barriers, which prevent host-country firms from duplicating this advantage, mean that direct foreign investment is frequently the preferred form of exploiting the advantage in foreign markets.

It is arguable, however, that the fundamental proposition of the Hymer–Kindleberger approach is not as easily applicable to established multinational firms as is to a firm becoming multinational. How far do the barriers to entry to a foreign market decline as the international spread of the firm widens? Established multinational firms have gained world-wide dominance and have developed techniques to "learn in advance" local conditions – products, processes, management style, marketing techniques are continually adopted to local markets. The ability of multinational to forecast and to adopt is one of the major competitive skills. It is now only the entry into unusually isolated markets where heavy "cost of foreignness" are still encountered. The advantage of locals in other instances can be discounted in advance by an experienced multinational firm.[24]

The Product Cycle Model

The product cycle hypothesis (PCH) chiefly associated with Raymond Vernor has yielded a large number of insights into the development of MNCs. The models rest on four basic assumptions:

  a) products undergo predictable changes in production and marketing;

---

[24] *Ibid.,* p. 4

b) restricted information is available on technology;

c) production processes change over time and economies of scale are prevalent;

d) tastes differ according to income and thus products can be standardised at various income levels.[25]

The original model suggested the new products would appear first in the most advanced country (the USA) because demand from (i) discretionary spending on new products arising from high income and (ii) substitution. Consequently, the *new product stage*, where an unstandarised product with a low price-elasticity of demand is produced on an experimental basis, occurs in the USA. The second stage is the *maturing product*. The product begins to be standardised and the need for flexibility on both supply and demand sides declines. The possibilities for economies of scale lead to expansion in production and this is matched by increasing demand as the product becomes cheaper. The market begins to appear in other advanced countries and is initially satisfied by exports from the USA. Eventually cost factors begin to dictate that these foreign markets should be serviced by local production and the emergence of investment by U.S. producers. So other advanced countries are the first recipients of U.S. direct investment. In the third stage, a *standardised product* emerges which sells entirely on the basis of price competitiveness. The imperative now is to produce the product at the lowest possible cost. Consequently, the labour-intensive stages of production are hived off and carried out, via foreign direct investment, in the less-developed countries, where labour is cheapest.[26]

Vernon's initial model thus has the virtues of simplicity and directness. It explains U.S. investment in other advanced countries and the phenomenon of "off-shore production" in cheap labour countries. Despite its virtues of integrating supply and demand factors, it has been outdated by events. Firstly, the U.S. is no longer totally dominant in foreign investment – European and Japanese multinational expansion also need further explanation. Secondly, MNCs are now capable of developing, maturing and standardising the product to suit a variety of needs without significant time lags.[27]

Internalisation and the Theory of Multinational Corporations

Two connotations of this concept exist. One aspect is the internalisation of a market where an arm's length contractual relationship is replaced by unified ownership. The other concerns the internalisation of an externality where a market is created where none has existed before.[28]

---

[25] *Ibid.*, p. 6

[26] *Ibid.*, p. 6

[27] *Ibid.*, p. 6

[28] *Ibid.*, p. 9

The theory of internalisation is now widely accepted as a key element in theory of the multinational enterprise. Internalisation is a general theory of why firms exist, and without additional assumptions it is almost tautological. To make the theory operational it is necessary to specify assumption about transactional costs for particular products and for trade between particular locations. It is typically asserted that:

a) It is very costly to licence unpatentable know-how, so that the market for know-how must be internalised. This leads to the vertical integration of production and R & D, and because of the "public good" characteristics of know-how, to the consequent horizontal integration of production in different locations.

b) It is difficult to specify and enforce long term future contracts, so that the market for raw materials used by capital-intensive production process must be internalised by backward integration.

c) Ad valorem tariffs, international tax differentials and foreign exchange controls create incentives for transfer-pricing, which are most easily exploitable through internalisation.[29]

The truth of the concept of internalisation is that the actions of firms can replace the market or alternatively can augment it. The explanatory power of the concept rests on an analysis of costs and benefits to the firm of internalised markets, particularly market in intermediate goods. The predictive power of the concept for the growth and pattern of MNCs is given by the statement of the likelihood of the internalisation of the various markets which the MNC faces. The advantages of internalisation (and therefore control by the firm versus the market solution) are given by:

a) the increased ability to control and plan production and in particularly to co-ordinate flows of crucial inputs;

b) the exploitation of market power by discriminatory pricing;

c) the avoidance of bilitater market power;

d) the avoidance of uncertainties in the transfer of knowledge between parties which may exist in the alternative (market) solution;

e) the avoidance of potential government intervention by devices such as transfer prices.

Costs arise from communication, co-ordination and control difficulties, and costs of foreignness. Three cases of empirical importance are (i) the advantages of vertical integration, (ii) the importance of situations where intermediate product flows in research intensive industries and (iii) the internalisation of human skills, particularly in areas with high returns to team co-operation such as marketing and financing.[30]

Underlying this internalisation approach is the view that internal solutions will be sought where international market imperfections would impose costs on firms

---

[29] *Ibid.*, p. 20
[30] *Ibid.*, p. 10

using those markets. Internalisation of markets also imposes severe barriers on new entry. The multinational is thus seen as both responding to market imperfections and creating them. Clearly, strong links with the Hymer–Kindleberger approach and the product cycle hypothesis are apparent. Attention to imperfections on intermediate markets should not obscure the role of imperfections in final goods markets, leading to competitive devices such as product differentiation and administered pricing. Multinationals are not passive reactors to imperfections, and internalisation decisions interact. The critical role of information as an intermediate product is an important synthesising element.[31]

This theory predicts the MNCs will predominate in R & D-intensive industries – particularly those where patents are difficult to register or enforce – in resource-based industries, and in situations where the international division of labour is inhibited by fiscal intervention which can be avoided by transfer-pricing.

It is apparent, however, that not all industries in which MNCs operate fulfil these conditions. MNCs occur in many low-technology manufacturing industries and are also quite important in the service sector. It is true that U.S.-based MNCs are predominantly R & D-oriented, but this does not apply to the same extent to European MNCs, and certainly not to Japanese MNCs.[32]

DIVERSIFICATION AND INTERNALISATION

It is possible to regard the MNCs not as an aggressive risk taker, investing heavily in R & D and diffusing fruits through an international network of subsidiaries and appropriating the returns, but as averse to risk, using multinationality to achieve stability of returns. Moreover, internationalisation may be regarded as an alternative to domestic diversification.

The typical MNC will be diversified in two ways – first, by its product – market position internationally, and second, it will be financially diversified, earning its returns in a variety of currencies. It is argued that the advantages given by international financial diversification have led to superior stock market performance by MNCs over purely domestic firms, even after allowing size and industry influences. Thus MNCs are regarded as an alternative vehicle for international financial diversification to individual diversification by the purchase of shareholdings. This argument rests on imperfections in the world capital market, which prevent individuals from enjoying the benefits of diversification. Such imperfections must (i) impede individuals from satisfactorily diversifying, and (ii) reduce the optimal diversification of intermediaries so that diversification through controlling interests is more

---

[31] *Ibid.*, p. 11
[32] *Ibid.*, p. 21

efficient than a large number of smaller shareholdings. Direct investment involves control and without such supporting argument control would involve a sub-optimal amount of diversification relative to the amount of each holding.[33]

The arguments adduced for such imperfections are that (i) transaction costs exist in the equity market in the form of costs of acquiring and disseminating the relevant mass of information and (ii) this results in the application by the market of a premium to the equity valuation of diversified firms. In addition, it can be argued that the divorce of ownership and control reinforces this tendency because managers in an imperfect capital market can pursue policies which enhance their own welfare, within the constraint that returns to shareholders do not fall below those which would make their shareholders receptive to a take-over bid. Managers may be averse to risk (preferring to safeguard their jobs to extra returns) and may therefore prefer a widely diversified company with the hoped-for stability which goes with this state. Diversification through foreign investment widens the scope of their discretion.[34]

Location Theory

Under the general interpretation already given, the MNC can simply be seen as a major vehicle for the transfer of mobile resources (technology, capital, management skills) to areas with immobile (or fixed) complementary inputs (markets, raw materials, labour). Thus Ricardian endowments (comparative advantages of countries) enter the theory.[35]

The location-specific endowments of particular importance to MNCs are (i) raw materials, leading to vertical FDI, (ii) cheap labour, leading to "offshore production" facilities and (iii) protected or fragmented markets leading to FDI as the preferred means of market servicing. Location factors therefore enter the theory not only in their own right, as an influence on the relative costs facing an MNC with a choice of locations, but also may provide the motives for international expansion.

The important connections between location factors and the (internal) organisation of MNCs should, however, be given due weight. First, the MNC will normally be a multi-stage, multi-function firm and the location of different stages and functions will be subject to different locational influences connected by international flows of intermediate products. Second, the internalisation of markets will affect location in two important ways:

a) The MNCs have incentives to minimise government intervention through transfer pricing, for instance, to reduce the overall tax liability by imputing high

---

[33] *Ibid.*, p. 11
[34] *Ibid.*, p. 12
[35] *Ibid.*, p. 13

mark-ups in lowest tax countries and possibly by altering their local strategy completely to take in a low-intervention "tax haven".

b) The increased communication flows in an internal market may bias high communication cost activities toward the "centre" – usually towards the source country where critical activities are focused on head office.

In his restatement of the product cycle hypothesis, Vernon gives a great deal of weight to the interplay between the stage of the industry's development and the relevant location influences upon it. The location of research activities (in centre) and the changing locational influences on production provide the dynamic for this theory.[36]

Synthesis – A General Theory of the Multinational Corporation

There are now several candidates for a general theory of the multinational enterprise. Amongst these are Dunning's eclectic theory, which relies on the so called OLI paradigm: ownership specific advantages, location endowments and internalisation advantages. The paradigm asserts that the extent, pattern and growth of value-adding activities undertaken by MNCs outside their national boundaries is dependent on the value of and interaction between three main variables:

- *Ownership-specific advantage of MNCs* (or comparative advantages elaborated by Hymer- Kindleberger): the extent and nature of the technological, managerial and marketing advantages of MNCs *vis-à-vis* indigenous firms in the country in which they are producing or contemplating value-added activities; these include those which arise from the ownership of geographically dispersed activity (see Table 5);
- *Location-specific advantages of countries:* the benefits of combining ownership-specific advantages with immobile factor endowments in a foreign or the home country to undertake value-adding activities; those benefits reflect the location-specific or comparative advantages of these countries (see Table 6); and
- *Market internalisation advantages*: the advantages of controlling and co-ordinating ownership- and location-specific advantages within a MNC hierarchy, rather than selling the right to use those advantages to indigenous firms located in the country of production (see Table 7).

It should be noted that those advantages are not necessarily independent of each other. For example, the fact that one MNC may choose a superior location to another may give it a competitive edge. Furthermore, it is accepted that the configuration of these ownership, location and internalisation advantages and the response to them by firms varies according to industry, country and region (of origin and

---

[36] *Ibid.*, p. 14

TABLE 5. Ownership-specific advantages (advantages particularly relevant to explaining TNC activities in service industries in bold)

1. Property right and/or intangible asset advantages

- Product innovations, production management, innovatory capacity.
- **Organisational and marketing systems.**
- Non-codifiable knowledge; "bank" of human capital experience; marketing, finance, know-how etc.; **ability to seek out, acquire, utilise and manage information; capacity to control quality of output and/or supply customised products;**
- **Trade marks or goodwill of brand names.**

2. Advantages of common management

a) Those which have branch plants of established enterprises may enjoy over de novo firms.
- **Those due mainly to size and established position of enterprise, for example, economies of scope and specialisation; monopoly power, better resource capacity and usage.**
- **Exclusive or favoured access to inputs, for example, labour, natural resources, finance, data-processing and transmitting equipment.**
- **Ability to obtain inputs on favoured terms (due, for example, to size or monopsonistic influence. Exclusive or favoured access to product markets.**
- **Access to resources of parent company at marginal cost.**
- **Economies of joint supply (not only in production, but in purchasing, marketing, finance etc., arrangements).**

b) Those which specifically arise because of trans-nationality.
- **Trans-nationality enhances the above advantages by offering wider opportunities.**
- **More favoured access to and/or better knowledge about international markets, (or example, for information, finance, labour, etc.**
- **Ability to take advantage of geographic differences in factor endowments, markets.**
- **Ability to diversify or reduce risks, for example, in different currency areas, and/or political scenarios.**

Source: J. H. Dunning, The Eclectic Paradigm of International Production: A Restatement and Some Possible Extensions. *Journal of International Business Studies* (1988).

destination) and firm-specific characteristics; the last of these factors incorporates the perceived competitive positions of firms and their strategies for growth. It also varies over time as changes in technology and entrepreneurial and economic environment may affect the competitive position of corporations and the location of their value-added activities.[37]

Several unresolved issues remain in this synthesising approach. First, the relationship between these three elements and their development over time is unclear and leaves a classification system which is bereft of a dynamic content. Second, the existence of separate and separable ownership advantages is doubtful and logically redundant because internalisation explains why firms exist in the absence of such advantages.

---

[37] *Transitional Corporations in World Development. Trends and Prospects, p. 426*

TABLE 6. Location-specific advantages (advantages relevant to explaining TNC activities in service industries in bold)

- Special distribution of natural and created resource endowments and markets.
- Input prices, quality and productivity, for example, labour, energy, materials, components, semi-finished goods.
- **International transport and communications costs (which in case of services can bc prohibitive.**
- Investment incentives and disincentives (including performance requirements etc.). Artificial barriers (for example, import controls) to trade in services.

- **Infrastructure provisions (commercial, legal, educational, transport and telecommunication).**
- **Psychic distance (cultural differences).**
- Psychic distance (language, business, customs, etc. differences). Economies of centralisation of information-gathering and interpretation. Economies of centralisation of R & D, production and marketing.

- Economic system and policies of Government; the institutional framework for resource allocation.
- **Regulation of markets and/or access to markets by Governments.**

Source: J. H. Dunning, The Eclectic Paradigm of International Production: A Restatement and Some Possible Extensions. *Journal of International Business Studies* (1988).

TABLE 7. Internalisation advantages (advantages particularly relevant to explaining TNC activities in service industries in bold)

- **Avoidance of search and negotiating costs.**
- To avoid costs of enforcing property rights.
- **Buyer uncertainty about nature and value of inputs (for example, technology) being sold.**
- Where market does not permit price discrimination.
- **Need of seller to protect quality of intermediate or final products.**

- To compensate for absence of future markets.
- **To avoid or exploit government intervention (for example, quotas, tariffs, price controls, tax differences etc).**
- To control supplies and conditions of sale of inputs (including technology).
- To control market outlets (including those which might be used by competitors).

- To be able to engage in such practices as cross-subsidisation, predatory pricing, leads and lags, transfer pricing etc., as a competitive (or anti-competitive) strategy.

Source: J. H. Dunning, The Eclectic Paradigm of International Production: A Restatement and Some Possible Extensions. *Journal of International Business Studies* (1988).

The "markets and hierarchies" approach associated with Oliver Williamson has also been advanced as a candidate for a general theory of multinational enterprise. Williamson suggests that his general theory of why firms exist explains the existence of the multinational firm as a special case. Without a theory of the conditions under which one ideal-type form (market and hierarchy) will be replaced by the other, only an arid comparative static framework remains. The transition from market to hierarchy may be explained by the minimisation of transaction costs once these have been carefully specified. The concept of bounded rationality in management decision-making utilised by Williamson is useful but sits awkwardly within an essentially neo-classical framework.[38]

The theory of the multinational firm therefore requires development in several directions before it can be seen adequate. First, the fusion between institutional and neo-classical elements must be made more secure. Second, the general area of the economics of business strategy needs greater attention. Third, the role of time must be more carefully defined in the relationship between the growth and decline of firms, technologies, products and industries. Finally, the formulation and testing of hypothesis from the theory is an urgent task.[39]

As there is not a generally accepted theory of MNCs, it may be reasonable to summarise the motives and driving forces to multinationals based upon the theories and practical experiences relating to the MNCs.

MOTIVES AND DRIVING FORCES TO MULTINATIONALS

Cross-border business has been driven forward by three main things: falling regulatory barriers to overseas investment; tumbling telecommunications and transportation costs; and freer domestic and international capital markets in which companies can be bought, and currency and other risks can be controlled.[40]

But the emergence and the growing role of the MNCs based upon on the one hand *on the very essential and specific features of modern capitalist market economy*[41] – having become into existence after the feudalism – especially on the following ones:[42]

a) *Market* in this economy – among other things – *is also an institution* that includes not only the introduction of a new process or product, entry a new market,

---

[38] Peter J. Buckley and Mark Casson, *The Theory of Multinational Enterprise,* p. 18

[39] *Ibid.,* p. 19

[40] Multinationals. *The Economist,* March 27th 1993, p. 4

[41] The modern capitalist market economy, in fact, is one of the main features of the Modern Western World. A good five hundred years ago, in the infancy of the capitalist mode of production, economics broke away from the traditional relation of the pre-modern societies and the Modern Western World started to develop. This Modern Western World has been living under the dominion of two institutions: *the Industrialised Market Economy* and *Modern Democracy.* See János Hoós, *The Unfolding New World and Economics* (Akadémiai Kiadó, Budapest, 1997) p. 5

[42] *Ibid.,* p. 5

access to new supplies of input, but a certain new organisation. *It has created factory system and efficient industrial, commercial and service enterprise, firms.* This organisation arrangement permits greater utilisation of productive resources; business firms of capitalism undertake investment strategies in response to new market and technological opportunities and they then put in place organisational structures to ensure economic success; the most important resources that the enterprise develops and utilises are not technologies embodied in processes and products, but the specialists on whom the organisation relies to develop and utilise its physical capital; and the essential role of the enterprise is the planned co-ordination of a specialised division of labour that develops and utilises the productive resources that have been committed to the enterprise; – results of all these enterprise as an institution, especially the large-scale enterprises, corporations and among them particularly the multidivisional, multiregional and multinational ones, have come to be the most powerful engine of economic progress.

b) *Today market means first and foremost world market*; the capitalist system, before the emergence of modern bourgeois society, already linked up the local, regional and national markets in a world market. Eventually all the aggregate forms of capital were globalised: commodities in the world trade, productive capital in the market for production locations, money and credit on the world money-market. The economic rationality of the market asserted itself against other, competing principles of order in the world society. So wherever market is involved today the main reference must be to world market – to the market for goods and services, capital, money and credit. Market-forced growth over time and expansion in space greatly enlarge the operational sphere of normal market rationality: this rationality strives toward world domination and supremacy over all expressions of human existence.[43]

On the other hand, *on the contradiction between these market features, especially the market as a world market and the other basic characteristics of the Modern Western World, namely it is based upon the Modern Democracy covering an English-type sovereign national state with elected Parliament , sovereign lawmaking body elected by territorial constituencies and by virtually universal suffrage.*[44]

These political forms of citizens, unlike the economic, are always nationally coloured. Economic freedoms relate to global space: they are universal, cosmopolitan. Economics and politics – along with their constitutive principles, the market and the democratic process – therefore constitute distinctive realms. National states dispose of differential power within the world system and make barriers for the free functioning and expanding of the market by creating special "market failures", efficiency losses in the international arena of the world market.[45]

---

[43] *Ibid.,* p. 21
[44] *Ibid.,* p. 6
[45] *Ibid.,* p. 22

Emergence of MNC has created an efficient institution to overcome or to decrease these failures originated by the contradiction between the international, global character of the market and the national character of the modern democratic process of national states, that is to ease those problems which are due to those phenomena that democratic procedures within a society held together by national-state are not congruent with the effects of economic processes and state activity within world society.

As Coase[46] has pointed out, the firm is an internal market, administratively organising production within itself, for transactions that would not have taken place in external markets and as a more profitable method of conducting some transactions that might otherwise have been at arm's length. Coase and his followers demonstrated that *there are often transactional advantages for a firm* when it makes use of its owned internal resources, some of which could not be bought in the market but their very nature were produced only within the firm in the process of growth; they have also showed that although there is no limit to the size of a firm as long as it can be administered as a coherent entity, there is a limit to its growth, but that as a firm grows there is no evidence that its administrative capacity cannot grow accordingly. *The MNC seems to be the most efficient form of firm within which the administrative organisation of production – internal market – has "transactional advantages" over the (external) market – both domestic and international market –, and in which managerial efficiency can be risen.*

If such an internal market has transaction advantages for the firm it implies either pure "market failure" or imperfect markets for other reasons. Such considerations do not, however, distinguish the MNC from domestic firms, but the MNC can cope with these failures and imperfections in a more successful way. Multinationals in many respects are creatures of market imperfection, or failures.

Broadly, two sorts of imperfection are relevant regarding the MNC.[47] One is the structural imperfection, which may be natural (transport costs, for example) or man-made. Examples of the latter include government restrictions on investment or import, taxes and subsidies, inadequate capital markets and monopolistic or oligopolistic markets.

The other sort of imperfection is inherent in transactions and markets themselves. Examples are the uncertainty that supplier will deliver on his promise; volatility of exchange rates; the difficulty customers facing evaluating unfamiliar products; the cost of negotiating deals; economics of scale in production, purchasing, R & D, distribution or marketing, which give advantages to exiting firms and impose barriers against newcomers; concerns about infringement of intellectual property rights; uncertainty about competitors' actions; opportunity to spread risk through diversification. Because of these and other imperfections firms locate their production and

---

[46] Ronald. H. Coase, The Nature of the Firm. *Economica*, 4 (n.s.) 1937, p. 40
[47] Multinationals. *The Economist*, March 27th 1993, p. 9

other operations internationally for reasons that are more complex than the simple minimisation of direct costs. The multinational firm is a much more complicated creature than that, whatever services or manufacturing it is involved in: released from its home-country cage by the demise of a structural imperfection, it spreads abroad in order to overcome or to exploit these imperfections.

The Main Concrete Motives to Multinationals

The most frequent reason to multinationalise is to make direct foreign investment is that entrepreneurs confront *foreign barriers to their exports*. Nationalistic sentiment leads most nations to try to build their own industrial capabilities. By rising barriers against imports of manufactured products, they induce foreign as well as domestic firms to establish domestic industries. (Large numbers of American corporations have become multinationals simply to maintain or expand market in Canada or in the European Economic Community (EEC) that could not be profitably served by exports.)[48]

Business firms also multinationalise because their presence as producers in a foreign nation enables them more effectively *to adopt their products to local demands*. (For example, during the nineteen-twenties General Motors acquired Vauxhall in Britain and Opel in Germany and opened assembly plans in fifteen foreign countries).[49]

There are many other causes as well.[50] The creation of larger free-trading regions, such as the EEC and European Free Trade Association, created opportunities to capitalise upon economic scale that American firms were prepared to seize more quickly than their European counterparts. The rapid post-war expansion of European markets, with spreading waves of mass consumption, opened doors to profit from the introduction of mass manufacturing and market methods. Another reason was that the dynamic of American business is expansion, and anti-trust laws and keen competition at home channelled the attention of corporate executives to opportunities abroad. Drawing confidence in the political stability and economic strength of the advanced nations appeared to reduce the risk of foreign commitments. Also, geopolitical diversification of a corporation's operations into many national markets offered a means of stabilising the growth of total earnings and thereby reducing the risk/reward ratio. (For example, if there is strike in Belgium, or a rise in German wage rate, or a 20 percent devaluation of sterling, then a spread of plants gives Ford the chance to cover a risk or exploit an opportunity.) Presence in a rival's home market – even the cost of building of this presence where a firm

---

[48] *The Multinational Enterprise in Transition*, p. 26
[49] *Ibid.*, p. 26
[50] *Ibid.*, p. 27

weak can be very high – might distract the rival or might lower the rival's profit, it might also yield valuable information about tactics or technology. If the firm has power of brand name and/or licence this firm can become a successful multinational exploiting advantages of unique cases, especially if the firm has been given a special monopoly position, at least for a period of time.

By multinationalising, a company also acquires certain competitive advantages. It can monitor technological developments in many countries. It can borrow at low interest rates in one country to finance working capital shortage in a high-interest-rate country. It is able to adjust intra-company transfer prices in a way that reduces total corporate tax liabilities. It can move surplus funds between its multiple bases to minimise the cost of borrowed funds or take advantage of predicted changes in the exchange rates of national currencies.[51]

A very important factor is the *development of management science*. Together with striking advances in communications and computer facilities, it makes the management of distant operation feasible. The enduring strength of any large firm – and especially that of a multinational one – lies in the quality of its "own" productive resource. Of these, perhaps the most important are the knowledge and experience of its personnel, for which the market is inherently as well as institutionally imperfect, its organisational capacity to formulate and implement strategies to utilise such resources, and the marketing advantages conferred by a long-established reputation. Technological expertise in production of goods and/or services, together with the monopoly power thus conferred, was in the first instance seen as the crucial element, but later the management skills required to develop new forms of administrative structures in order to maintain the efficiency of administration as firms grew large and controlled increasingly diversified activities was seen to be important.

Both the managerial structure and the managerial function have undergone fundamental changes that have profoundly affected the nature of the organisation itself. Chandler's history[52] of large American industrial enterprises superbly showed the relationship between growth, strategy and structure.

According to Chandler, as a result of the regulatory, increased volume, and greater speed of flows of goods and materials made possible by the new transportation and communication systems, new and improved processes of production developed that, for the first time in the history, enjoyed substantial economies of scale and scope. Large manufacturing works applying to the new technologies could be produced at lower unit costs than the smaller works.

In order to benefit from the cost advantages of these new, high-value technologies of production, entrepreneurs had to make three sets of interrelated investments. The first was an investment in production facilities large enough to exploit a tech-

[51] *Ibid.,* p. 28

[52] A. D. Chandler, Jr, *Scale and Scope, The Dynamic of Industrial Capitalism* (The Belknap Press of Harvard University Press, Cambridge, 1990) p. 102

nology's potential economies of scale. The second was an investment in a national and international marketing and distributing network, so that the volume of sales might keep pace with the new volume of production. Finally, to benefit fully from these two kinds of investment, the entrepreneurs also had to invest in management: they had to recruit and train managers not only to administer the enlarged facilities and increased personnel in both production and distribution, but also to monitor and co-ordinate those two basic functional activities and to plan and allocate resources for future production and distribution. It was this three-parted investment in production, distribution, and management that brought the modern industrial enterprise into being.

The first entrepreneurs to create such enterprises acquired powerful competitive advantages. Their industries quickly became oligopolistic, that is, dominated by a small number of first movers. These firms, along with the few challengers that subsequently entered the industry, no longer competed primarily on bases of price. Instead they competed for market share profits through functional and strategic effectiveness. They did so functionally by improving their product, their processes of production, their marketing, their purchasing, and their labour relations, and by strategically moving to growing markets more rapidly, and out of declining ones more quickly and effectively than did their competitors.

Such rivalry for market share and profit honoured the enterprise's functional and strategic capabilities. These organisational capabilities, in turn, provided an internal dynamic for the continuing growth of enterprise. In particular, *they stimulated its owners and managers to expand into distant market in their own country and then become multinational by moving abroad.* They also encouraged the firm to diversify by products competitive in markets other than the original one and so to become a multiproduct enterprise.[53]

This modern industrial enterprise contains a number of distance operation units, and carries out modern production processes. It has more than a production function, however. It is a "governance structure" to use Oliver Williamson's term.[54] It governs units that carry out different production as well as commercial and research functions and so integrates these activities. In such an enterprise each unit – factory, a sales or purchasing office, or a research laboratory – has its own administrative office, its own managers and staff, its own set of books, as well as its own resources (physical facilities and personnel) to carry out a specific function involved in the production or distribution of a specific product in a specific geographical area.[55] Modern multiunit enterprises became multifunctional, multiregional, and multi-

---

[53] *Ibid.*, p. 104

[54] Oliver E. Williamson, *Markets and Hierarchies: Analysis and Antitrust Implications.*(Free Press, New York, 1975)

[55] A. D. Chandler, Jr, *Scale and Scope, The Dynamic of Industrial Capitalism*, p. 106

product because the addition of new units permitted them to maintain a long-term rate of return on investment by reducing costs of production and distribution, by providing products that satisfied existing demands, and by transferring facilities and skills to more profitable markets when returns were reduced by competition, changing technology, or altered market demand.[56]

Williamson[57] analysed the way in which firms can expand their ability to manage growth efficiently with minimum interference with ongoing operations, and he outlined the types of structural change that permit it to avoid rising managerial inefficiency and to develop and implement coherent strategies in a world where competition in technological innovation and in the ability to influence consumer demand are often more prevalent than price competition. The "organisation theorist" of the firm developed the advantages to be obtained by a firm when production, marketing, research and development, and financial management could be linked and formed into a coherent administrative organisation with the objective of capitalising the rent generated at each level.

The MNCs are the entities that can use these opportunities and possibilities in the most successful way. They buy, produce, employ, distribute, research, develop, raise finance, advertise and thus compete in a lot of different countries, all at once. Some of the operations of a typical multinational are more global than other. Chief among the global ones is finance, which big firms can now raise from wherever it is cheapest to do so, and many will also lend or invest globally. In 1988–1991, more than half of world flows of foreign direct investment were in industries classified as services. A sizeable chunk of that investment came from the financing affiliates of multinational manufacturers or traders, such as IBM, General Motors, Matsushita or Mitsubishi Corporation. Another function that exhibits more of a global tendency is marketing, since this applies both to local production and to export. With some consumer brands becoming well-known around the world, more and more firms have started to use a single campaign, saving on creative costs and identifying the brand more strongly with a single culture (usually American). Some firms are making their R & D efforts global. Having originally built their expertise at home, they are seeking to remain competitive by building or buying R & D facilities wherever the expertise exist.[58]

Manifestly, *the forces behind corporate multinationals are so potent that there is a high probability that multinational business will continue to expand relative to domestic business long into the future.*

---

[56] *Ibid.*, p. 107

[57] Oliver E. Williamson, *Markets and Hierarchies: Analysis and Antitrust Implications*, 1975, p. 16

[58] Multinationals. *The Economist*, March 27th 1993, p. 17

The Strategic Alliance

This development has been intensified by the most widespread trends in international business in the recent years. The *strategic alliance* of the MNCs can be experienced in car, computer hardware, computer software, aerospace, drugs, telecommunications, defence and other industries as well. The simplest way to think of an alliance is that they accept a firm's limitations: geographical, financial, technological or some other sort. A survey made by the University of Limburg in Holland concluded that 4,182 technological alliances in 1980–89 were concentrated in biotechnology and information technology (see Table 8). The number of the interfirm agreements has been growing dynamically (see Table 9). According to the main studies on strategic alliances, interfirm agreements are intended to provide the following advantages:

    a) sharing of the large investment needed for specific activities such as in R & D;

    b) accelerating of return on investment through a more rapid diffusion of firms' assets;

    c) spreading risks;

    d) enhancing efficiency through economies of scale, specialisation and/or scope;

    e) coping with the competition.

At the same time, strategic business alliances often involve substantial set up and monitoring transactional costs. Those include the possibility that one's partners may behave in a way detrimental to one's interests, and – this is particularly important where one's partner is also a major rival – that he may overall be in a competitive position relative to one's own.[59]

The recent study has found the three reasons most commonly cited for alliances were to gain access to a market, to exploit complementary technology, and to reduce the time taken for innovation. Alliances are generally used to help a firm leapfrog its competitors (or catch up with them) or plug a technological or product gap that would otherwise be too costly to fill. The pace of innovation is rapid in many industries, but the costs of keeping up are high, so some can be defrayed through an alliance.[60]

The strategic alliances can intensify the advantages of ownership, location and internalisation, particularly in the R & D field as Figure 5 shows it.

In many industries, the introduction of new technologies has essentially become a pre-condition for remaining in business. The need for the continuous introduction of technological innovations and the speed with which even basic technologies are changing have dramatically increased the cost of new investment, while simultaneously reducing the expected life span of any innovation in production or of any

---

[59] John H. Dunning, *The Globalisation of Business* (Routledge, London, 1993) p. 194
[60] Multinationals. *The Economist*, March 27th 1993, p. 20

TABLE 8. Strategic alliances by sector and fields of technology, 1980–1989

		Main reason for alliance, percent of total						
	Number of alliances	High-cost risks	Lack of financial resources	Technological compatibility	Reduced innovation time-span	Basic R&D sharing	Market access/ structure	Technology monitoring/ market entry
Biotechnology	847	1	13	35	31	10	13	15
New materials technology	430	1	3	38	32	11	31	16
Information technology	1660	4	2	33	31	3	38	11
Computers	198	1	2	28	22	2	51	10
Industrial automation	278	nil	3	41	32	4	31	7
Microelectronics	383	3	3	33	33	5	52	6
Software	344	1	4	38	36	2	24	11
Telecommunications	366	11	2	28	28	1	35	16
Other	91	1	nil	29	28	2	35	24
Automotive	205	4	2	27	22	2	52	4
Aviation/defence	228	36	1	34	26	nil	13	8
Chemicals	410	7	1	16	13	1	51	8
Consumer electronics	58	2	nil	19	19	nil	53	9
Food and beverages	42	1	nil	17	10	nil	43	7
Heavy electric/power	141	36	1	31	10	4	23	11
Instruments/medical technology	95	nil	4	35	40	2	28	10
Other	66	35	nil	9	6	0	23	8

Source: Hagedoorn and Schakenraad, Maastricht Economic Research Institute in Innovation and Technology. *The Economist,* March 27th 1993

TABLE 9. The globalisation of business. Evolution of co-operative agreements established annually 1974–1989

	a)	b)	c)	d)	e)	f)	g)
1974			37				169[1]
1975	3		14				
1976	7		16			31	
1977	7		15				
1978	7	2	14				
1979	13	1	27				317[2]
1980	22	4	34	85		94	
1981	28	22	40	169			
1982	23	19	35	197			
1983	39	16		292	46		
1984	66	42		346	69		1504[3]
1985				487	82		
1986				438	81		
1987					90	180	
1988					111		
1989					129		2629[4]

Sources:

a) Jacquemin et al. (1986): data on 212 co-operative agreements formed between 1978 and 1984 by at least one EC firm.

b) Haklisch (1986): Co-operative agreements formed by the world's 41 major semi-conductor producers.

c) Hladik (1985): US international Ns created in high income countries between 1974 and 1982.

d) Cainarca et al. (1989): Arpa data base on 2014 agreements formed between 1980 and 1986 in the information technologies sectors (semi-conductors, computers and telecommunications).

e) Commission's Reports on the EC's competition policy. See, for example, Commission des Communautés Européennes, 1989.

f) Hladik and Linden (1989): McKinsey Studies on US international JVS created in 1976, 1980 and 1987.

g) Hagedoorn and Schakenraad (1990): Cati data base on 9,000 agreements formed until July 1989.

[1] Before 1974,   [2] 1975–1979,   [3] 1980–1984,   [4] 1985–1989.

new product. Some MNCs have channelled considerable resources into speeding up their internal innovation process, with the idea of using rapid product change and introduction to gain competitive advantages. The combination of rising investment costs and shorter product life cycles has the risks associated with new investment. MNCs have adopted several strategies in order to cope with those enhanced risks.[61]

---

[61] *Transitional Corporations in World Development. Trends and Prospects*, p. 57

Technological Innovation

- Emergence of new technologies
- High risks
- Rapidity of Innovations
- Rent of returns' period reduced

Convergence of Technologies

- New borders of industrial activities
- Mastering simultaneously several technologies
- New structure of the markets

Advantage

Ownership

- Rapidity of new advantages' development
- Rapidity of existing advantages' exploitation
- Higher flexibility
- Advantages based on the combination of non-similar assets
- Advantages based on the supply of complete range of systematic and compatible products
- Advantages based on products with a dominant standard

Location

- Access to complementary asset based on the nations' competitive advantages, originated in the partners' home countries
- Access to the main worlds markets and outputs when a go-it alone solution is not possible because of the high capacities needed to exploit them alone

Internalisation

- Sharing the costs and spreading the risk in high uncertainty situations
- Transaction costs less important because of the technological diffusion rapidity
- Benefit from scales economies
- The launching of projects with high sunk costs
- New oligopolistic reactions to replace traditional oligopolistics strategies which are inadequate because of the concentration, unstability and asymmetry of oligopolies

Globalisation

- Concentration, asymmetrical and unsuitable oligopoly
- World's products adapted to local demand
- Products based on world's accepted standards
- Systems product

FIGURE 5. The value of strategic alliances. Technology based cross-border alliances

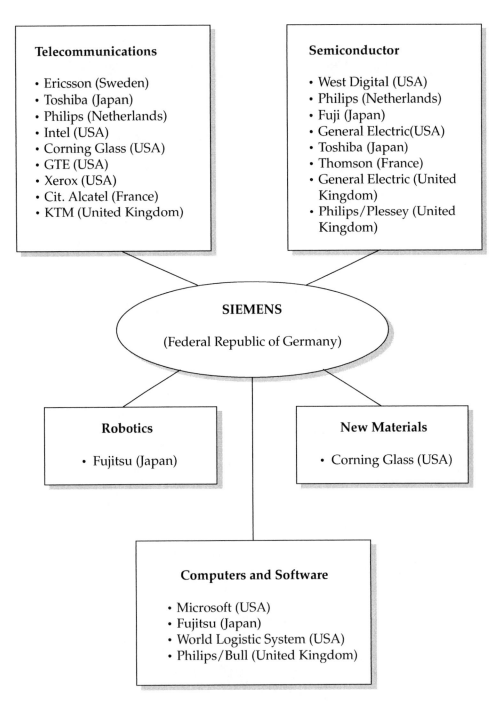

Telecommunications

- Ericsson (Sweden)
- Toshiba (Japan)
- Philips (Netherlands)
- Intel (USA)
- Corning Glass (USA)
- GTE (USA)
- Xerox (USA)
- Cit. Alcatel (France)
- KTM (United Kingdom)

Semiconductor

- West Digital (USA)
- Philips (Netherlands)
- Fuji (Japan)
- General Electric(USA)
- Toshiba (Japan)
- Thomson (France)
- General Electric (United Kingdom)
- Philips/Plessey (United Kingdom)

SIEMENS

(Federal Republic of Germany)

Robotics

- Fujitsu (Japan)

New Materials

- Corning Glass (USA)

Computers and Software

- Microsoft (USA)
- Fujitsu (Japan)
- World Logistic System (USA)
- Philips/Bull (United Kingdom)

FIGURE 6. Siemens AG and its main international co-operative agreements, 1984–1987
(*Source:* UNTST, based on company annual report and other public documentation. Includes joint ventures in R & D and in production, licensing and sub-contracting)

One response is that companies are increasingly adopting global strategies, designed to penetrate simultaneously the world's major markets with or updated products in order to amortise large fixed R & D expenditures and to maximise the impact of the new products before competitors can follow suit. The traditional methods of expansion, whereby firms first produced domestically, then exported to foreign-based production, are too slow, as they allow domestic and foreign competitors time to enter new foreign markets first. Strategies emphasising global marketing and global product development imply that MNCs need to have a significant presence in all of their major markets and are a stimulus to increase FDI within the developed market economies.

Such global strategies have been aided by, but have also helped foster, the increasing world-wide integration of information transmitted and of financial markets and financial institutions. In addition, *the increase of cross-border mergers* in publishing, public relations and advertising is another implication of the importance of global strategies, as marketing activities associated with global product strategies are themselves becoming increasingly internationalised.

The second major strategic response to the new technological environment is that many corporations have sought to reduce their risks through *various forms of cooperations, including strategic alliances*, especially with regard to R & D and the introduction of new production methods (see Figure 6). The new technologies are encouraging intricate network among firms to pool specialised services, share the high costs of R & D, and spread investment risks arising from heightened competition and shorter product life cycle.[62] Figure 7 shows the simplest possible representation of N. V. Philips, a multinational company headquartered in the Netherlands. The company has its own operating units in 60 countries. With only minor alterations, Figure 7 could also be a representation of an American multinational such as Procter & Gamble, or other European companies or Japanese companies, and Figure 7 could be even more complicated if we take into consideration the different inter-firm agreements.

Major innovation in products and processes is generally expensive, time-consuming and highly risky. Innovations in sciences are often disseminated rapidly through the publication of scientific papers and holding international conferences, and through the process of reverse engineering, where competitors purchase and disassemble a product to learn how it was constructed in order to be able to copy, and possibly improve upon, its most significant features. This "public goods" aspect of product innovation makes it difficult for firms to capture enough of the potential returns from a new idea to justify the frequently substantial amount of investment required.

---

[62] *Ibid.*, p. 57

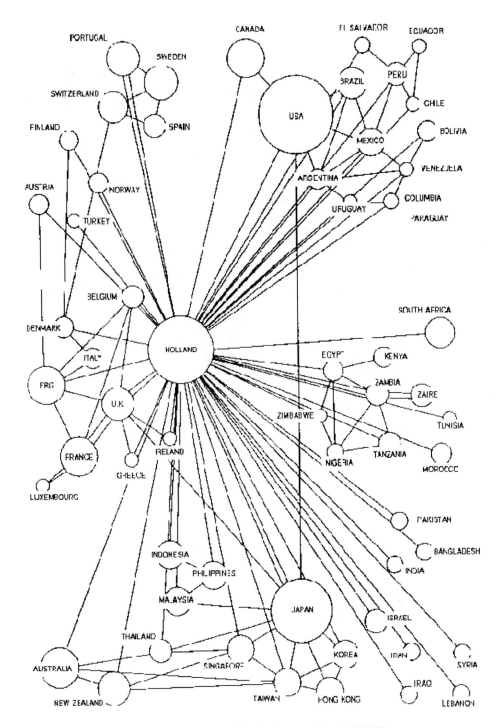

FIGURE 7. Organisational units of the linkages within N. V. Philips

105

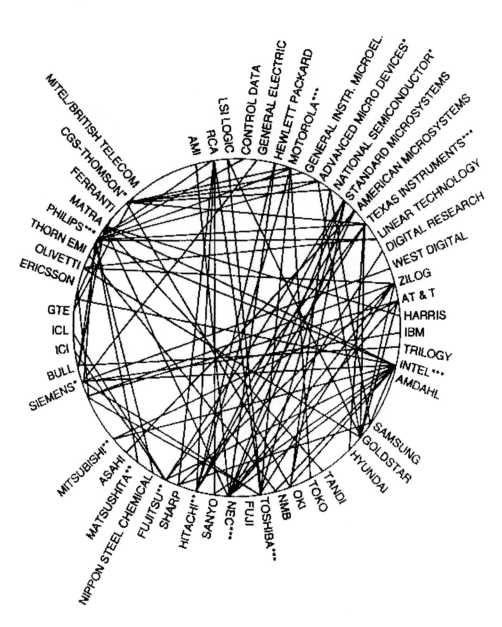

FIGURE 8. Alliance networks in the semi-conductor industry 1990
(*Source:* Gugler, 1991)

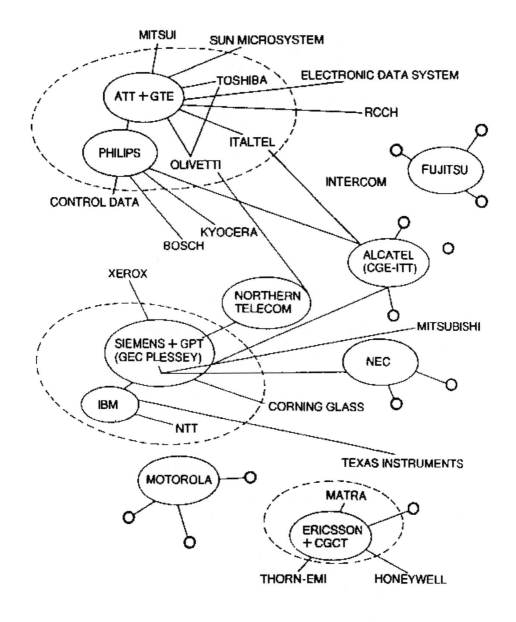

FIGURE 9. Interim clusters and networks in the telecommunication industry
(*Source:* Gugler, 1991)

The spread of micro-electronics into both product and process technologies has increased the extent of technological cross-fertilisation, as technologies originally developed for one industry are being increasingly applied across a wider range of activities. In telecommunications, for example, computer technology is central to the new generation of telephone switching and transmission equipment; similarly, linkages with national telephone systems are essential to the international transmission of computerised data bases and information retrieved and processing systems. As more countries are reducing their regulation of national telephone systems, encouraging the modernisation of national systems and supporting increased competition in the provision of equipment, the market for telecommunications equipment and services is growing rapidly. MNCs with substantial investments in telephone equipment, computers and semiconductors have entered into a variety of alliances in order to assimilate rapidly needed technologies, share huge development costs, spread risks and gain access to markets in foreign countries.[63]

One form of such technologically motivated alliances is the *acquisition of a firm*, with its technology and markets, by MNCs. In such cases, the acquired firm is usually relatively small, but is in possession of a technology that the MNC sees as important to its own development and for which it is willing to pay an attractive price. In some cases, large MNCs have acted as venture capitalists and have provided start-up equity capital to spur the development of key technologies, receiving, in return, licenses or contracts to utilise the technology. This has been a practice used in biotechnology, as established pharmaceutical firms have sought access to gene splicing technology, yet also want to limit their risks and exposure in as yet untried area. For their part, new firms are willing to provide access to their technology in return for needed capital and in order to gain experience in product development. Alternatively, some corporations with a view to combining technological and marketing skills to develop a single set of products, or improve upon an existing set, do not merge activities across each firm's entire range of products.

In recent years, co-operation agreements involving two or more MNCs, and usually involving corporations from different countries, have become increasingly popular. While co-operation agreements between different MNCs have long been common in petroleum, they are a recent phenomenon in high-technology sectors. Such agreements stop short of outright merge or acquisition. They can involve some equity participation, usually with a specific objective. (For example, IBM purchased a significant minority stake in Intel, a United States-based semiconductor manufacturer, in order to provide the latter with capital for a major expansion programme. Intel produces microprocessors for IBM's personal computers. Later, when Intel's business outlook improved, IBM reduced its equity stake. In another example, AT & T

---

[63] *Ibid.*, p. 57

purchased a 25 percent equity stake in Olivetti and is marketing Olivetti-produced personal computers under the AT&T name-plate.)[64]

International joint ventures and non-equity arrangements have been used in the past by MNCs, especially in mature, low-technology industries in the manufacturing and extractive sectors of the developing countries. In recent years, such agreements have occurred increasingly among two or more MNCs in the developed countries in different areas of specialisation. The growth of international co-operation agreements among MNCs is due primarily to attempts by firms to assimilate a new technology that is itself changing rapidly. In most instances, each party seeks to gain some competitive advantage that it can employ in its activities outside of the particular co-operative venture. Those agreements include joint ventures, where two or more MNCs establish a separate entity, cross-licensing and consortia, where a number of companies contribute to joint research efforts, frequently with government backing. The number of international joint ventures among MNCs in the developed market economies has been substantially higher since the late 1970s than it had previously been. International co-operation agreements have been concentrated in high-technology industries and in mature manufacturing industries that are seeking a technological infusion. The use of such agreements has been dominated by the largest MNCs.[65]

Strategic alliances are visible in all areas of activity, be it specific projects, single product lines or marketing. Previously formed mainly by firms in the primary and manufacturing sectors, alliances will be increasingly common in the services area, especially with the emergence of fully integrated world markets, as exemplified by the round-the-clock trading on financial exchanges. Even "go-it alone" companies are re-evaluating their strategy.

Spanning countries and continents, strategic alliances could significantly modify the character of trans-nationalisation. Although mainly among MNCs of equivalent size and market power, they also take the form of *corporate galaxies* in which a large MNC is linked via joint ventures, sub-contracts, marketing agreements and the like. Such links usually involve little or no transfer of equity, hence they need not result in increased consolidation of firms. Nevertheless, smaller MNCs and national firms, particularly from developing and former socialist countries, may need to join an alliance, or form their own, in order to enter international markets.

In many industrial sectors (aeronautics, telecommunications, computers, semi-conductors, etc.) it is possible to identify hierarchical or heterarchical galaxies, with a pivotal group of firms being surrounded by satellite partners. For example, as illustrated in Figure 8, the major world producers of semi-conductors have a focal position in a *complex web of alliances*. At the same time, new coalitions may induce

---

[64] *Ibid.*, p. 58
[65] *Ibid.*, p. 59

new market structure. Figure 9 shows that, at the end of the 1980s, the market for international telecommunications equipment was dominated by a limited number of closely linked interfirm clusters.[66]

Transnational corporate strategic alliances add a new dimension to global inter-dependence, and force a re-thinking of current approaches in many key areas, such as national antitrust and industrial policy, and international monetary policy. Corporate alliances are distorting the effects of exchange-rate adjustments on global trade imbalance, and motivating the governments of major countries to agree on new mechanisms for international co-ordination.[67]

---

[66] John H. Dunning, *The Globalisation of Business*, p. 212
[67] *Transitional Corporations in World Development. Trends and Prospects*, p. 497

IMPACT OF THE MULTINATIONAL CORPORATION ON THE ECONOMY

The MNCs have profound positive impact on the economy mainly through technology transfer, promotion of structural adjustment, reducing burden of debt, redressing debt-equity imbalance, but they exert influence on employment practice and the environment in many favourable ways, too.

TECHNOLOGY TRANSFER

An important contribution of MNCs to development is in the area of technology and perhaps the most important contribution the MNCs can make to the development process and modernisation is in the field of technology[1] transfer. MNCs are responsible for a large share of the world's technological innovation, they are at the centre of an accelerating pace of technological innovation. MNCs are playing a key role in the development of the new technology. Most technological innovations are the result of either the R & D activities of MNCs or of research undertaken by others, but funded by MNCs. Even in the numerous cases where innovations are made by smaller national firms on their own, those firms are often eventually taken over by MNCs, or sometimes they grow rapidly and become MNCs in their own right. The role of MNCs in technological change can be more readily appreciated when one begins to view technological innovation not as something exogenous or disembodied, but as one of the competitive pressures and to other stimuli stemming from

---

[1] Technology is commonly understood to mean the stock of knowledge, which permits the introduction of new or improved machinery and equipment, products, processes and services. In a wider sense, it includes additional elements, such as management and marketing skills. Technology, therefore, takes a number of different forms; "software", such as blueprints, formulae or process specifications; and the "services" of technicians and professionals for quality improvements, management and marketing know-how, process and product design etc. The software and service components of technology have become increasingly important since the advent of information technology as the central element in the production methods of most goods and services. (The various elements of a typical technology transfer package are briefly summarised in Figure 10.) *Transitional Corporations in World Development. Trends and Prospects* (United Nations, New York, 1988), p. 178

the environment in which they operate. Thus, technological innovations are highly firm-specific intangible assets, which tend to diffuse throughout the economy only with passage of time. Moreover, since technological innovations require large volumes of resources, only firms of a certain size are able to undertake or fund them.[2]

Technological innovations have been concentrated in the developed market economies, which are home to innovating MNCs. Most modern commercial technologies originate within MNCs. This has become even more apparent at the present time, when technological transformation has accelerated. The ability of a country's producers to generate or absorb foreign technologies continuously has become an increasingly important determinant of international competitiveness. A great appreciation of those technological considerations has also contributed to relaxation of laws and regulations towards FDI in several developing countries. At the same time, several countries have been applying regulation on the unpacked transfer of technology more flexibly.

Technological developments and the way they have affected the behaviour of MNCs are having other consequences. Because of large research and development costs, MNCs have sought to co-operate with each other by forming joint ventures, sharing research, cross-licensing new products and technologies, and in other ways. Often, such co-operation arrangements involve companies based in several home countries and having investment in dozens of host countries. Each one of the corporations belonging to a cluster of companies joined together by common research interest can overwhelm the regulatory capacity of many individual national governments, particularly in developing countries. By avoiding unnecessary and wasteful duplication of effort, technology-driven co-operation agreements can be cost efficient and can lead to significant productive gains and lower product prices.[3]

MNCs can increase productive efficiency through technology transfer. Most host countries seek the co-operation of the MNCs in expectation that those firms will contribute to the modernisation of their economies. MNCs adopt different mechanisms in the commercial transfer of technology. A listing of these include the following: *a)* FDI; *b)* joint ventures; *c)* licensing; *d)* franchising; *e)* management contracts; *f)* marketing contracts; *g)* technical service contracts; *h)* turnkey contracts; and *i)* international sub-contracting. Of these, FDI and joint ventures inevitably involve equity participation by MNCs; and others generally represent arm's length transactions between MNCs and independent enterprises in the host countries.[4]

The possession of firm-specific intangible assets, of which technological ones are among the most important, is considered to be one of the principle factors underlying the ability of MNCs to engage profitably in production abroad. Such assets – for

---

[2] *Ibid.,* p. 21
[3] *Ibid.,* p. 7
[4] *Ibid.,* p. 176

example, ownership of industrial property rights, unpatented know-how, product differentiation and promotion capabilities – provide competitive advantage over domestic enterprises in the economy of the host country and over other transitional rivals. The appropriation of the economic rents derived from those advantages is a principle motive for FDI. In any cases, corporations that own such intangible assets would find it difficult or impossible to earn the same rents on them in foreign markets in forms other than through the establishment of an affiliate abroad.

However, FDI is not without cost, since it involves the commitment of capital and managerial resources to a foreign venture. Foreign firms may encounter difficulties operating in an unknown economic environment, and they may find it advantageous to take on a domestic firm as a partner, which may bring to the joint venture some intangible assets of its own (for example, knowledge of local conditions). If the project involves risks which are perceived as large by the foreign firm – as many projects in the developing world undoubtedly do – it may wish to shift some of those risks to firms in the host country. Where the perceived benefits of internalisation of technology transactions clearly exceed the perceived costs, the foreign firms will be inclined to establish an affiliate. On the other hand, if costs exceed benefits, they will opt for either a joint venture or for non-equity forms of involvement.[5]

The process of technology transfer can be construed to consist of three stages: a) the acquisition of existing technologies relevant to the production of specific goods or services; b) the assimilation and diffusion of those technologies in host economies; and c) the development of indigenous capacities for innovation. MNCs can contribute to this process under different modes in different circumstances.

The technological transfer is especially important for the developing countries. The vast majority of the technology transferred from developed market economies to developing countries involves MNCs, either as foreign investors or as sellers of technology in contractual forms (for example, licensing, management contracts, turnkey projects etc.).

There are four different aspects to the transfer of technology through FDI that are of particular importance to developing countries:

a) Transfer of skills to the employed labour force. The methods for transferring and developing skills would, in principle, include formal in-house training programmes, an active promotion policy aimed at facilitating "learning" by nationals through exposure to progressively higher levels of responsibility, and sponsorship of the job training through provision of scholarships and support for technical and professional training institutes. The transfer of skills is most complete from the point the dependence on foreign manpower is phased out over time and full localisation of staff occurs.

---

[5] *Ibid.*, p. 179

Many MNCs prefer to use as many local managers and skilled workers as possible. The assignment of expatriates to overseas is often very expensive. In addition, the foreign investor may need to employ national managers, who have a better grasp of local conditions than expatriates do. Finally, the employment of nationals of the host country in visible positions is certain to improve the country's image in the host country.

b) The simulation of local technological activities. The impact of MNCs in this area could occur through undertaking R & D activities directly within their subsidiaries and through contracting with local R & D institutes, manufacturers of machinery and equipment, and engineering firms for the supply of technological goods and services. This is especially likely where the purpose of FDI is to exploit the parent transitional corporation's technological advantages through production within the host country.

In most situations, adoptive engineering and product design are required, and such work is evidently not without cost. None the less, the marginal cost of the basic technology is effectively zero, since it draws upon the R & D already undertaken by the parent company. Therefore, it is not unreasonable to expect that the affiliate will undertake relatively little R & D itself and will rely on the locally-developed technologies to a very limited extent.

c) The diffusion of technology throughout the economy. FDI can be hypothesised to contribute to the diffusion of technologies throughout the economy in a number of ways. Linkages to suppliers of inputs may result in the upgrading of product quality or reductions in cost. And the establishment of new foreign firms could lead to new investments in supplying industries. In countries with sufficient market size, a second channel for the diffusion of technology is the effect of FDI on competition within the industry. Domestic firms already operating in the industry may, therefore, be impelled to bring about technological improvements in their own operations. A third channel of diffusion is through the training of labour and management personnel by foreign enterprises. Some of these personnel may eventually take up employment in domestic enterprises or set up their own enterprises. A fourth possible source of diffusions is a kind of "demonstration effect": the presence of MNCs creates an opportunity for local enterprises to become aware of the existence of improved process and product technologies.[6]

Not all technologies are available in arm's-length markets. When it comes to up-to-date or sophisticated technologies, MNCs are singularly unwilling to transfer them through licensing or even to enter joint ventures with domestic firms that may lead to a loss of control over the intangible assets that are the basis for their competitiveness. On the other hand, a number of industrially more advanced developing countries have shown a marked preference for non-equity forms of technology trans-

---

[6] *Ibid.*, p. 182

fer or for joint ventures as ways to encourage the development of dynamic domestic enterprises. Equally significantly, those countries are bargaining for access to core technologies in their dealing with MNCs as arm's-length suppliers or as foreign investors. The willingness of individual MNCs to transfer core skills is an increasingly important determinant of whether they win a contract or are allowed to invest. When the desired technology is unavailable in forms other than fully- or majority-owned FDI, the insistence on non-equity forms or on joint venture could result in a diminishing inflow of new technologies.[7]

There are several features of the technology market, which introduce a great deal of complexity into the determination of prices of technologies transferred through non-equity channels. Technology takes a number of different forms. Market imperfections exist in each of these sub-categories of goods and services; and these forms of technology are often brought together in a single package by a supplying firm in a way that increases the degree of imperfection, since no firm's package is exactly like that of any other firm. These imperfections associated with technology as product are further aggravated by imperfect information on part of recipients.

In consequence, technology transactions between MNCs and unrelated parties have normally been analysed in term of a model of imperfect market, and within the specific context of a bargaining model. In a typical bargaining model, the licensor has a minimum (or floor) price, which is made up of the direct costs of effecting the technology transfer, plus the opportunity costs of doing so (such as loss of market opportunities, if any). The licensee has a maximum (or ceiling) price that he is willing to pay, which can be either *a)* the costs of developing the technology on his own, or *b)* the cost to obtaining the technology from an alternative supplier, or *c)* the increment returns (or cost savings) derived from using the technology, whichever is the lowest of the three. The actual price will be established in the range between the licensor's floor and the licensee's ceiling. The result will depend on the relative bargaining power of the two parties and the negotiation process.

Since the purchaser has less knowledge of the technology and its value than the supplier, the latter is often in a superior bargaining position. The buyer's disadvantage stems from what has been called the "information paradox": in order to bargain effectively, a buyer needs information about the value of the technology to him, the costs of developing it independently, and the direct costs to seller; however, in order to obtain this information, he would have to know the technology, which would then become worthless to seller. With a view to redressing this structural imbalance in technology markets and strengthening the position of domestic firms *vis-à-vis* powerful foreign technological suppliers, several developing countries have introduced a number of restrictions on the conditions of technology contracts that will be allowed.[8]

---

[7] *Ibid.*, p. 183
[8] *Ibid.*, p. 184

Accepting the importance of the technology transfer for economic development and modernisation, it has to be emphasised that the high degree of complexity of the new technologies has made it imperative for countries to strengthen their domestic technological capabilities, regardless of whether the technology transfer takes place through FDI or in unpacked forms. Only countries with sufficient skills will be able to obtain technologies with a high information component. For example, whether computers are produced by foreign firms, domestic firms or are imported, their widespread use in production requires the availability of sufficient computer programmers and technicians. This is particularly true if developing countries wish to obtain engineering and design know-how. One of the reasons why domestic capabilities are so important is exactly that. For all technologies that have a large information component, the "software" aspects are just as important as (or even more important than) the "hardware". Whether a country is able to obtain new technology through licensing and joint ventures or whether the technology comes as part of the FDI package, a greater degree of co-operation between MNCs and host-developing countries is likely to be needed today than in the past.

In making FDI and technology-transfer choices, policy-makers should also keep in mind that important innovations have been taking place in the area of organisation. Many companies have adopted the new methods, but many have not. Since these new methods can be introduced within any change in equipment, a country could experience significant gains in productivity at minimum cost. And this opens another potential area of co-operation between, and mutual gain for, MNCs and host countries.[9]

Technology transfer by MNCs also holds out the prospect of minimising or correcting adverse environmental impacts. Today, transitional corporations are frequently held to legally enforceable environmental standards in their home countries, following the upsurge of popular interest in this issue over the last two or three decades. They also tend to process superior financial, technical and management expertise of relevance to environment management. Thus, technological innovations in developed countries are likely to embody more effective measures to control pollution, for example. The environmental and occupations safety performance of transitional corporations is considered to be better, on average, than that of local firms in developing countries.[10]

---

[9] *Ibid.,* p. 192
[10] *Ibid.,* p. 229

Technology

Process technology	Product technology	Management technology	Quality control

• Determination of the type processing to be used
• Identification of economically and technically efficient machines and tools
• Raw materials specification
• Plant and design lay-out
• Identification and organisation of blueprints, specification sheets, operating manuals etc. of all sub-systems
• Cataloguing the documents, checking for text completeness, translating them for local use
	• Product specification
	• Product design
	• Identification of locally produced equipment and materials, and adapting them
		• Personnel management:
		  • skill identification
		  • training
		  • motivation
		  • design of rewards and penalties
		• Financial management:
		  • monitoring sales
		  • prioritising capital spending
		  • managing revenue expenditure
		  • distribution of dividends
		  • generating financial data useful for management decisions
		• Marketing management:
		  • processing information to guide product development and production planning
		  • training of sales personnel
			Ensuring appropriate design and standards of:
			• materials
			• equipment
			• end products

FIGURE 10. Elements of a typical technology transfer package

MULTINATIONAL CORPORATIONS CAN FACILITATE STRUCTURAL ADJUSTMENT

The sustainable economic growth and/or the resumption of economic growth after economic crisis require adjustment in the structure of production. The structural adjustment implies a change in structure of the economy towards the production of tradeable goods and services, which could take the form of exports or domestic production that substitutes previously imported goods. In case of the more industrialised developing countries, structural adjustment involves primarily an increase in manufactured exports and the building up of internationally competitive manufacturing production for the domestic market. The development of internationally competitive modern service is also an important component of structural adjustment.

MNCs have a global outlook and, therefore, they are able to respond rapidly to changes in international competitiveness. Thus, in certain sectors (for example, textiles and electronics), MNCs have been an important conduit for shifting production from the developed market economies to the more industrialised developing countries. They have done so not only through increasing production by affiliates, but also through subcontracting arrangements with independent firms in the developing world. Several developing countries have taken actions to enhance the contribution of MNCs to structural adjustment by revising their investment regulations and by setting up export processing zones (EPZs) aimed specifically at attracting export-oriented FDI.

The economic growth and structural adjustment for the low-income countries implies a set-up in the rate of growth of agricultural production and a diversification in the commodity composition of exports. In those areas, MNCs can play a useful role. MNCs have long been involved in exporting minerals and agricultural commodities from the developing countries and can be expected to continue to do so. In fact, given the paucity of alternative sources of financing mineral development, it can be predicted that MNCs are likely to increase their share in the mineral exports of developing countries in general. Likewise, MNCs can make a contribution to the growth of exports based on agricultural products and to the development of agribusiness in general. MNCs have been significant exporters of manufactures from some newly industrialising developing countries. Therefore, they can be expected to make a contribution in this respect in the future. While most FDI in the manufacturing sector in developing countries was intended originally for domestic market, where conditions have been right, MNCs have been willing to reorient a part of their production facilities in developing countries to international markets. Those countries, which have been successful in coaxing already established MNCs to sell in international markets, have done so mainly by correcting a chronic overvaluation of their exchange rate or by maintaining an internationally competitive exchange rate in real terms in the presence of strong domestic inflation. Other incentives to exports have also played a role.[11]

Adjustments in the structure of production to increase the supply of exportable and import-substitutes is an inescapable element of policy for a great many developing countries, especially the heavily indebted countries. It seems quite reasonable to suppose that MNCs may be particularly well suited to contribute to this process. Apart from their familiar advantages as vehicles for the transfer of capital and technology, their international connections assure access to the distribution and marketing channels of foreign countries; and their power to lobby with legislative bodies gives added meaning to such access in a period of rising projectionist pressures. Wherever MNCs are prominent in domestic manufacturing industry they are no less to the fore in exports of manufactures. Their share of exports has quite often been higher than their share of total domestic production. For many industrial MNCs – as for many domestic enterprises – the dichotomy between investment in production for the domestic market and investment in production for export should probably not be drawn too tightly. Many affiliates of MNCs straddle both markets.[12]

It would be a serious mistake, however, to equate the contribution of MNCs to export growth simply with the performance of their affiliates in developing countries. MNCs have been developing new forms of contractual arrangements with suppliers in developing countries, which are far more flexible and complex than those that could be realised with a conventional, majority-owned foreign affiliate. Those arrangements have been immensely influential in expanding the volume of manufactured exports of some newly industrialising countries, particularly the Southeast Asian countries. Through those arrangements, MNCs have enjoyed the advantage of lower-cost supplies without incurring the financial and managerial costs of setting up and operating their own affiliates. Those arrangements have been a feasible alternative, however, only because the climate of industrial competition in those countries has created a body of domestic manufactures who can be relied upon – as much as many direct managed affiliate – to meet quality standards, delivery dates and agreed prices. When combined with realistic exchange rates, these have powerfully boosted exports. Two kinds of arrangements have been of particular importance: *sub-contracting by the large retail chains* in industrial countries and *original equipment manufacturing*.[13]

Firms in developing countries seeking to expand their export to the developed market economies face immense difficulties in setting up a distribution network, keeping in close touch with the rapid change in consumer tastes, mastering the technicalities of industrial norms and safety standards and building up a new prod-

---

[11] *Ibi d.*, p. 133
[12] *Ibid.*, p. 158
[13] *Ibid.*, p. 159

uct image. Those problems of marketing and distribution are further compounded by geographical distance and considerable differences in culture.[14]

The role of marketing and distribution skills is vital for actual export performance. Those skills constitute a key link between production units and the final buyers, and the export performance of the newly industrialising countries undoubtedly has been considerably influenced by the effectiveness of that link. Of particular interest in this context are the Japanese trading corporations and the large department store chains in the developed market economies. Japanese general trading companies, also known as the *sogo shosha* (for example, Mitsubishi Corp., Mitsui and Co. Ltd.) play a critical role in identifying and developing new outlets for their clients' outputs. These companies operate in diverse products, ranging from primary commodities to high-technology products. In consequence, a large part of Japan's trade with developing countries is handled by the sogo shosha. They often provide trade credit for financing their customers' raw material purchases, intermediate imports or working capital requirements. The sogo shosha have also contributed to developing countries' exports of both resource-based and manufactured products by participating in joint ventures.

Some department stores in the developed market economies are true MNCs with outlets in several countries. Others have begun to develop their foreign activities more recently and are still selling very largely in their home countries. Many are very large and account for a substantial share of retail business in their countries of operation. What is more, their concentration rate appears to be increasing. These chains generally sell a very wide range of consumer goods; and a growing proportion of those goods is being imported from developing countries. The large department store chains in developed countries have emerged as a significant means of penetrating the consumer markets of industrial countries.

But perhaps no less important is their impact on trade, their indirect influence on the industrialisation process itself in the exporting countries. That influence operates at several different levels, from marketing and quality control to management and innovation. One of the most important and least-known channels of influence is the effect of such contractual arrangements with developing-country firms on the latter's managerial focus. An Asian or Latin American enterprise, working exclusively as a supplier to big European, United States or Japanese department stores, is in a position to focus most of its top managerial resources on production problems, and notably on quality control, manufacturing efficiency and technological innovation. The enterprise is in effect relieved of the marketing, distribution and after-sales functions that in other firms account for a large share of manpower and, most important, managerial attention. It may even be relieved of the product-design function and of the risks associated with rapid changes in fashion. In the textile and

---

[14] *Ibid.*, p. 164

garment industry, for instance, the purchasing agents of the big department stores specify not only the final product's design, but also the fabric down to the button and zippers. The effect on efficiency are probably considerable: a firm's senior managers, who can devote maybe 80 or 90 percent of their time and attention to production issues taken in widest sense, will tend to be much more efficient in their tasks than senior managers of the same quality, who might be spending no more than 10 or 20 percent on the same issues.[15]

The result of this single-minded focus on manufacturing is not only greater production of technological learning process, but also an acceleration of the technological learning process: a pure production firm of this type can devote a considerable amount of its production-oriented attention to the improvement of its production process and to technological innovation. This may be part of the explanation why many firms from newly industrialised countries have managed to bridge the technological gap more rapidly than could have been expected from the normal interplay of international competition.

The relationship of developing-country suppliers with the major retail chains in the developed market economies has also had a number of other important effects. The best known relates to quality control. The big department stores whether they sell their foreign made products under their own brand name or more anonymously, tend to be extraordinarily quality conscious, and impose very strict quality-control standards on their suppliers. This quality consciousness, motivated both by the strong competition between the various retail chains in the industrialised countries themselves and by the high financial penalties involved in large purchases of poor-quality goods, has had very obvious positive effects on their developing country suppliers. It has contributed to developing among those suppliers a much greater sensitivity to quality, in general, and the management of quality control, in particular.

The quality-control mechanisms set up by the big retail chains play another important if less conspicuous role: they serve in effect as a complement to the still poorly developed national agencies responsible for checking the quality of export products. As the experience of Japan in the early decades of this century clearly shows, a newly industrialised country can easily fall prey to the temptation of exporting cheap low-quality manufactured goods. In the short-run, it may achieve significant export successes, but the poor international image which develops as a result of such practices will then take years, if not decades, to overcome. Such a negative image, furthermore, operates as a major obstacle to the export efforts of the country's industrial transition towards more sophisticated products with higher value added. (After the Second World War, Japanese planners and the main industry associations made enormous efforts to build up effective quality-control mechanisms for exported goods, and largely succeeded in overcoming the poor reputation established by the shoddy exports of the 1920s and 1930.)

---

[15] *Ibid.*, p. 165

Building up effective export quality-control mechanisms at the national level can be a very long and painstaking effort, especially if it has to start with the legacy left by massive exports of poor quality manufacturing goods. In the case of the newly industrialised countries, there are good reasons to suspect that the quality-control standards imposed by the big retail chains have allowed those countries to develop an industrial quality-control culture at a much faster pace than would probably have been the case in the absence of this symbiotic relationship between purchasers and suppliers. The standards set by large foreign purchasers are obviously no substitute for quality-control mechanisms at the national level. But the existence of the former can stimulate the development of the latter, and the indirect role of the big department stores may well have been to help the newly industrialised countries to gain 10 or 15 years, if not a whole generation, in the quality-control learning process.[16]

Another major variant of new forms of subcontracting relationships is the *original equipment manufacturing arrangement (OEM)*. This type of long-term contractual relationship between a manufacturing firm and its main suppliers of components and sub-assemblies is nothing very new: its origins can be traced back many years – most obviously to the United States in the 1920s. Those arrangements, concluded for a limited period of time but with an option for renewal, are one of the major ways in which a manufacturing firm can ensure a certain stability in its sources of supply: prices are usually fixed for the duration of the contract (and usually very competitive, given the size of the orders, delivery dates are clearly specified, quality standards can easily be maintained, and the manufacturers can concentrate on their main line of business rather than having to invest in the production of goods which lie beyond their sphere of technical competence. This stability is also to benefit the supplier, who can plan his production schedule accordingly and count on a predictable cash flow for a relatively long period of time. What is more, such an arrangement can be very beneficial to the competitive standing in the industry: a small firm which lands a major OEM contract with a big manufacturer known for his quality standards and hard bargaining will almost immediately have established itself as a serious and reliable enterprise with a strong technological capability and this will, in turn, facilitate its penetration of other markets.

Original equipment manufacturing, once limited to a region of origin of the main contractor (for example, the Detroit region in the case of the United States automobile industry or the Midland in the case of British firms), gradually expanded to the level of an entire country and, in the last 20–30 years, to the whole world. OEM contracts today account for a significant share of world trade in manufacturing goods, and are a central factor in the internationalisation of industry and expansion of MNCs.

---

[16] *Ibid.*, p. 166

OEM arrangements offer some major advantages for manufacturers in developed market economies. They allow then to take advantage of lower production costs in the developing country without deployment of their own resources. They neither have to utilise capital in equity investment nor to use managerial staff in overseeing the operations of affiliate in an unfamiliar business and cultural environment. Interestingly, some of MNCs have used OEM arrangements to respond to foreign competition. (The arrangements of Ford and General Motors with enterprises in the Republic of Korea, for instance, have allowed them to challenge Japanese-made imports of small cars with competitive Korean-made products.) Others have used the arrangements to diversify their product range. (In the case of Olivetti or AT&T, for instance, the arrangements with Samsung have facilitated their penetration of the computer market by providing them with a supply of monitors that lay somewhat away from their main line of business.)

By no means would all manufacturers in developed market economies, however, find OEM arrangements advantageous or even feasible. Numerous MNCs produce highly differentiated products using patented, in-house technologies, which they are not willing to licence other to employ. Indeed, it is a characteristic of OEM arrangements that are found in industries at a phase in the product cycle where their technologies have become largely standardised.[17]

It is also notable that the Republic of Korea and, to a lesser extent, Taiwan Province, have been the main participants in OEM arrangements. From the viewpoint of the importing corporations in the developed countries, essential condition for an OEM arrangement is the availability of producers who not only have the necessary technical or managerial capacity but who can be relied on to meet delivery deadlines and quality standards and who can do so at previously agreed prices. In the absence of the competitive industrial milieu, which fosters such producers, MNCs may prefer the greater reliability that would come from establishing their own affiliates in developing countries. Thus, the phenomenon of OEM may be both regional-specific and industry-specific.[18]

For a considerable number of developing countries, an important initiative taken in the last 10–15 years has been the establishment of *export processing zones (EPZs)*. Though distinctly different from the new constractual arrangements, they have been similar in their intended effect of promoting exports.

The central features of EPZs are that imports and exports are free of tariffs and other trade restraints, that infrastructural production is provided, and that regulatory and administrative procedures entailed in the establishment and operation of enterprises are simplified. Fiscal and financial incentives may also be provided.[19]

---

[17] *Ibid.*, p. 167
[18] *Ibid.*, p. 168
[19] *Ibid.*, p. 170

EPZs may stimulate a flow of foreign investment by corporations, which might not have otherwise been prepared to consider the risk of producing in another country. What those foreign firms have sought has been access – under favourable financial, administrative and physical conditions – to low-cost supplies of labour. It is quite consistent with the dominance in EPZs of industries with a large labour-intensive element in their manufacturing processes. Most EPZs have, in fact, tended to be dominated by either the electronics or the textile industry. Since those are industries whose products are high in value relative to their weight, their location is not greatly affected by transport costs.

It would be quite wrong to suppose, however, that EPZs have been filled solely by the affiliates of foreign enterprises. Domestic firms account for about one quarter of total employment in EPZs and there are numerous joint ventures between domestic and foreign enterprises. Sub-contracting by the large retail chains in the industrial countries is an important source of business for those domestic firms in EPZs, so too are OEM arrangements in some countries (as, for instance, in the export of motor-vehicle components from firms sited in Mexican EPZs to the United States).

Understandably, domestic enterprises have often pressed for permission to locate in EPZs and, especially when aided by sub-contracting arrangements, they have often proved able to compete effectively on the international market. From the national viewpoint, their establishment in EPZs has also had advantages. For one thing, the success of an EPZ as an economic proposition depends on early and full utilisation of its capacity; otherwise, the heavy infrastrucural costs cannot be amortised. For other, locally-owned enterprises, by virtue of their local knowledge and connections, are perhaps more likely to develop backward linkages with industries in the domestic economy.[20]

There are also certain other, less tangible potential benefits that should be part of any broad assessment of EPZs. Those take the form of demonstration effects. The sale of a portion of EPZs output on the local market, for instance, creates a form of controlled competition for local industries. Perhaps more important is the evidence that EPZs provide an example of how industrial investment can be stimulated by the removal of cumbersome regulations governing the establishment and operation of industrial enterprises.[21]

---

[20] *Ibid.*, p. 171
[21] *Ibid.*, p. 172

REDUCING THE BURDEN OF DEBT AND REDRESSING EXISTING DEBT-EQUITY IMBALANCES BY AUGMENTING THE FLOW OF EQUITY CAPITAL TO DEVELOPING COUNTRIES

An important aspect of the problems facing developing countries has been the growing imbalance between foreign equity and foreign debt. A part of the redressing of that imbalance can involve higher level of FDI. But stimulating larger flows of FDI requires considerably more than liberalising host country laws and regulations. One of the steps that could be taken by the countries concerned, perhaps with the aid of appropriate international agencies, is to make efforts to tap the potential of MNCs including the small and medium size ones. Those corporations have become increasingly important foreign investors.[22]

In relation to this, the recognition that foreign equity and foreign debt are by no means perfect substitutes is important in arriving at correct policy conclusions as to how to deal with debt problem. Indeed, many projects, particularly in the natural resource sectors, are financed partially with foreign equity and partially with debt-creating flows. To the extent that there is a margin for substitution, however, *future emphases ought to be in favour of equity rather than the further accumulation of debt*. It is not just a matter that bank loans are unlikely to be forthcoming in the foreseeable future. It can be argued that an excessive accumulation of debt detriment to equity flows (either FDI or of a portfolio nature) is undesirable. The unsuitability of bank lending (an essentially medium-term flow at floating interest rates) for financing development projects, which usually have long gestation periods, has clearly been demonstrated during the debt crisis. Bank lending exposes a country to the decisions of a small group of large creditors, whose behaviour is pro-cyclical and herd-like. Thus, when sentiments in international financial markets about a country's future prospects deteriorate, that country may encounter difficulties in obtaining access to new credits and even in rolling over maturing loans. Moreover, debt contracted at floating interest rates leaves the economies of large borrowers unduly exposed to the effects of unpredictable fluctuations in international interest rates.[23]

While borrowing from international financial markets certainly has a role to play in financing development, it can be argued that the equity flows have certain advantages over debt-creating flows. In the first place, while foreign loans can be used to finance excess consumption (public and private), *equity flows, at least in principle, are invested in projects that are expected to generate positive returns*.

Debt-service payments are inflexible, regardless of the use to which the foreign resources are put, the success or failure of projects financed with loan, or of the

---

[22] *Ibid.*, p. 7
[23] *Ibid.*, p. 129

balance-of payments situation of the borrowing country. On the other hand, dividend remittances are directly related to the success of the venture financed with foreign resources. If foreign equity investments are directed to the production of tradeable goods or services (they are export or competitive import substitutes), a successful venture will generate or save the foreign exchange required for dividend remittances. Undoubtedly, in the past too many investments made by MNCs were undertaken under the protection of excessively high tariff walls, which resulted in projects that consumed more foreign exchange than they produced. In addition, transfer-pricing abuses and payments of various fees by affiliates to parents have often led outflows of foreign exchange before projects began to yield any concrete positive results for the host country. However, FDI need not have an adverse balance-of-payments impact. A project's foreign exchange earnings or savings can be considerably improved through the adaptation of trade policy that do not discriminate against the sectors, which produce tradeable goods and services. And foreign exchange remittances that are unrelated to actual profits can, in principle, be monitored and restricted.

It is easier to regulate profit remittances than interest payments. For example, a host country in balance-of-payments difficulties can give affiliates of MNCs incentives to postpone profit remittances or to reinvest profits. This is not an option when the outflow in question is interest payments. In addition to these, MNCs have a world-wide network of affiliates, which facilitates the expansion and diversification of exports. New ventures financed with loan capital have greater difficulties in penetrating foreign markets.[24]

Thus one kind of structural adjustment that the heavily-indebted countries must make – and which is often overlooked – is to redress the imbalance between debt and equity. Since in the short to medium term equity flows are not likely to rise at a pace that is fast enough to make up for the disappearance of bank lending, the process is likely to be protracted. In principle, the needed external financial adjustment can be brought about in three different but complementary ways. In the first place, there must be resumption of FDI flows to developing countries, and new ways of attracting portfolio investments should be considered. A second contribution to financial adjustment could come from the outright conversion of debt into equity. And debt relief would be the appropriate remedy for over-borrowing and over-lending. Whatever the relative weight of these three elements turns out to be in practice, there is no doubt that FDI must assume a more important role in providing external finance to developing countries.[25]

However, it should be recognised that, even under the most optimistic circumstances, FDI is highly unlikely to reach significant levels in the low-income coun-

---

[24] *Ibid.*, p. 130
[25] *Ibid.*, p. 131

tries, which are largely bypassed by MNCs. In addition, the sectors in which they most urgently need to invest (primary economic and social infrastructure) do not attract private capital, either domestic or foreign. Therefore, those countries will continue to depend heavily on official development assistance to supplement their low level of domestic saving. If they were to increase the size of the markets they offer to MNCs, for example, through regional integration schemes, they might be able to attract larger volumes of FDI. Of course, such policies are desirable on other grounds as well.[26]

While recognising that FDI can make an important contribution to reactivating economic growth, that contribution will necessarily have to be of a supplementary nature. The major effort will have to come from the domestic private and public sectors. And this means that there will be a continuous need for external financing from sources other than MNCs. Portfolio investment could be one such source. Another possibility could be for developing countries to attempt to break into securitised international financial markets that have developed in the recent years, perhaps with the aid of the multilateral financial institutions. However, these new forms of financing are unlikely to be forthcoming unless potential lenders and investors – among them MNCs – in international financial markets perceive that the debt crisis is on the way to being overcome.[27]

EMPLOYMENT, HUMAN RESOURCES DEVELOPMENT, EMPLOYMENT PRACTICE

Until quite recently, the world of work has been shaped by local and national factors. At least since the Second World War, the level of employment has been a major consideration influencing the policies of national governments. The quality of employment depended on the sectoral distribution of production and the behaviour of individual firms with respect to wages, working conditions and training programmes, albeit in the context of wider government policies relating to the labour market and education and training. Most people, at least in developing countries, expected a lifetime employment, if not in the same company, then likely in the same locality or country. Trade union and employer organisations bargained within an established framework of national relations. All that now is changing under the pressure of globalisation, as the increased mobility of capital meets the more location-bounded asset that is labour.

---

[26] *Ibid.*, p. 132
[27] *Ibid.*, p. 133

More specifically, the growth and organisation of international production under the governance of MNCs has several implications for the organisation of domestic labour markets:

- The conditions underlying firm-level competitiveness are changing, relying less on traditional natural assets and more on created assets, above all assets in the form of skill and knowledge. Such assets are therefore an important factor influencing the locational advantages of countries hosting MNCs.
- The importance of skilled human resources, as well as the proliferation of cross-border production linkages via FDI, subcontracting arrangements and strategic alliances and adaptation of complex integration strategies by MNCs create both challenges and opportunities for mutually beneficial relations between employers and employees.
- As the organisation scope of MNCs widens, both geographically and functionally, and as the mobility of capital increases, labour and governments must adopt quickly to changes in the international competitiveness of their industries and firms.
- Increasing reliance on market forces redefines the relationships of firms, labour and governments with one another, including those in the areas related to employment and the workplace.

In addition, the recent increase in unemployment has refocused the attention of policy makers on the link between MNCs and the generation, location and upgrading of jobs. Although the fundamental factors underlying current unemployment problems relate to macroeconomic and structural imbalances in developed countries and resource constraints in developing countries, MNCs, as major forces in the internationalisation of economic activities, influence the quality of jobs available world-wide. The influence is particularly important in manufacturing and services and, within these, in certain industries and countries.[28]

MNCs are estimated to employ some 73 million persons at home and abroad (see Table 10). Although this represents only around 3 percent of the world's labour force, employment in MNCs accounts for nearly 10 percent of paid employment in non-agricultural activities world-wide, and close 29 percent in developed countries considered alone. In addition, the indirect employment effects of MNC activity are at least equal to the direct effects and probably much larger. Backward linkages, such as the purchasing of raw materials, parts and components from subcontractors and external suppliers, are among the principle channels whereby MNCs can indirectly contribute to employment generation. The importance of these effects has grown in recent years, as firms have progressively focused on smaller but higher-value segments of the production process, relying increasingly on national and international out-sourcing for technological, cost or flexibility reasons. (An example

---

[28] *Transitional Corporations*, Vol. 3, No. 2 (August 1994) p. 89

TABLE 10. World foreign-direct-investment stock and estimated employment in transnational corporations, 1975, 1985, 1990 and 1992 (millions of dollars and millions of employees)

Item	1975	1985	1990	1992
Outward FDI stock	282	674	1649	1932
Estimated employment in TNCs	40	65	70	73[a]
Employment in parent companies at home		43	44	44[a]
Employment in foreign affiliates		22	26	29[a]
Developed countries		15	17	17[a]
Developing countries			9	12[a]
China			3	6[a]
Memorandum				
Employment in United States	26[b]	25	25	
Of which:				
Employment in foreign affiliates	7	6	7	

Source: UNCCAD, Division on Transnational Corporations and Investment, *World Investment Report 1994. Transnational Corporations, Employment and the Workplace* (United Nations publication, Sales No. E.94.II.A.14).

[a] Preliminary estimate.

[b] 1977.

is the footwear company Nike whose core staff consists of 9000 persons but, through subcontracting, employs an additional 75,000 located in different countries.) Overall, however, it is estimated conservatively that each job in MNC generates at least one additional job elsewhere in the economy. Thus, at a conservative estimate, the total number of jobs associated with MNCs may be paced at 150 million at the beginning of the 1990s.[29]

Perhaps even more importantly, MNCs often provide labour with the opportunity to acquire additional knowledge and skills, and this is particularly so in the case of affiliates operating in developing countries. Indeed, the essential characteristic of MNCs is that they bring together in the workplace international knowledge and skills with the human resources present in a particular location. Accordingly, host country employees and the host economy as a whole can benefit from the upgrading of skills already passed through employment in MNCs and, especially, the acquisition of new vocational and management skills through formal and on-the-job training in foreign affiliates.

The major role of MNCs in human resource development stems form the learning opportunities and training that they provide for their employees. The extent and nature of training varies according to country, industry and activity in which a MNC is engaged, as well as firms-specific strategies with respect to FDI and human

---

[29] *Ibid.*, p. 91

resource management. On the whole, MNCs provide at least as much, if not more, training for their workers in developed and developing countries as domestic firms. Because of their size and international character, MNCs are able to offer formal and non-formal training programmes that are, in some respects, better than those provided by many domestic firms, especially in developing countries.[30]

MNCs have been responsible for the introduction of new categories of employment into many developing countries over the last few decades, and this has intensified in the 1980s. The most obvious examples of this are in the fields of consumer electronics and the information technology industries. The automobile, toy and sports goods industries are others in which component assembly of subsidiaries of MNCs has had a substantial impact in recent years. This has had repercussions all through the labour force, including the training of operatives, who had never previously held factory jobs, the process of replacing expatriate with indigenous managerial and technical personnel, and the growth of indigenous capacity in unfamiliar and/ high technology industries.

One of the important consequences of the international division of labour has been the establishment of many new types of industries by MNCs in developing countries. While the rate of increase of MNC job creation in the developing countries levelled of somewhat in the 1980s, the growth of employment in EPZs, largely due to increased FDI by newer and relatively small MNCs, has been rapid in some developing countries. It has been claimed, since many MNCs embark on offshore sourcing precisely to escape from their domestic unions, that the right of workers to organise is severely curtailed in some EPZs, and that trade unions are either suppressed or manipulated. Others argue that MNCs tend to bring more progressive labour relations that had previously been the case in such countries. Irrespective of the fact that many, perhaps most, of those jobs are low-paid, dirty and monotonous by domestic standards, they are very widely sought and carry high prestige.

There are several dimensions to being employed by an affiliate of an MNC, which contribute to the prestige of those jobs. One is, of course, the fact that wages and salaries tend to be higher than in domestic firms. At the lowest level in the firm hierarchy, the operatives, there is clearly a reputational element at work, in so far as working for a company that has an international name means something positive for most people. Further, employment with an affiliate of a MNC often promises skill enhancement and promotion. At the managerial level, large numbers of developing country nationals have entered international business careers through employment with MNCs. There is a growing body of evidence to suggest that, in recent years, more MNCs have seen the benefits (or, in some country, accepted the inevitability) of employing host-country managers and technicians to run their plans. It is likely that the chief executive of a MNC plant will still be from the home coun-

---

[30] *Ibid.*, p. 96

try, but it is now quite common to see host-country nationals occupying salaried positions at all levels.

Employment practices of MNCs compared with those of domestic firms vary widely. There are many MNCs that have been operating in specific countries for so long that they are almost indistinguishable from domestic companies. Most MNCs operate outside the EPZs, of course, and for them plant size and branch of industry are more important determinants of their employment practices than the bare fact of foreign ownership. The larger MNCs often take the question of corporate identity very seriously and their wages, facilities and non-wage benefits frequently tend to be superior. Such firms strive, though not always successfully, to inculcate feelings of membership in a global family among their employees in different countries through magazines, competitions related both to production and non-work activities, and widespread uses of company logos on small gifts and prizes.[31]

However, MNCs are among the first to introduce new work and employment norms and to use the advantages of the new labour market conditions. The feminisation of the labour market is the most dramatic visible evidence of the gender revolution that has marked this new work world. Throughout much of the economy, firms now rely on non-standard female workers. Work without job security has become the norm for the young and the old.

Jobs are no longer full-time, but part-time, casual and contractual. With working time reorganised, the pay structure is being revised downward. The better-paying good jobs have disappeared in record numbers as companies have downsized and laid off workers in the hundreds of thousands in North America and Europe. The new jobs are for the most part at the low-end of pay scale.

The union representation has also suffered a dramatic reversal of fortune everywhere. The shift from goods production to service industries has encouraged employers to de-unionise the workplace whenever the opportunity presents itself. The unionised workplace of the Fordist variety has been overtaken by the aggressively non-unionised work world of K-mart, named appropriately after the large U.S. discount consumer outlet chain. Its practices are emblematic of the new capital-labour accord now taking shape. Management's rights have been strengthened, work rules tightened, job security reduced and wages hover as close as possible to the minimum set by law. In such an environment unions are not welcome. With the huge resources of business and employer-friendly governments, the changes of any successful unionisation drive are light even when protected by law. For example, László Pasztérnak, Hungarian trade union leader complained that European and American MNCs – General Motors, General Electric, Audi, VW and others – exerted a considerable pressure to make a union-free zone in Hungary.[32] In addition, the most

---

[31] *Ibid.*, p. 221
[32] William Greider, *One World, Ready or Not* (Simon and Shuster, New York, 1998) p. 62

dramatic change is in the service sector where the majority of the jobs are to be found. Working time is becoming more skewed as part-time work becomes the norm. Part-time employment in Canada, for instance, is three times more common in this sector than in the goods economy. The Canadian situation is by no means unique. Throughout Western economies, more people are working longer hours than ever and for less pay.[33]

UNFAVOURABLE, NEGATIVE IMPACTS OF MULTINATIONAL CORPORATIONS ON THE ECONOMY AND THE SOCIETY

The MNCs have not only favourable impacts on the economy and the society but they are responsible for some very essential unfavourable impacts too, from which the following deserve distinguished attention:
- They have given rise to fresh concerns about the vulnerability of economies to disturbances in financial markets and about the world-wide growth of speculative activity;
- Unintended impact on the environments;
- An impact on social and cultural values in host countries;
- Political influence.

Concerns about the Vulnerability of Economies

The extensive changes in financial institutions and markets which have taken place over recent years have given rise to new prudential and macroeconomic concerns. The central authorities have long engaged in the regulation and supervision of financial institutions, particularly the banks, in order to ensure that those institutions conduct their business prudently. Since the banks are principal providers of the means of payments, a failure of the banking system could have devastating consequences for the economy. Financial institutions and markets, moreover, are key intermediaries through which the central authorities bring their macroeconomic policies to bear on real economic activity. The changes of recent years, which have been brought about in a large part by the dismantling of regulations, have both altered the nature of the prudential concerns and the effectiveness of macroeconomic policies. One consequence has been a continuing effort to revise regulatory and supervisory framework and, in particular, to conform the regulations of the leading

---

[33] *States against Markets*. S. Robert Boyer and Daniel Drache, ed. (Routledge, London, 1996) p. 45

developed market economise more closely. Another has been an awareness of the vulnerability of real economic activity to the behaviour of international financial markets and of the added limitation imposed on the pursuit of independent macroeconomic policies.[34]

In addition, the sharp fluctuations in exchange rates have played havoc with MNCs. Indeed, the very meaning of a balance sheet, composed of assets denominated in several currencies, has been called into question. Those fluctuations, together with sharp swings in interest rates, have often made it more profitable for companies to devote resources and talents to speculations on the direction of change in these prices than to nurture productive investments that yield long-run results. Speculative international capital flows have experienced a huge increase in the 1980s and 1990s, and this has stimulated foreign and domestic investments in banking and finance in the world's major money market centres.

A set of concerns turns on the issue of prudent behaviour by the financial institutions, including MNBs, themselves. It is nothing new that financial markets may run heavy risk if individual financial institutions succumb to the temptation of engaging in speculative transactions and ignore accepted rules of prudent financial management. In times of general unease about financial and economic conditions, the failure of an individual institution can touch off panicle responses by other institutions, generating a succession of liquidity crises which destabilise interest rates and exchange rates and depress real economic activity. Individual countries have long had their own arrangements for regulation and supervision of financial institutions – mainly the banks – in order to safeguard against such a situation. But there are new elements in the present situation. First, the internationalisation of financial markets has multiplied the links between institutions and market in different countries; chain reactions may run not only through different institutions in the same country, but also through different institutions in separate countries. Secondly, the compartmentalisation of the banking and securities markets has been breaking down, and the links between institutions operating in the two segments are growing. There is also the further complication that national arrangements for regulation and supervision vary considerably. Some are more lax than others, although all countries are exposed to risks arising in any of them.

The spread of transitional banking has caused problems for the regulation and supervision of financial markets. This has been recognised for some time. The central banks of several developed market economies have met from time to time since 1975 to reach agreement on the co-ordinated application of national regulations and even on common standards regulating capital requirements. However, while there is more interlocking today of banks and non-bank financial institutions both within and between countries, the non-bank institutions are often very lightly regu-

---

[34] *Transitional Corporations in World Development. Trends and Prospects*, p. 120

lated, and no action has been taken so far to begin the construction of a common international regulatory framework. Yet, as the global plunge in equity prices in October 1987 amply underlined, for example, securities markets have many direct links with each other, and imprudent conduct by a financial institution in one nation market may have almost immediate repercussion elsewhere. Greater regulatory co-ordination appears to be a necessary element in the protection of the international financial system.[35]

One of the new prudential concerns has arisen from the movement of the banks into off-balance sheet activities. It will be recalled that, partly to comply with bank supervisors' requirements that the banks raise their capital-to-assets ratios, banks have been active in generating new sources of income through off-balance sheet activities. Their participation in a securities markets through such new financial instruments as note issuance facilities, stand-by letters of credit, swap and options, has been extensive. Back-up commitments alone have grown to levels several times the capital pledged to them. However, the trouble with those off-balance sheet activities is that they carry risks, which may sometimes be obscure and that are not embraced in conventional balance-sheet analysis. This has raised uncertainties about the capital adequacy of the banks.

Another change giving rise to prudential concerns is that the banking system and the securities markets have ceased to be largely insulated from each other. The distinction between banks and non-bank financial institutions, has, indeed, become blurred. One consequence is that, as the various institutions are linked through their mutual borrowing and lending, the banking system is more vulnerable to imprudent conduct by institutions in securities markets. Traditionally, firms operating in securities markets have been subject to relatively light regulation and supervision; the intent has usually been no more than to protect the individual investor and to prevent fraud (including "insider" trading). But the trend in the very recent past has been to give greater weight to prudential considerations.

A further source of prudential concern has been the differences that exist among developed market economies in their regulations and tax regimes. Those differences have provided financial institutions with a way of escaping from the more stringent, and costly, regulations in their home countries. So long as cross-border transactions remained relatively small, the anomalies in regulatory disciplines were not of great consequence. But, with the huge expansion in international financial transactions, particularly since the dismantling of exchange controls in Japan and European countries, the sensitivity of markets world-wide to the failure of financial institutions anywhere has increased, and the need for more uniform regulatory and supervisory standards has become more urgent.[36]

---

[35] *Ibid.*, p. 4
[36] *Ibid.*, p. 120

International co-operation on regulatory matters was begun among the central banks of the countries of the Group 10 in middle-1970s under the auspices of the Bank for International Settlements. Their first agreements, known as the two Basle Concordats, laid down rules concerning the jurisdictions to which the subsidiaries and branches of MNBs should be subject. In subsequent years, central banks have sought to broaden their co-operation.[37]

Besides such prudential concerns, the recent trend towards the internationalisation of financial markets has undoubtedly complicated the task of policy-makers in managing macroeconomic activity. It is clear that, with the closer integration of financial markets, countries have lost a degree of autonomy in their domestic economic policies. Instability in international financial markets – notably in exchange rates and interest rates – is worsened if the lending countries pursue discordant policies; but for industrial countries, the co-ordination of policies with others may be possible only at the cost of foregoing the pursuit of domestic-policy objectives.[38]

In principle, the freedom of financial flows to respond to price signal worldwide should imply enhanced economic efficiency in the international allocation of capital. It can also act as a market-disciplining device working against inappropriate or inconsistent macroeconomic policies. But these results presume that private capital invariably moves to eliminate any discrepancies that arise between the currently quoted value and the fundamentally correct value of financial assets; this is demonstrably not so. The greater freedom of private capital movements in asset price of the 1980s has not moderated the fluctuations in asset prices, including the price of assets denominated in foreign currencies, but has given rise to wider gyrations around their fundamental values. The most striking instance was, for example, the strong and steady appreciation of dollar up to 1985, which took place even as the United States current-account deficit rose to record levels.

It is an old observation that participants in financial markets tend to act on the basis of views about what are the conventionally accepted values. This can cause a deviation from fundamental values which, when widely perceived, may bring about a large and sudden revision of prices. The difficulty for macroeconomic policy-makers is that those volatile swings, if large enough and broad enough, can have sufficiently disruptive effects on asset prices, particularly interest rates and exchange rates, as to jeopardise real economic activity. Their tasks, it may be said, is therefore clear enough: it is to prevent asset prices from becoming distorted in the first place or, if they do, to moderate the market revolution. But it is not as simple as that. First, the policy-makers themselves may be part of the problem, pursuing macroeconomic policies, which are themselves unsustainable in the longer run. Second, in the present-

---

[37] *Ibid.*, p. 121
[38] *Ibid.*, p. 4

day world of more internationally integrated financial markets, the macroeconomic policies of the leading market economies have to be co-ordinated with others if each intent of theirs is to be realised.[39]

The Unintentional Impact on the Environment

Affiliates of MNCs can have an adverse effect on the environment of the host countries. New technologies may embody new ecological risks, as it is the case with genetically engineered micro-organisms. In addition, actual practices may be lax in individual situations. At the Bhopal plant, for example, a number of the safeguards were not functioning at the time of the accident. Many MNCs in the chemical and related hazardous industries have increased their awareness of safety procedures and community relations; they have started risk-assessment studies to examine hazards associated with their products and their production and delivery operations and proposed a variety of changes in risk-control system. Despite this, the response has been uneven, with most of the changes coming from large firms with plant operations in their home countries rather than abroad.

The logic of the process of trans-nationalisation also suggests the presence of systematic negative impacts on the physical environment from the expansion of transitional corporations. The process of trans-nationalisation involves a greater proportion of economic activity within the organisational framework of transitional corporations, as opposed to being carried out via arms-length between buyers and sellers. For the MNCs, the internalisation of economic activities involves a judgement that revenues can be internalised to a greater extent than costs. There is, in effect, a strong incentive for firms to adopt strategies to capture revenues while keeping costs external. The incentive to externalise adverse environment impacts is well known, and phenomena like air and water pollution are among the most widely cited examples of negative externalities.

The externalisation of adverse environmental impacts is, of course, not unique to transitional corporations. But transitional corporations may have greater scope than purely national firms for avoiding the burden of environment costs. In cases where transitional corporations are involved with local partners in joint ventures, or have transferred technology through licensing or franchising agreements, the bargaining power of transitional corporations may allow them to shift the burden of dealing with environmental impacts onto the local enterprise.[40]

There is a need to strengthen the capacity of national regulatory agencies in developing countries to monitor both domestic and foreign enterprises. In this re-

---

[39] *Ibid.*, p. 121
[40] *Ibid.*, p. 229

136

spect, there is need for the development of an international system of norms and rules. There is also a need for more self-regulation at the international level by individual groups: companies have a shared interest in protecting the environment and reducing the costs of environmental damage. And greater international co-operation at the governmental and industry level could facilitate the agreement on suitable international environmental standards.[41]

In many instances, however, it may be difficult for developing countries to establish and enforce an independent set of environmental standards and regulations. Relative scarcity of both scientific personnel and financial resources to devote to technical pursuits means that people with the skills to undertake such endeavours have a high opportunity cost. Moreover, to the extent that developing countries are dependent on transitional corporations to provide technical training, the creation of an independent perspective necessary for an effective regulatory function can be difficult.[42]

Impact on Social and Cultural Values

The MNCs can also have an impact on social institution and cultural values. Because of their size, MNCs can potentially exert a significant social and cultural influence in countries, especially in developing countries, in which they operate. This has frequently been a concern in developing countries, where the impact of "modernisation" can come in conflict with traditional values. But such issues may be more universal, as evidenced by concerns over the impact of United States-based MNCs in Canada and Western Europe and the concern over the role of Japanese MNCs in the United States.

MNCs have been criticised for fostering consumption patterns in developing countries that are inimical to the interests of population as a whole. For the most part, consumers in host developing countries willingly purchase products sold by MNCs, and often in preference to products produced by locally-owned business. The consumption patterns that emerge in developing countries are, to a significant extent, the result of choices made by consumers. Thus, the influence that MNCs may exert over consumption patterns is, at least in part, because their products are in demand or pushed. Moreover, the consumer goods that are in demand are not necessarily those produced by affiliates of MNCs, but those that are advertised by the local (and, increasingly, by the multinational) media. Most of those products are produced by domestic firms, although often under licence from MNCs.[43]

---

[41] *Ibid.*, p. 7
[42] *Ibid.*, p. 230
[43] *Ibid.*, p. 222

However, there are a number of aspects of the actual practices of MNCs in developing countries, which suggest that the determination of consumption patterns is a more complex phenomenon. For one thing, consumption is more class-specific in developing than in developed societies. MNCs produce for upper-income groups. In the case of pharmaceutical products, the bulk of promotional efforts by MNCs in developing countries is directed towards the relatively expensive drugs originally designed for markets in developed countries and the promotion of general personal-care products that are frequently of doubtful medical value, instead of the relatively simple and inexpensive preparation needed to cope with diseases most common in poorer populations. But here, the host country's income distribution may be responsible, rather than the practice of MNCs. The problem is that, outside of upper-income groups, in most developing countries the market is too small to justify significant efforts by MNCs or by domestic private firms, for that matter.[44]

It is also the case that choices that consumers make are shaped by the cost and availability of products and there is clearly an interaction between the consumer sovereignty exercised by those who demand goods and services and the characteristics of the products made available by MNCs. Advertising plays a prominent role in the marketing of products by MNCs, both in term of their attempts to expand into new markets and in their efforts to differentiate their products and compete against other MNCs. For the wide variety of consumer goods, advertising involves not only emphasising the objective characteristics of products, but the subjective ones as well, including those that purportedly link the product with life style objectives. For those reasons, there is a strong tendency for MNCs to infuse their products with subjective characteristics different from those prevalent in developing countries. Thus, products from automobiles to toothpaste to beverages and cigarettes are marketed by identifying them with culture images drawn from Western Europe and North America. For example, the world's best selling brand of cigarettes is sold everywhere with the same white and red package supported by the same cowboy images. Although not all companies have the resources to undertake global campaigns, global merchandising techniques are being developed to encompass an increasing number of consumer products.

Advertising, of course, can impart useful information, and many of the products sold by MNCs in developing countries are beneficial. It remains an issue, however, whether the fostering of upper-middle-class lifestyles that are inaccessible to most of the population, and the sale of products that are superfluous to the needs of this large group, are the most effective use of scarce resources in developing countries.

It has also been claimed that advertising by MNCs has an impact on the mass media in developing countries. Many governments, conscious of the possible sociocultural effect and of the strategic importance of radio, television, magazines and

---

[44] *Ibid.*, p. 223

newspapers, have restrained FDI in this sector. Nevertheless, MNCs more than domestic companies, have become an important element in determining the shape and content of the media, especially radio and television, by means of their large advertising resources. Transitional advertising has been found to represent as much as 84 percent of total advertising in radio, 77 percent in television and 60 percent in magazines in developing countries.[45]

Television programmes are frequently imported from developed countries. This practice has been reinforced by lower costs of imported culture, journalistic or entertainment programmes as compared to domestically produced ones. (In one instance, a four-hour programme was sold to a television network in the United States for $5.3 million, in Australia for $307,000, and in Singapore for $5,000. Obviously, a Singapore television production firm cannot produce a domestic programme comparable to an imported one at that cost.) These price variations occur because production companies recoup their costs in the home market and then sell the rights for the transmission or reproduction of their programmes on a country-country base, depending on what each country can pay. That amount is, in turn, determined by the size of the audience reached in the importing country.

Industries which produce cultural goods such as television programmes, films, comic books, magazines, records, books and scientific textbooks are often MNCs that establish subsidiaries in developing countries. In many instances, they have incorporated domestic culture into their goods. In others, they reproduce the cultural contents from the home country without any concession to social or cultural differences. It has been argued that those goods by providing accounts of the contemporary world and image of a certain lifestyle, can play a pivotal role in shaping social consciousness. It is a special relationship between their economic and cultural content, which has made it the issue of a continuous concern by developing countries and some developed countries as well.

It has been argued that it is, in the last instance, the responsibility of governments and not of MNCs to protect national culture. This is a highly controversial matter, which ranges from discussions of corporate social responsibility to the debate on the free flow of information. Governments trying to regulate the flow of cultural goods and FDI in this sector might have to face criticism for preventing freedom of expression. Those trying to leave the solution of those problems to the forces of the market might have to face conflicts over the protection of the natural culture and identity.

Those problems are bound to become more complex with the introduction of new information technologies to the cultural life of developing countries. MNCs are the world leaders in the production, distribution and utilisation of information technology. Their overseas operation will increasingly require a domestic labour

---

[45] *Ibid.*, p. 224

force trained in new managerial and technical skills. This will affect the social structure of the developing countries in which they operate.

The increase in the activities of MNCs in the service sector opens to them new spheres of investment in developing countries, which are intimately linked to the social and cultural life of the host countries, such as education, engineering, law and a myriad of other information services as data processing, videotext and satellite broadcasting. At least two elements are of importance here: the question of cultural identity, especially with respect to language, and the classification and codification of information, data banks and data bases. MNCs in data services organise their information according to their own criteria, usually ones dictated by economic rationality; and in the language of the home country.

One of the main concerns is that subsidiaries will cater to urban affluent minorities, disregarding the needs of other segments of the population. The information goods and services made available to developing countries by MNCs may be of a quality unimagined one or two decades ago, but their availability may be affected by a selection process tied to the wealth and income of the user. It is claimed that activities of MNCs in information technology may bring about a major redefinition of the concept of modernity, whereby a modern corporation is one which increasingly relies on information technology and services for the conduct of its worldwide operations, and a modern consumer is one, who increasingly utilises information goods and services. This will leave out a large number of domestic firms and most of the population of developing countries.

For good or for ill, a world culture is emerging, and MNCs both in the cultural industries and in the production of goods are important agents for the transmission of cultural attributes. The increasing use of information technologies is speeding up that process. The cultural implications of economic activity have, therefore, become increasingly evident, and they render policy decisions that are vital to economic modernisation more complexity.[46]

In the world culture a so-called "global consumer culture" has been emerging in which the MNCs have been playing a major role as well. For global consumer culture such value-laden terms as "Americanisation", "Western cultural imperialism" and "Coca-colonisation" are often employed, and not without good reason. These terms imply that the consumer culture that was developed in the USA in the middle of the twentieth century has been mass mediated to all other parts of the world.

It should be stressed, however, that consumer culture means more than simple consumption. An interest in consumption is historically and cross-societally universal. However, in a consumer culture the items consumed take on a symbolic and not merely a material value. It arises in societies where *powerful groups* usually those seeking to accumulate capital, in caricature, *encourage consumer to "want" more than they "need".*

---

[46] *Ibid.*, p. 225

Indeed such groups will seek to confound the meanings of these two terms. Under a consumer culture, consumption becomes the main form of self-expression and the chief source of identity. It implies that both material and non-material items, including kinship, affection, art, and intellect become commodified, that is their value is assessed by the context of their exchange, rather than the context of their production or use. An advanced consumer culture experiences hypercommodification in which minute differences between products or minute improvements in them can determine variations in demands, and in which consumption is differentiated on the basis of the signifiers known "brand names". Here consumption, or more precisely a capacity to consume, is itself reflexively consumed. This tendency is captured in such terms as "taste", "fashion" and "lifestyle" that become key sources of social differentiation, displacing class and political affiliation. The consumer culture is created through the advertising and simulatory effects of the mass media. In its original form it was probably a deliberate creation but under global world conditions it is hypersimulated, having a life of its own that is beyond the control of any particular group.[47]

Because it is symbolically mediated, consumer culture liberates values and preferences from social and geographical locations and indeed invalidates the social and political structures including states. Bourgeois domination might have been legitimated by its claim to have special knowledge of cultural standards in art, morality and justice but in a consumer culture these standards merely become some of a range of opinions accepted or rejected at will. Indeed, the delegitimation of such standards has meant a more widespread and popular dissemination of what previously would have been regarded as high or elite cultural products. To just give one highly globalised example, the "three tenors" concerts linked opera music to the popular sport of soccer, set it up as a spectacle as much as a concert, and marked it by the mass media to a huge global audience.

If the original American version of consumer culture depended on mass mediated advertising and simulation, that process entered a global phase with the expansion of communication technologies – telephone, record-and playback machine, radio, television, PC, Internet and their most modern and sophisticated variants – beyond the nation-state-society. The examples are numerous but a few may suffice to illustrate the point. In the 1930s the German car industry built a Wagen for its own Volk, and the Model T and Austin 7 were similarly conceived of as cars for the people of their respective nations, but now manufacturers build and market "world cars", the latest Ford appropriately called the "Mondeo". The "many colours of Benetton", stressed presumably because colour is one of the few minute variations offered in their standardised clothing products, Nike and Reebok casual shoes, and

[47] Malcolm Waters, *Globalisation* (Routledge, London, 1995) p. 140

Levi's jeans infuse global popular culture. In food and beverage products, global branding has been so effective that the examples are almost too obvious to mention: Coca-Cola and its rival Pepsi are the paradigm cases; McDonalds and its revals, Pizza Hut, Sizzlers, and KFC fast-food restaurants engorge the world with vast quantities of sanitized and homogenised food.[48] As we have seen in these examples they are all well-known MNCs.

The consumer culture can be considered as an extension of Western rationalisation process first identified by Weber. Weber had broadly been interested in the ways in which the rational calculability of capitalism was extended beyond material issues to human relationships, especially those to do with production in its broadest sense of global-attainment. Ritzer's view is that society and thus the world, is afflicted by "McDonaldisation": the process by which the principles of the fast-food restaurant are coming to dominate more and more sections of American society as well as the rest of the world.[49]

The principles are the following:
- efficiency: McDonaldisation compresses the time span and the effort expended between a want and its satisfaction;
- calculability: it encourages calculations of costs of money, time and effort as the key principles of value on the part of the consumer, displacing estimations of quality;
- predictability: it standardises products so that consumers are encouraged not to seek alternatives;
- control of human beings by the use of material technology: this involves not only maximal deskilling of workers but control of consumers by means of queue control barriers, fixed menu displays, limited options, uncomfortable seats, inaccessible toilets, and "drive-through" processing.

Clearly, to the extent that the social technology of McDonaldisation can penetrate the globe and to the extent it can include consumers to enter the premise, it can convert apparently sovereign consumer into docile conformists. McDonaldisation represents a reordering of consumption as well as production, a rationalisation of previously informal and domestic practices, that pushes the world into the direction of greater conformity.[50]

Under such a culture, political issues and work can equally become items of consumption. A liberal-democratic political system might be the only possible political system where there is a culture of consumption precisely because it offers the possibility of election. But even a liberal democracy will tend to be McDonaldised, that is leaders will become the mass mediated images of photo-opportunities and juice

[48] *Ibid.*, p. 141
[49] *Ibid.*, p. 143
[50] *Ibid.*, p. 144

one-liners, and issues will be drawn in starkly simplistic packages. Equally, work can no longer be expected to be a duty or a calling or even a means of creative self-expression. Choice of occupation, indeed choice of whether to work at all, can be expected increasingly to become a matter of status affiliation rather than of material advantage.[51]

In the framework of globalised consumer culture the modern communication technologies have three major effects. First, they export this culture via mass media, the "culture-ideology of consumerism" as Sklair calls it, from the centre to the periphery of the world-system. This is because most of the news, information, entertainment programming, sport, information and advertising flows in that direction. Not only the programme producers, but the advertising agencies and news agencies, as well as the companies that manufacture consumer products, are owned in advanced capitalist societies – and they are mostly belong to MNCs. Advertising, in particular, seeks to sell products by depicting idealised Western lifestyles, often under the universalising themes of sex, status and the siblinghood of humanity – the world sings a hymn of harmony to a soft drink of doubtful nutritional value.[52] They mimic to the opportunities for simulation already given in soap operas, sitcoms and action thrillers.

Second, as well as absorbing new nations into what some might call the network of cultural imperialism, cultural flows via the mass media dissolve the internal boundaries of that network and help to knit it together. These cultural flows are primarily examples of transnational connections, links between collective actors and individuals that subvert state frontiers. Satellite broadcasting in particular denies the possibility of national sovereignty over the airwaves. A specific consequence is that, insofar as much of the hardware is American-owned and much of the programming is American in origin, English is becoming the *lingua franca* of the global communications systems. This has proved a particular problem for the territorially small nations of Europe but the failure of Euronews, a multilingual satellite news channel, to dent the market shares of CNN and Sky News that broadcast exclusively in English, indicates that English may well become the common public language of the globalised system and that vernaculars may be restricted to localised and domestic contexts.

However, the mass media knit the global culture together by means of content as well as by means of language. They do this not merely by offering common simulation opportunities but by magnifying global problems and global events. We can say, with appropriate apologies, that we now look at the world through global spectacles. (When an American fighter pilot bombs a building in Baghdad we are there with her seeing what she sees and war becomes a spectacle; the demolition of the

---

[51] *Ibid.*, p. 145
[52] *Ibid.*, p. 148

Berlin wall, a major political event, becomes a rock concert.) These deliberately constructed, stylised mass entertainment can be collective representations of global commitments to good things (to democracy, for example,) and to harmful things as well (like uneconomical consumption, or one-sided national interests).[53]

Insofar as the mass media convert the contents of human relationships into symbols or tokens, they can connect people across great distances. This is the third globalising effect of the mass media. So effective can this process become that communities of interest or value-commitment can develop between people who have never met, much less joined as simulated communities or simulated power blocs because they are based on behavioural cues given in the mass media. (For example, many women feel a sense of global sisterhood in relation to patriarchal oppression even if they are not participants in the women's movement.) This effect also can beneficial and harmful consequences if, for example, a pressure group uses this possibility for lobbying.[54]

Political Influence

MNCs have been charged with exercising unique influence on the domestic politics of the host developing countries. Fewer such charges have been levied in recent years, and there are reasons for thinking that the political influence of MNCs could be on the decline, but certainly it will remain very decisive.[55]

First, in three decades after the Second World War, the U.S. MNCs exercised a substantial degree of hegemony in world economy. This was also the period during which specific MNCs from the United States were said to have exercised a political influence on host developing countries. In fact, most of the evidence cited to demonstrate the undue and adverse political influence of MNCs refers to American companies during their period of ascendancy in world economy. Since the mid-1970s, with the emergence of Japanese corporations as significant foreign investors and the strengthening of Western European firms, the international investment scene has become more pluralist, and international competition between firms from different developed market economies, and even from some developing countries has substantially increased. At the same time, and perhaps partly owing to these developments, instances of political interference appear to have declined noticeably.

Second, host developing countries have become more cognisant of the need to limit the political activities of MNCs, while at the same time fostering inflows of FDI. Much effort has been expended in enhancing the benefits and minimising the

---

[53] *Ibid.*, p. 149
[54] *Ibid.*, p. 150
[55] *Transitional Corporations in World Development. Trends and Prospects*, p. 225

negative effects of FDI in developing countries. In many instances, the relationship between MNCs and host countries has become more mutually beneficial, and less antagonistic, than it had been in the past.

Third, the 1980s have seen the continuation of efforts to formulate principles to govern the relations between MNCs and host countries. Home country laws and regulations and international codes of conduct have been formulated to prohibit or restrict certain types of behaviour, and to make the right and obligations of MNCs explicit when they operate in developing countries.[56]

In addition to these, transnational activities are forcing governments to face up to the challenge of international governance. Technological change in financial services and world-wide telecommunications are making traditional national regulatory mechanisms obsolete. Global corporate alliances are modifying the play of world market forces. International movements of trade and capital have substantial impacts on the domestic economies of even the largest countries; the impacts on developing countries can be overwhelming. These and other transitional trends undercore a common theme: the successful pursuit of national policies in an interdependent world economy requires a global view.[57]

* * *

Having seen all of these tendencies presented in the preceding part of this book, it is not accidental, that there are such forecasts that :"in the future business would be dominated by vast-company alliances, which is called 'relationship enterprise', coming together to handle big complicated projects" and "by the end of the decade, our industry will be dominated by a few giant firms, world-wide".[58] Even if these predictions can be judged as exaggerations, it is unquestionable that the emergence of MNCs has fundamental impact

- on the economics as on a science including its three main branches, that is, on micro-, macro- and public economics;[59]
- on the former socialist countries including Eastern and Central European Countries,[60] and in Asian socialist countries, especially China, which were outside the globalisation process and/or were only partially part of the globalised world economy for a long time.

---

[56] *Ibid.*, p. 226

[57] *Ibid.*, p. 499

[58] Multinationals. *The Economist*, March 27th 1993, p. 1

[59] For example, different type of competition is emerging, there is modification in the crowding-out and -in effects, and there are the modifications in the so-called market and government "failures".

[60] For example, in Hungary 110 companies of the 200 largest ones are under foreign control, they produced 10.4 percent of the GDP in 1994, this figure means in the industry 36.7 percent – and

By analysing and investigating these impacts useful lessons can be drawn for better understanding of the economics as a science by redefining its paradigm according to the new reality having been created by the impact of the MNCs, for the policies, which could and/or should be elaborated and implemented by the respective governments and MNCs in order to exploit the huge potentialities for economic development[61] provided by the MNCs and to eliminate and/or decrease the negative effects, problems and tensions[62] caused by the activities of the MNCs.

in the food industry 49.2, chemical industry 73.0 percent, engineering industry 53.3 percent, and in the finance sector 78.5 percent. These companies have already played a key role in the Hungarian export, import and finance market and by these in the economic growth and equilibrium condition of the county that the economic policy of the government should take into consideration.

[61] For example, quick spreading of the new innovations in a global worldwide scale.

[62] For example, negative effects of restructuring, downsizing or monopolistic position.

IMPACT OF THE MULTINATIONAL CORPORATION ON THE ECONOMICS

We can detect significant impact of the MNCs on all main branches of the economics, that is, on the micro- macro- and the public economics as well.

IMPACT OF THE MULTINATIONAL CORPORATIONS ON THE MICROECONOMICS

In the microeconomics as a consequence of the changing conditions and circumstances of the real economic life many important new tendencies and phenomena have been started to develop a long time ago and in the last decades they – mainly due to MNCs – have got determining and paradigmatic characteristic modifying basically the teaching of the classical microeconomics.

As we know, the basic model of the microeconomics consists of rational, self-interested individuals and profit-maximising firms, interacting in competitive markets; and according to this model, *the profit motive and private property* provide *incentives for rational individuals and firms to work hard and efficiently.*[1]

That is, this traditional or "neo-classical" approach assumes that the decisions are made under condition of perfect knowledge, and *the objective of the firms is to maximise profits.*[2]

The Change of the Firm's Objectives

In the practice, however, these theoretical assumptions are rarely to be found and this is due to MNCs in a great extent, which have intensified those reasons that can be offered as justification for abandoning these assumptions. These relate to the following:

---

[1] Joseph E. Stiglitz, *Economics* (W.W. Norton and Copany, New York, 1993) p. 47

[2] Joseph G. Nellis and David Parker, *The Essence of Business Economics* (Prentice Hall, New York, 1992) p. 100

THE GROWTH IN OLIGOPOLY

Oligopoly is the most common form of the market structure in reality and yet it is the structure to which the traditional assumptions fit least. Empirical evidence of the growing importance of oligopoly can be found by measuring the degree of concentration across industries. When industry is concentrated, but not a monopoly, it displays the characteristics of oligopoly. Empirical studies of countries have shown a general trend across many industries towards this type of market structure throughout the last century.

There are two reasons why the traditional theory of the firm, based on the assumptions of perfect knowledge and profit maximisation behaviour, fails to provide a satisfactory explanation of market behaviour under oligopoly. These concern:

- the extent to which firms are interdependent, and
- the degree of uncertainty that exists in oligopolic market.

Mutual interdependence arises in oligopoly because each firm produces a sufficiently large proportion of the industry's output for its behaviour to affect the market share of its competitors. Uncertainty arises because the behaviour of one firm is conditioned not just by what its rivals are doing but also by what it thinks its rivals might do in response to any initiative of its own.[3]

THE GROWTH OF MANAGERIAL CAPITALISM

The traditional assumption of profit maximisation implies that the "firm" somehow has a mind of its own, capable of arriving at independent, rational decisions. In reality, of course, firms do not make any decisions – it is the entrepreneurs and managers (i.e. individuals) who make business decisions. A "firm" is nothing more than an abstract concept covering owners, managers and employees.

Over time, the relationship between ownership and control in firms has changed substantially. In their earliest form business units or firms were owned and managed by the same people, therefore the assumption of profit maximisation did not seem unreasonable. Over time, however, with the growth of large corporations – and among them MNCs – and with the dominance of public joint-stock companies, there has emerged a shareholder who may or may not exercise his voting rights at board meetings. Control, however, is largely in the hands of the managers and directors of the firm. This situation is described as managerial capitalism and has given rise to "managerial theories" to explain the behaviour of firms. With manag-

---

[3] Uncertainty and interdependence are best tackled through a game theory approach to market behaviour. *Ibid.*, p. 101

ers in control it is easy to question the validity of the profit maximisation assumption of the traditional theory. Some managers may seek to keep shareholders happy by reporting a certain level of profit while leaving themselves the flexibility to achieve, perhaps personal objectives (such as business growth, diversification, salary, etc.). Even if profit maximisation is stated as the key objective of the firm as a whole, it is unlikely that every individual within the firm, even within senior management, will pursue this objective consistently.[4]

Once we acknowledge that managers in the private and perhaps more especially in the public sector are able, to some degree, to pursue their own goals rather than that of profit maximisation, the question arises as to what are these goals and what is their effect on prices and outputs. We shall consider the following three possible goals:

- sales revenue maximisation;
- manager utility maximisation;
- corporate growth maximisation.

Sales Revenue Maximisation

The idea of sales revenue maximisation as a management goal was first put forward by William Baumol in 1959. The argument is based on Baumol's own research into managerial behaviour and is couched in terms of oligopolistic industry, in which there is a divorce of ownership and management of resources. Baumol argues that managers are likely to attach a great importance to achieving high sale revenues for the following reasons:

- high and expanding sales revenues help to attract external finance to the firm – larger firms generally find easier to raise capital, while financial institutions may be less willing to deal with a firm suffering declining sales;
- high sales assist the distribution and retailing of products – resulting in economies from selling in bulk;
- consumers may view a firm with falling sales in a less favourable light – this may deter consumers from buying and reduce sales even further;
- the distributive trade may be less co-operative, for example, to extend credit lines, when a firm's sales are declining;
- falling sales may result in reductions in staffing levels, including managerial staff, as costs are cut;
- last, but not least, managers' salaries may well depend on fast growth of sales revenues – managers are rewarded for expanding business.

---

[4] *Ibid.*, p. 102

Baumol's theory does not ignore profit altogether, but it is presented in terms of sales revenue maximisation subject to a minimum profit constraint on the firm. As long as this constraint is met, based on the assumption that this will be sufficient to pacify shareholders, the firm will aim to maximise sales revenues. The needs of shareholders cannot be ignored but the minimum profit constraint will usually be less than the maximum profit feasible.

In later formulations of his model Baumol substituted the objective of management as the maximisation of the growth of the firm for the maximisation of sales revenue. The goals are, of course, related, though growth maximisation is a more dynamic concept. Also, whereas in the sales revenue maximisation model the profit constraint could be at any level (whatever keeps the shareholders happy), in the growth model it is set by the "means for obtaining capital needed to finance expansion plans", i.e. by the need to attract finance for investment. The "optimal profit stream" is that which is consistent with raising adequate investment funds to achieve the highest rate of growth of output over the firm's lifetime.[5]

Managerial Utility Maximisation

Baumol's model implies that management has some choice in the trade-off between profit and sales revenues in business decision-making. This recognition has led to the development of other models that explain firm's behaviour in terms of managerial discretion. One important approach was developed by Oliver Williamson in the 1960s. He argued that managers in large firms have enough discretion to pursue those policies which give them personally most satisfaction. Whereas shareholders are assumed to equate their level of satisfaction (i.e. "utility") with profit, management is considered to have utility functions which include a number of personal goals and personal measures of "well-being". These goals may include the achievement of a plush office, a large company car, a high salary, etc. In fact, the goal of sales revenue maximisation could even be interpreted as a special case where that single goal dominates all other managerial goals or is even the means by which the other managerial goals are realised.[6]

Williamson suggests that managers' self-interest could be seen in terms of the achievement of goals in four particular areas, namely:

1. High salaries. This includes not just take-home pay but also other forms of monetary income such a bonus and share options. The desire for large salaries reflects a desire for a high standard of living, and a high status.

---

[5] *Ibid.*, p. 109
[6] *Ibid.*, p. 110

2. Staff under their control. This refers to both the number and quality of subordinate staff as a measure of status and a measure of power (reflecting the "I hire them. I fire them" type of management philosophy).

3. Discretionary investment expenditure. This does not refer to investment that is essential for success of the firm but rather to any investment over and above this amount. This includes any pet projects of the management that are excused as necessary to the general development of the firm (such as sponsorship, say, of Formula One motor racing in the case of a petrol company). The manager may be able to further his or her own personal interests and hobbies (sponsoring staff tennis outings, for example). The extent of the manager's authority over discretionary expenditure may be taken as an indication of his or her status.

4. Fringe benefits. Managers might strive for an expense account, a lavishly furnished office, a company car, free club memberships, etc. These perks may be part of the "slack" in the organisation – i.e. non-essential expenditures that force up the firm's costs.

Profit is not ignored by Williamson. Like Baumol, he recognises that a minimum profit must be paid to shareholders, but argues that managers will strive to increase their utility as long as this profit constraint is being satisfied. Equally, however, it is possible to conceive of management desiring higher profits because they drive satisfaction from business achievement. Profitability is a measure of business success and buoyant profit provides a fertile environment in which managers can then pursue other goals.[7]

Corporate Growth Maximisation

This variation of the managerial theory of firms's behaviour also sees managerial motivation in terms of striving to maximise a target. This time target is growth. The model assumes that competition is limited, with ownership divorced from management so that there is scope for managerial discretionary behaviour. The theory stems from Morris's view of the institutional framework and organisation of the modern corporation. He sees the firm as typically a bureaucratic organisation – self-perpetuating structure – where corporate growth and the security that it brings is seen as a desirable end in itself. Managers are expected to see a relationship between the growth of the company and hence profits ploughed back into investment, and their own personal goals (such as increased status, power, and salary). At the same time, managers are expected to balance growth against the impact on profits and dividends – they must be aware of the danger of low dividends depressing share prices, which may leave the firms vulnerable to a hostile take-over bid. Therefore, growth

---

[7] *Ibid.*, p. 111

and security compete as objectives and each requires a different approach to risk in terms of investment and capital raising.

In particular, there may be a trade-off between securing profits to pay dividends and taking risk when investing to increase the growth of the firm. At the same time, while profits provide the retained earnings to help finance new investments, which leads to growth, excessive company liquidity may attract predators. Cash-rich companies attract take-over bids. In Marris's model this conflict is summarised as management seeking the optimal dividend to profit retention ratio.[8]

There appears, therefore, to be a potential division between the goal of shareholders and the goals of management in reality. This issue has been approached through the agency theory.

Agency Theory

The broad thrust of agency theory as a basic understanding of the behaviour of firms is summarised in Figure 11 which[9] shows the agent-principal relationships that exist in the private and public sectors. In the private sector, the principals are those who ultimately have the right to the assets or who "own" the firm. In joint-stock companies these are the shareholders and they appoint directors as agents to manage these assets in the interest of the principals, but in practice this cannot be guaranteed. In practice, therefore, the agent-principal relationship may involve costs in terms of lower efficiency. This is likely to mean that principals face costs, not least in terms of the time and effort involved in monitoring the work of their agents.

There is, however, a "control mechanism" in the private sector. Shareholders may attend company annual general meetings to question and, if necessary, replace the directors. Perhaps more importantly, the shareholders can exercise their right to sell their share holding altogether. Many economists argue that the existence of such a control mechanism acts as a major constraint on private sector management. If management pursues a quiet life or other objectives which reduce profitability, then shareholders can react by disposing of their shares. This will tend to drive down the share price, making the company vulnerable to a take-over by new management.

On the other hand, some economists question the significance of shareholder power, arguing instead that shareholders are fairly inert to management performance. Most shareholders rarely attend annual general meetings and the existence of transactional costs and capital gains taxation may reinforce a tendency to hold onto share hoping that things will get better. If things do get better those who have held on to their shares benefit and this produces a "free rider" problem. Shareholders

---

[8] *Ibid.*, p. 112
[9] *Ibid.*, p. 104

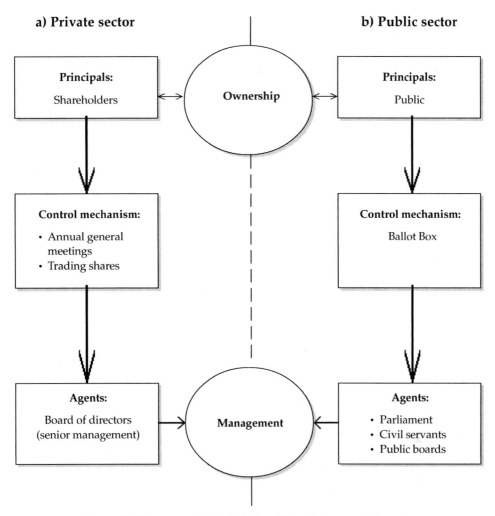

a) Private sector   **b) Public sector**

| Principals: | Ownership | Principals: |
| Shareholders | | Public |

Control mechanism:		Control mechanism:
• Annual general meetings		Ballot Box
• Trading shares		

| Agents: | Management | Agents: |
| Board of directors (senior management) | | • Parliament • Civil servants • Public boards |

FIGURE 11. The agent-principal relationship: private vs. public sector

may be reluctant to sell, hoping, however, other shareholders do sell. Further, it is not obvious that it is necessary the less profitable firms will succumb to a take-over. Sometimes what appear to be profitable, well-managed firms face hostile take-over bids.

Figure 11 also illustrates the agent-principal relationship, which exists in the public sector. In this case, civil servants and public boards manage industries and services on behalf of the public. Since there are no shares to sell or annual general meeting to attend, the public are unable to indicate directly dissatisfaction with management performance. Voters can express their views on government performance through the ballot box, but this is a crude indicator of satisfaction and dissatisfaction with particular state activities (such as postal service, police, education, etc.). Voters reflect broad manifesto pledges and not, usually, views about the quality of service from one particular public industry or state sector. For this reason there appears to be greater scope for managerial discretionary behaviour by management in the public sector compared with the private sector.[10]

A further constraint on managerial discretionary behaviour relates to the product market. Firms, whether of the private or the public sector (unless backed by considerable taxpayers' funds), must be efficient to survive in competitive markets. Any inefficiency that leads to higher prices will be penalised through a loss of market share and eventual bankruptcy. In a perfectly competitive market in the long run only normal profits are earned by firm, the less efficient one will make losses and goes out of business. Therefore, that non-profit goals, which raise costs are likely to be more prevalent in firms operating where product market competition is imperfect, since if the market was perfectly competitive the firm would not be able to afford the luxury of non-profit goals. And as we have seen the competition is far from perfect in globalised economy.

Difficulties Surrounding Profit Maximisation in Practice

In practice, businesses may have insufficient accurate information about demand and cost conditions to be able to use the concepts of marginal revenue and marginal costs as the basis for determining the profit-maximising output. Pricing policies in practice are often determined by other methods, such as on the basis of a mark-up over average unit costs subject to the achievement of a "required" profit margin. As much of the output as possible will then be sold on the market at this price.

Other guidelines of pricing may be followed for different firms in different industries. (For example, over the years two basic pricing guidelines for state industries have emerged: marginal-cost pricing, and mark-up pricing to achieve a target rate of return.) So the traditional theory of the firms does not provide a particularly useful framework for analysing the behaviour of state firms.

THE ORGANISATIONAL COMPLEXITY OF FIRMS

With the growth of managerial capitalism and as the globalisation has been gaining place, firms have increased in size, they have become much more complex in terms of their organisation structure too. This structure will reflect the often conflicting

---

[10] *Ibid.*, p. 105

154

views of owners, managers, workers and consumers. Within each grouping there will be more complex structures: perhaps different categories of shareholders with different share holdings who are interested in different objectives (short-term versus long-term profits perhaps); different managers at different levels with different aims and aspirations; blue-collar workers and white-collar workers with different career expectations and reward packages, perhaps represented by different unions; finally, there will be different groups of consumers to be satisfied (such as the one-off consumer versus the long-term, loyal consumer).

Given the degree of complexity of organisational structures today, some economists argue that it is unlikely that a useful theory of business decisions can be based on a single objective and that, instead, the subject should be approached through a study of individual or group behaviour within the firm. Such an approach should start from the position that people in firms, including mangers, do not aim to maximise anything – they simply aim to "satisfy" a range of objectives.[11] So *this "behavioural" approach based upon the behaviour theories* goes well behind the simple notion of profit maximisation. The "behaviourist" rejects the whole notion of maximisation in favour of a less strong goal of "satisfying". Whereas the traditional profit-maximising model and the alternative theories, which have been concerned with how firms should behave to maximise profits, sales revenue, etc., the behaviourist approach (the behavioural theory) is concerned with how firms actually behave with attention focused on the internal decision-making structure of the firm. The aim is to understand this decision-making process rather than to try and make predictions about price and output.[12]

The idea of "satisfying" was initially introduced by H. A. Simon in the 1950s. He argued that, faced with incomplete information and uncertainty, individuals are more likely to be content to achieve a satisfactory level of something rather than to strive to maximise goals, and that this level will be revised continuously in the light of experience. This notion was further developed by R. M. Cyert and J. G. March, who established a behaviourist model of the firm. According to Cyert and March, the firm can be thought of as several levels of management, different groups of workers, suppliers and consumers, shareholders, etc. Hence, a complex process of bargaining must take place between groups within the firm to determine their collective goals. Some of the goals could be related to the following:

- production: a goal that output must lie within a certain satisfactory range;
- sales: a goal that there must be a satisfactory level of sales;
- market share: a goal indicating a satisfactory size of market share as a measure of competitive success as well as growth;
- profit: still an important goal, but one amongst many rather than necessarily of overriding importance.

---

[11] *Ibid.*, p. 103
[12] *Ibid.*, p. 112

Consequently, there is no single objective of the firm; instead, there are multiple goals, which emerge from the potential for conflict amongst interest groups within the firm. In addition, these goals can be expected to alter over time as circumstances change. Different managers from different departments or sections of the organisation will have a strong affiliation for targets in their own areas. For example, sales personnel will tend to identify with the goals of marketing and sales departments, while the accountants will tend to identify with financial outcomes and the interests of the finance department. It is not necessary that the goals of these different interests should be the same or easily reconcilable. In these circumstances the objectives of the firm are eventually determined by factors such as the following:

- bargaining between groups and the relationship between groups within the firm;
- the methods by which objectives are formulated within the organisation;
- how groups and, therefore, the "firm" react to experiences and make adjustments.[13]

Hence, the various goals set by different departments within the organisation may well conflict and it may arise that managers will be prepared to sacrifice some profit to achieve other goals. The way in which such conflicts are resolved draws attention to the process of decision-making within organisations.

The goals may be inconsistent, but it is possible to see how they can be reconciled if we introduce the idea of satisfaction in the place of maximising behaviour. The aim will be to achieve a satisfactory performance for each goal. For example, sales staff might accept what they regard as a "satisfactory" level of sales growth to maintain an agreed profitability, while finance staff agree to the firm forgoing some immediate profit by raising spending on advertising. With such compromises within the organisation, Cyert and March argue that different groupings can be bought off by "side payments" when their particular goals are not being met. This side payments can take pecuniary or non-pecuniary forms, such as higher pay for a section of staff or plusher offices for production managers. Similarly, disgruntled shareholders might be bought off by a rise in dividends per share. Naturally, there are groups that are able to exert a greater influence on objectives from time to time. Psychology plays a key role in the management of the firm in the way just described since people's actions are to a degree a result of their aspirations, which, in turn, stem from their perception of how well they feel they ought to be doing within the firm.

So the essence of the behaviourist approach lies in the study of human beings in term of their relationship with their environment. Within the complex environment of the firm, behaviour can be seen as a compromise between conflicting views and

---

[13] *Ibid.*, p. 113

interests. In achieving a compromise so that the firm can function it is unlikely that any goal could ever be maximised, at least for long.[14]

The behaviourist approach to the firm has won many adherents, because it appears to be most descriptively realistic. Rather than simply assuming some maximisation objectives (profits, sales, etc.), it seeks to explore the internal decision-making of the firm and the process by which the goals emerge. It allows for and copes with conflicting and changing goals that the other theories avoid. Also, it is concerned with how firms reach decisions and why. Its weakness, however, lies in its lack of generality and thus predictive ability. Clearly, maximising of something is easier to model than satifying behaviour. Since every firm is different, we may need a different "behavioural theory" for each firm.

The other approaches to the firm provide interesting variations on the traditional profit-maximising assumption. In the sense that they highlight managerial discretionary behaviour, the choice of goals, goals conflict and the constraints upon management decisions, they have considerable value. However, as with the behavioural theory, most economists regard them as supplements to the profit-maximising model, at least in relation to the private sector; in the public sector where there are often no profit goals they are clearly appropriate.

The profit-maximisation model still prevails. Even within the alternative models put forward, profit exists as an important constraint upon management and it is still the case that the profit-maximising model serves us well in predicting how price and output will change when, for example, product taxes are raised, costs of production increase or market price is lowered. Moreover, some economists stress that profit maximisation and the other models of the firm can be reconciled through a more careful definition of profit maximisation which stipulates the time period concerned. Sales revenue growth, for example, may be a target set to achieve a greater market share with a view to making larger profits in the longer term.[15]

The importance of these different theories arises from the insight they provide into the impact of different managerial objectives on the behaviour of firms and from reasoning they give about the complexity of goals of firms existing in real life, in practice.

The Change of the Ownership

The content, characteristics of the ownership have undergone major changes as well, especially as regards private ownership of corporation, and in this respect there is a need to modify the teaching of classical economics, the basic model of economics

---

[14] *Ibid.*, p. 114
[15] *Ibid.*, p. 115

according to which private property provides incentives for rational individuals and firms to work hard and efficiently. It was already realised in the 1930s that the modern corporation is characterised by the separation between shareholders, owners of the company, and the managers who control the assets and activities of the firm.[16] Since then a very complex *corporate governance* has developed that means on the one hand the concept "governance" related to words like influence, power, ruling, leading, guiding, directing and inspiring in the corporation and that is, on the other hand, the concept "corporate" which refers to ways of organising business, the formation and management of joint stock companies, company law provisions on capital, regulation by law and statutes of manager/shareholder relations, procedures for the appointment of supervisors' boards, definition of the respective responsibilities of managers, board members, auditors, etc.[17]

The corporate governance can be defined as the outcome of the relationships and interaction between the different economic agents that operate within a corporate, limited-liability institution. Corporate governance determines both the long-term strategy of this institution and the use of its income. Typically, shareholders, management, employees, creditors, and suppliers/customers are the main actors and, to varying degrees, exert influence on the corporation within a framework given by existing laws, regulations and institutions, as well as firm-specific governance structures.[18] In this respect there is a need to make a distinction between *"stakeholder" and "shareholder"*. There is a growing perception that managers have become insufficiently accountable to shareholders and other individuals or institutions that have stakes in companies (i.e. the stakeholders). The concept stakeholder is broader than the concepts "owner" or shareholder. Employees, trade unions, suppliers, tax authorities and other public authorities can be important stakeholders in companies, but they will not normally be shareholders. To have something "at stake" means in this connection having a direct interest in the proper conduct of the affairs of the business.

Most stakeholders want to play a role in the "governance" structure – they want to influence corporate decision-making in accordance with their own interests, and some of the stakeholders who are not owners do have the power to exert a certain influence. In some countries, for example Germany, The Netherlands, Luxembourg and Denmark, employees of big companies have a right to elect members of the supervisory boards, and in Scandinavia the government has the right to appoint one board member in banks and other financial institutions.[19]

---

[16] A. Berle and G. C. Means, *The Modern Corporation and Private Property* (MacMillan, New York, 1932) p. 38

[17] *Corporate Governance, Financial Markets and Global Convergence.* Morten Balling, Elizabeth Hennessy and Richard O'Brien, ed. (Kluwer Academic Publishers, Dordrecht, 1998) p. xi

[18] *Ibid.,* p. 42

[19] *Ibid.,* p. xii

There is also a reasonable argument beginning with the premise that it is the society that grants firms the right to exist, it follows that the manager's responsibility is not just to maximise shareholder returns, because shareholders are not the only ones responsible for the firm's existence. Managers must consider the legitimate concerns of other stakeholders in the firm, including the following: customers, employees, suppliers, communities, society at large, as well as shareholders. Customers have special standing within these stakeholder constituencies, because they are the providers of the revenue and subsistence for the firm. Shareholders are also given special status, but in the stockholder approach, shareholders are viewed as providers of risk capital rather than as principals. Consequently, shareholders are entitled to a reasonable return on the capital they put at risk, but they are not entitled to a maximum return, because not only they are responsible for the existence of the firm. To maximise return to shareholders would take away returns owned to other constituencies. Thus, managers must make decisions and undertake actions that provide a reasonable return to shareholders balanced against the legitimate concerns of customers, employees, financiers, communities, and society at large.

The fundamental process of stakeholders and corporate relations is an exchange and influence. For example, customers receive product and services for which they exchange money. Employees exchange work for wages. Because there is a two-way exchange, corporations can influence constituencies but can also be influenced by them. If a MNC that emits pollution into a river may lower its costs and thereby benefit customers, but may hurt surrounding communities that use the water for drinking. Communities can use tax, permits, fees, and so on to influence the firm to stop pollution or to pay for water treatment. The community might also manipulate the local press and influence public opinion, which, in turn, could influence purchases. Because customers, employees, financiers, communities, and society at large can take actions which effect firms, in turn, firms may benefit shareholders by responding to, as well as proactively considering, the needs of other constituencies. Not only can firms avoid or reduce the negative consequences that can result from ignoring the concerns of influential constituencies, but also by responding to and proactively considering their concerns, firms may endanger support from customers, employees, financiers, communities, and society at large. This support can lead to greater efficiency in transaction costs and leverage in negotiations with these constituencies.[20]

Since the work by Berle and Means[21] and the one by Coase,[22] not only the traditional view of the firm as a profit maximising entity has been questioned, but the

---

[20] Anant K. Sundaram and J. Steward Black, *The International Business Environment* (Prentice-Hall, New Jersey, 1995) p. 144

[21] A. Berle and G. C. Means, *The Modern Corporation and Private Property*, p. 38

[22] Ronald. H. Coase, The Nature of the Firm, *Economica*, 1937

emphasis has been shifted to the contrasting interest of different stakeholders. Berle and Means argued that due to the dispersion of ownership rights that characterised the modern corporation, shareholders' control over managers is relaxed, and managers are free to pursue their own interests, which often are in contrast with those of the shareholders. Dispersed ownership rights have thus been associated with managerial discretion and with divergence from profit maximisation.[23] A more solid theory of firm, founded on the study of the interaction among stakeholders, was thus needed. As Jenson and Mackling put it:

> "The firm is not an individual. It is a legal fiction which serves as a focus for a complex process in which the conflicting objectives of individuals (some of whom may 'represent' other organisations) are brought into equilibrium within a framework of contractual relations. In this sense the behaviour of the firm is like the behaviour of the market; i.e. the outcome of a complex equilibrium process."[24]

Ownership structures vary considerably from country to country. But enterprises in almost all countries have mixed ownership in the sense that there are everywhere examples of companies owned by the government, by banks and other financial institutions, by institutional investors, by non-financial companies, by personal investors and by foreign companies and investors. It seems in fact to be difficult to find a country, in which one single type of owner completely dominates the company ownership structure. Tables 11 and 12 provide an international comparison of ownership of common stock in a sample of OECD countries.[25] Traditional company legislation generally gives owners/shareholders (including individuals who have major influence on implementing and exercising of the property right) mastery of the firm. However, as Tables 11 and 12 show, other agents have staked to claims to exercise some control and the individuals have a minor role (except in the non-financial sector of the United States). In Anglo-Saxon countries, company management has emerged as a powerful control agent. In continental Europe, employees and banks have acquired an important say in how firms are run. In several countries, including Japan, there is a pattern of interlocking control between large industrial companies, and in some countries public-sector ownership plays a significant role, particularly in sectors deemed to be "sensitive" or "strategic".[26] There are still some wealthy and influential individuals on the corporate governance scene, who sit in boards of directors or at least influence the composition of these boards, but on the *whole the influence of wealthy individuals is diminishing, while the influence of institutional investors is growing.*

---

[23] *Corporate Governance, Financial Markets and Global Convergance,* p. 165

[24] M. C. Jensen and W. H. Meckling, Theory of the Firm: Managerial Behaviour, Agency Costs and Ownership Structure. *Journal of Financial Economics,* 11, 1976, p. 311

[25] *Corporate Governance, Financial Markets and Global Convergance,* pp. 51, 95

[26] *Ibid.,* p. 50

160

TABLE 11. The structure of shareholding in selected countries (percentage of total, as at end of year)

	G 1990	F 1992	I 1993	UK 1993	U.S. 1992	J 1992	NL 1995
Institutional investors	22	23	11	60	31	47	24
Banks	10		10	1	0	26	2
Pension Funds/Insurers	12		1	52	24	17	22
Others (Unit trusts)			0	7	7	4	
Households	17	34	34	19	48	23	19
Private Companies	42	21	23	4	14	25	19
Public Authorities	5	2	27	1		1	
Foreign Investors	14	20	5	16	7	4	37

Note: The figures do not necessarily add up to 100 because of differences in definitions used by the providers of the data and differences in regulatory structures. A bank is a universal bank in Germany and a high-street bank in the UK.

Sources: Lannoo (1995; see Table 3; data for Germany, France, Italy, UK, U.S. and Japan) and Annual Report of De Nederlandsche Bank (data for the Netherlands).

In a market economy the manager, the bank, the institutional investors and personal investors share the responsibility for the functioning and efficiency of the governance system. It is a common feature that the big institutional shareholders are called upon to remember their responsibilities and to involve themselves in systematic analysis of company information, to participate in shareholder meetings and to criticise weak corporate performance. These recommendations are reinforced by the fact that institutional share ownership has been rising all over the World. It should also be kept in mind that foreign shareholders in many cases are institutional investors.[27]

The growth of the institutional sector (pension funds, insurance companies, investment companies) has been a driving force behind structural changes in both the process of corporate governance and the structure of world capital markets. The expansion of the institutional sector has had a growing influence on financial governance channels, including the market for corporate control. First, institutional investors have enhanced their corporate governance role in the form of an increase in market control via equity and debt. Second, an increase of direct control via equity in the form of an increase in shareholder activism by institutional investors has been an important characteristic of the change in corporate governance in the last decade. Third, direct control via debt is an important mechanism of corporate control in Continental Europe and Japan.[28]

---

[27] *Ibid.*, p. xxi
[28] *Ibid.*, p. 42

TABLE 12. Ownership of common stock – an international comparison (percent at year end)

	United States (1994)	Japan (FY 1994)	Germany (1993)	France (1993)	United Kingdom (1993)	Italy (1993)	Sweden (1993)
Financial sector	45	44	29	8	62	19	24
of which:							
Banks	3	26	14	3	1	10	1
Insurance companies	4	16	7	1	17	2	8
Pension funds	22	0	0	0	34	0	0
Mutual funds	12	0	8	2	7	6	6
Other financial institutions	4	2	0	2	3	1	8
Non-financial sector	55	46	71	92	38	81	76
of which:							
Non-financial enterprises	0	24	39	59	2	32	34
Public authorities	0	1	4	4	1	28	7
Individuals	48	24	17	19	18	17	16
Foreign	6	7	12	11	16	5	9
Other	1	0	0	0	2	0	10
Total	100	100	100	100	100	100	100

Note: Due to rounding, the figures may not add up to the total. Pension funds in Japan are managed by trust banks and insurance companies. The assets in these funds are included under banks and insurance companies. No data are available on the extent to which mutual funds own shares. Security houses do manage such funds. These companies are included under other financial institutions.

Source: Flow of Funds, Board of the Federal Reserve System. Round Table, of National Stock Exchanges, 'Survey of Stock Ownership Distribution', August 1995. Deutsche Bundesbank, Banque de France, CSO, Consob, Banca d'Italia, Statistika Centralbyran, Sweden. Quoted in OECD (1995b). Annual Security Statistics (1995).

The Change of the Pricing Strategies

Pricing has become a very complicated process in the MNCs dominated economy. While choosing the appropriate price to charge for goods or services remains one of the most important challenges facing management of the firms, the assumption is made by the basic model of microeconomics that decisions are being made with full or perfect information available to managers about demand, competitors' reactions, supply costs, etc., are even more highly unrealistic in today's globalised world economy than they were in the less globalised one. Although price keeps to serve two broad functions: price raise revenue for the firm (price multiplied by the quantity sold determines the firm's total revenue and, depending on production costs, ultimately the firm's survival) and price is a rationing device (it rations out the available production amongst consumers on the base of their ability and willing-ness to pay), the implementation of these functions have undergone a very substan-tial change and modification. These can be summarised in the following way.

Pricing is driven by managerial objectives. The precise objectives pursued by man-agement ultimately determine the kind of pricing strategy that is adopted. Manage-ment might pursue profit maximisation, or corporate growth maximisation, sales revenue maximisation, or they might attempt to maximise their own sense of well-being, perhaps subject to a minimum profit requirement to keep shareholders con-tent. Equally, firms may not maximise anything, preferring instead to achieve a satisfactory outcome to a range of objectives (satisfying policy). In some industries, notably where there are state-run firms, the target could be breakeven or perhaps involve a negative mark-up. That is to say, the price is set so as to produce a politi-cally acceptable rate of loss, the burden of which is borne by taxpayers. Equally, private sector firms may, from time to time, adopt for short periods a pricing policy which leads to no profits or even losses, perhaps to win some market share or to fight off a competitor in the place. Occasionally, products may be used as "loss leaders" (for instance, to attract consumers into the store, some goods could be priced very low and displayed in the shop window). Firms also need to keep a wary eye on important considerations in market, such as the state of current demand, the market growth rate, the stage in the product's life cycle, its price elasticity, and the prices set by competitors.[29]

Whatever objective is being pursued, however, will have implications for pric-ing. The firm which endeavours to maximise its profits adopts a different price to one that is more concerned with maximising its market share or sales.

The pricing strategies applied by a firm have changed. Usually four pricing strategies can be distinguished:

a) marginal cost pricing,
b) incremental pricing,
c) breakeven pricing and
d) mark-up pricing.[30]

Marginal cost pricing involves setting prices, and therefore determining the amount produced, according to the marginal costs of production, and is normally associated with a profit-maximising objective. This strategy is mostly applied in highly competitive market and as in the MNCs dominated economy the market is rather oligipolistic the emphasis has shifted towards other strategies, especially to-wards incremental and mark-up pricing.

Incremental pricing deals with the relationship between larger change in rev-enues and costs associated with managerial decisions. The proper use of incremen-tal analysis requires a wide-ranging examination of the total effect of any decision

---

[29] Joseph G. Nellis and David Parker, *The Essence of Business Economics*, p. 120
[30] *Ibid.*, p. 121

rather than simply the effect at the margin. It will appreciate that fixed costs are irrelevant to both marginal cost and incremental pricing since costs are "sunk" and therefore do not change with output (unless the firm is already working at full capacity and therefore can only be increased by investing, i.e. by incurring more fixed cost). The decision to supply then simply reflects whether the change in total revenue is greater or less than the change in variable costs (i.e. the marginal or incremental costs from raising output). Because most of the MNCs have a very substantial fixed cost due to their size they incline to use this pricing strategy.

> A good example of incremental pricing involved Continental Airlines in the United States, which in the late 1950s decided whether to add or conceal flights according to whether the increase in total revenue from a flight covered the incremental cost of the flight. If fixed costs (the aircraft, management overheads, etc.) were ignored and the costs of keeping a plane parked at an airport were reflected in the opportunity costs of not flying, it made sense to fly a route even if flying losses results. In other words, a smaller loss resulted from flying than from not flying. Hence, Continental's operating rule was, in effect; "Does the flight at least cover its incremental costs?" Where a flight covered more of these costs, but still operated at an overall loss, it, of course, made a useful contribution towards the fixed costs.

That is the case regarding the mark-up pricing strategy too. The mark-up pricing is similar to breakeven pricing (which requires that the price of product is set so that total revenue earned equals the total costs of production), except that a desired rate of profit is built into the price (hence this pricing is also sometimes referred to as cost-plus pricing, full-cost pricing or target-profit pricing.) The particular mark-up will be what management consider appropriate or necessary to achieve a profit which satisfies the shareholders. It appears to guarantee the desired profit, but to realise this the output produced should be sold at the mark-up price or even the output should be sufficient to satisfy demand. In most cases the MNCs have such a strong market position that can meet these requirements.

As we know, the nature of the market in which the product is sold will have a major influence on the pricing policy adopted. Markets can be divided into four broad kinds:

1. perfectly competitive markets,
2. monopoly markets,
3. monopolistically competitive markets and
4. oligopolic markets.[31]

This nature of the market has substantially changed according to the dominance of each of these four characteristics: the markets have become more and more monopolistically competitive and less and less perfectly competitive in a large ex-

---

[31] *Ibid.*, p. 126

tent due to the growing influence of the MNCs. As markets become less competitive – i.e. as *the degree of monopoly power of the firm increases, suppliers will have more discretion when setting the prices*. Perfectly competitive and pure monopoly markets are rarely found – most firms are subject to competition but to a lesser extent than what would arise under perfect competition. More commonly, most firms are faced with a large number of competitors producing highly substitutable products, thus an attempt to achieve product differentiation is a dominant feature of the market place. This situation, referred to as monopolistic competition, means that firms still have some control over the price of the output. In monopolistically competitive markets, firms put considerable marketing effort into segmenting their markets and thereby reducing competition.

When markets are monopolistically competitive, firms are more likely to make decisions without explicitly taking into consideration competitive reactions. While this may be more appropriate for some industries than others, it is less applicable in an oligopoly market where an individual firm's is very likely to provoke a competitive reaction.

In oligopoly markets it is crucial to know how competitors are likely to react to a price change. Will they follow suit or not? Or will they react in some other way, for example, with an intensive advertising budget to preserve their market share? Oligopoly markets, therefore, reflect various competitive strategies in which price may or may not be critically variable. They are also prone to collusion and the formation of cartels (if firms co-operated in setting their prices uncertaintly faced by firms would be reduced) and to price leadership. In markets where there is a price leader, pricing policy may have similarities to pricing in highly competitive markets with the going rate set by one firm being important and with less attention paid by other firms their own demand and cost functions.[32]

Pricing strategies require a strong integration of pricing into a wider *marketing mix*, which takes into account other factors than price, which determine demand. Some firms may be reluctant to change price because of the uncertain effects on rivals' actions, so the other marketing variable take on added importance. At the same time, consumers may only have a vague idea of the price of products they buy, which appears to relegate the importance of price in demand, though it does not remove it altogether. At the very least pricing should complement the other factors in the marketing mix.

The most important elements of the marketing mix are product, place, promotion and price. These four elements of market mix determine what is called the "offer" to the consumer.[33]

The *product* raises the issue of consumers' perceptions of the product's characteristics. The perceived value or utility to the consumer rather than the supplier's costs

---

[32] *Ibid.*, p. 128
[33] *Ibid.*, p. 129

of provision becomes the key to pricing strategy with non-price factors used to increase the perceived value. Whereas breakeven and mark-up pricing emphasise costs as a basis of price, attention to the marketing mix places the emphasis more squarely on demand, with products perceived to be of high quality or status than the nearest competition-attracting "premium prices". (When the founder of Revlon cosmetics proclaimed that "In factory we make cosmetics, in the store we sell hope" he was well aware that his marketing success had opened the road to high profit margins.)

Place relates to the distribution of the product. How well a product is distributed is important to its success. Hence, successful suppliers put considerable time and resources into distributing the product effectively. Such questions should get proper answer: can the product be moved quickly from warehouse stores to retail outlets? Is the product best displayed in the supermarkets? Are distribution costs controlled to enable competitive pricing? A marked trend of the post-war period has been the manufacturer's loss control over his own product's marketing at the point of sale.

Product promotion involves effective marketing including the provision of adequate credit (very important for consumer durables) and advertising. Brands with intrinsically average quality but with high advertising budgets may achieve premium prices. Advertising shapes consumer perceptions of the product and increases consumer demand at all prices. Thus more can be sold at constant price or for the same amount at a higher price, leading to healthier margins. There is also some evidence that successful advertising by increasing market segmentation reduces price sensitivity. It therefore enables suppliers to gain a differential advantage by distinguishing themselves from the competitors. In effect, the firm gains a "quasi-monopoly" position. Segmentation and differential advantage involve aspects of product positioning, in which price is just one variable contributing to that positioning.

Product, place and promotion all leave their mark on both a firm's demand and cost relationships. *Price* has to fit with the remainder of the marketing plan because together they determine the product's "positioning" in the market place.[34]

The positioning of some kind of goods or service in the market has major implications for pricing policy. There is no point in marketing a high-quality product and then selling it at a down-market price. Equally, product perceived to be of low value must be priced accordingly. When a firm is competing for consumers and wants to earn high profit margins, it must try as far as it is possible to ensure that its and its competitors' "offers" are not compared on price alone.[35]

The impact of the product life cycle on pricing policy has changed, too. The notion of the product life cycle raises important issues for pricing since it implies that there may

---

[34] *Ibid.*, p. 130
[35] *Ibid.*, p.131

be a case for adopting different strategies at each stage of the cycle. The powerful MNCs can apply a very aggressive promotional or penetrating pricing in which the price is set low to enter the market against existing competitors, attracting consumers to the new product and gain market share. They also use a "skimming policy" more efficiently than the non-MNCs do. This price policy arises when price is set high initially to cover large unit costs in the early stage of the product life. Skimming policy will be attractive where a new product has a monopoly position in the market for a short period. Producers attempt to maximise the present value of the future profit stream by charging a monopoly price in the early years of the product's life and lower price later once competitive pressure begins to emerge.

The high initial price under a skimming policy implies a lower rate of growth of the sales than under a penetration pricing strategy. And because of the shortening of the product's life cycle due to the accelerating technological development pushed the MNCs, there is a need for a more rapid diffusion of the product in the market and to achieve that there is a very intensive incentive for the firms, especially for the MNCs to use their monopolistic position (which exists at least for a short period) to exploit as much as possible the promotional and skimming price policy for their special advantages.

The possibility of applying price discrimination has increased as a result of the high rate of monopolisation. It represents the practice of charging different prices for various units of a single product when the price differences are not justified by differences in production/supply costs. The critical factor for successful price discrimination is the ability of the firm to control its own prices. In other words, there must be imperfect competition so that an effective barrier exists to stop consumers from being able to buy the product at low price and to on-sell at a higher price. Also, there must be different elasticities of demand in the various markets. These differing elasticities may reflect different preferences, information and perceptions of the product and incomes and tastes. Where different price elasticities exist there is scope for price discrimination. (An obvious example is the pricing of seats on public transportation.) The so-called second-degree price discrimination involves charging a uniform price per unit for a special quantity or block of output sold to each consumer, as in pricing of water, gas and electricity. Most frequently found is the so-called third-degree price discrimination, which simply involves charging different prices for the same product in different segments of the market. The markets may be separated in the following number of ways: by geography – when an exporter charges a different price abroad than at home; by type of demand – as in the market for, say, textile where demand by households differs from the bulk purchase demand by large firms; by time – with a lower price charged for off-peak periods (as in case of the electricity and telephone sectors). By charging different prices to the various market segments for the same product the so-called price discriminator will be able to increase his total profits above the level that would have existed in the case of uniform pricing. This is because he is soaking up as much consumer surplus as possible and hence transforming it into producer surplus – i. e. higher profit margins for himself.[36] MNCs due to their special position are the good candidates for being price discriminators, in many cases they have opportunity to apply all of the above-mentioned discriminations.

Pricing in multi-plant and multi-product firms. In practice, most firms of any real size, and especially the MNCs, produce a range of products and on more than one site. The majority of large corporate enterprises are multi-business, multi-market, transnational firms; the scope of their operations is by no means limited to selling a single, well-defined item in a small, mostly local market. Today, most firms operate in a number of different markets and different countries. The existence of more than one production point facilitates price discrimination between different geographical areas served. This will be especially so where the production occures in different countries and national markets are protected by import controls. Where a firm's output of the same product is produced on more than one site, the profit-maximising output rule, that marginal supply costs must equal marginal revenue, is unchanged, but in this case marginal cost is the sum of the separate plans' marginal costs and production must be allocated between the plans so that the marginal supply cost at each plant is identical.

When producing and pricing a product, the multi-product firms have to take into consideration not only the impact on the demand for that product of the price change (its own price elasticity of demand), but the impact on the demand for the other products in the firm's range (the relevant cross-price elasticities). In other words, pricing now involves obtaining the desired rate of return from the full product range rather than individual products. Such a full-range pricing means that the firm may be content to earn little or no profit on certain products, preferring to use them as "loss leader" to attract consumers who then (hopefully) buy the higher-profit items. (This has been the strategy of some supermarkets for a long time.) In multi-product firms the products can be complementary, such as Kodak which sells cameras and film, or substitutes, such as Procter and Gamble's detergents. In both case demand for the products is interrelated. This means that profit maximisation requires that the output levels and prices of the products produced are determined jointly (in some firms the marketing departments of the various products may compete to increase efficiency and drive down costs, but this risks ignoring the high cross-price elasticities with damaging results for overall profitability).

In addition to demand interdependencies, multi-product firms may have production interdependencies. The most obvious example relates to a production of by-products. In such cases, complex "joint-costing" rules must be introduced and economic of scope recognised (cost reduction resulting from supplying together two or more products). Product can be produced jointly in fixed or variable propor-

---

[36] *Ibid.*, p. 135

tions. Hence, the costs of supply cannot be meaningfully apportioned between the two outputs.[37]

Pricing in multi-plant and multi-product firms has two other important features that need to be mentioned: *transfer pricing and the internalisation of market transactions.*

Large-scale multi-product, multinational firms are often decentralised by being split into semi-autonomous divisions, with each responsible for its own price and output decisions as well as profit performances. However, decentralisation brings with it problems of resource allocation, one aspect of which is the pricing of products which are transferred between divisions. This gives rise to the need for *transfer pricing* and problem of determining the transfer price which maximises overall company profits. For example, it may be possible for one division to raise its own reported profits by raising the transfer price but this may be at the expense of profits made by the receiving division. In such situations the general answer to the transfer-pricing problem is that the product being transferred between divisions should be priced at marginal cost.

Furthermore, when divisions are located in different countries with different tax systems, transfer pricing can be used to redistribute profits between countries in order to minimise the overall tax liability. This could be achieved, for example, in situations where one country, A, has high profits tax relative to another country, B. By setting the transfer price artificially low in country A, the profits could be realised in country B. It should be noted, however, that under fiscal regulations such arrangements are usually illegal – though they are also difficult to police.[38]

Internalisation means that bypassing the market, the firm performs the function of the market itself by internalising market transactions. Outside the firm, price movements direct production, which is co-ordinated through a series of exchange transactions on the market. Within a firm, these market transactions are eliminated and in place of the complicated market structure with exchange transactions it has substituted the enterpreneur-co-ordinator, who directs production.[39] It is clear that these are alternative methods of co-ordination and take place in the hierarchical organisation of the firm. "Hierarchical organisation replaces market first of all, because economies of scale arise from team production; ... and ... will also replace market transactions where specialised human or physical capital investment makes the principals vulnerable to post-contractual opportunism because of imperfect enforcement. Vertical integration can reduce the likelihood of hold-up where substantial quasi-rents are approprable."[40] The most obvious example of such internalisation is vertical

---

[37] *Ibid.*, p. 138

[38] Joseph G. Nellis and David Parker, *The Essence of Business Economics*, p. 140

[39] Ronald H. Coase, The Nature of the Firm, *Economica,* Vol. 4 (November, 1937) pp. 386–405

[40] Douglass C. North, *Structure and Change in Economic History* (W. W. Norton and Company, London 1981) p. 41

integration in which a firm decides to control either its own sources of supply or the destination of its output. In both cases, the functions of independent material suppliers or of wholesale and retail merchants are absorbed – internalised – within the firm.

The major incentive for a firm to internalise market is uncertainty. The greater the degree of uncertainty – whether over the availability, price or quality of suppliers or of the price obtainable for the firm's product – the greater the advantage for the firm to control these transactions. It is generally agreed that internalisation is especially likely to occur in the area of knowledge. Innovation and technological change are vital elements in a firm's ability to remain competitive and profitable. Many firms, especially large ones but also all those in high-technology industries, spend huge sums of money on R & D. To ensure a satisfactory return on such investment and to protect against predators, firms have a strong incentive to retain the technology and its use within their own boundaries. Rather than sell or lease the technology to other firms abroad the firm sets up its own production facilities and exploits its technological advantage directly.

More economic activity occurs within firms, than between firms; that is, companies produce intermediate products that are used as inputs for goods the company eventually sells, and firms may even produce the inputs that are used in these intermediate products. Such activity is known as vertical integration; by contrast, the horizontal integration involves bringing together firms producing the same goods. Table 13 shows that the output of several large, vertically integrated firms is as large as the entire output of several medium-sized countries.* Within these firms, relationships are controlled by commands – direct decisions by managers, hierarchies replace markets[41] – though those commands themselves may be effected by accounting profits and prices which can differ significantly from market prices and profits. In external markets, prices are charged on an "arm's-length" basis between independent sellers and buyers.

In the internal market, on the other hand, transactions are between created prices – units of the same organisation; the rules of the external market do not apply. The firm itself sets the accounting (or in the case of MNC the transfer) prices its goods and service within its own organisational boundaries. Potentially, at least, this gives the firm very considerable flexibility in setting its accounting (transfer) prices to help achieve its overall goals, as we have already seen it in the case of MNCs. And if we take into consideration the decisive role of the MNCs this internalisation is

---

* The comparison is not perfect. The appropriate comparison would be between the value of U.S. corporations added to the difference between their sales and the goods and services they purchase from other firms. Even in these terms, General Motors and Exxan are larger than Egypt and Greece.

[41] Oliver E. Williamson, *Markets and Hierarchies: Analysis and Antitrust Implications* (Free Press, New York, 1975) p. 55

TABLE 13. Comparing large corporations and small countries

1990 sales of large U.S. corporations	
General Motors	$ 125 billion
Exxon	$ 107 billion
Ford	$ 97 billion
IBM	$ 69 billion
Mobil	$ 64 billion
1989 national output of medium-sized economies	
Norway	$ 95 billion
Thailand	$ 70 billion
Argentina	$ 53 billion
Greece	$ 40 billion
Egypt	$ 32 billion

Sources: Business Week, March 18, 1991, p. 52; *World Development Report* (1991), pp. 208–209, Table 3.

taking place in global scale because their foreign affiliates located in different countries tend to be specialised, and flows among them are internalised to reduce the transactional costs, that is, they substitute the market in global scale.

In addition to all of these summarised above, *the role of the government in pricing* has changed moving from taxation and subsidies to regulation. All market economies have some state intervention in pricing in the form of taxation and subsidies, and direct controls, such as regulations and licensing. Also, in many countries state-owned industries, in many cases with MNCs, exist at central and local government levels and some decision must be taken on the pricing of their output.[42]

In a private market the price consumers are willing to pay reflects the benefits they receive from marginal consumption. However, in some cases the price consumers are willing to pay may not accurately reflect the true social benefits and costs of consumption – i.e. externalities – in which case the price could be altered through taxes and subsidies. For example, a pollution tax based on the principle that the polluter should pay and equally, in so far as public transport has wider social benefits by reducing congestion on the roads, demand for it can be encouraged by state subsidies to keep price low. Governments very often provide subsidies to MNCs to give the incentive for investment and technological transfer; these subsidies can make the prices of the MNCs more competitive.

Government direct controls on pricing arise out of prices and income policies, anti-monopoly and restrictive practice legislation, and other forms of regulation and licensing. The latter has grown in importance in recent years following the privatisation of some major public utilities, namely telecommunications, gas, elec-

---

[42] Joseph G. Nellis and David Parker, *The Essence of Business Economics*, p. 140

tricity and water industries. The monopoly suppliers now operate under licensing granted by the state, which regulates, amongst other things, price regulations.[43]

Rate-of-return regulation is ultimately an indirect form of price regulation since the price charged is an important variable in determining profits. Where the price is directly or indirectly regulated, competition must centre on some other aspect of the market mix. In airlines, for example, where prices are heavily regulated, competition is often focused on the level of service, in flight catering and movies.

Price in public sector has a special character. The public sector may well have different objectives since it is concerned with the wider public interest rather than profits. If this is the case, state enterprises should set their prices with an eye to the marginal social benefits (MSB) from the additional output and marginal social costs (MSC) of producing that output. The MSB reflects the benefits to the immediate consumer plus any external benefits (wider social gains) and the MSC is calculated to reflect not only the normal costs – wages, raw materials, etc. – but any external (social) costs, such as environmental effects. By pricing in this way, a public utility can maximise the difference between the social benefits of production from the output and the social costs of producing that output. The result, however, may be losses which have to be met through taxpayers' subsidies and taxation distorts employment, investment and spending decisions. Also, subsidies imply a welfare transfer between payers of taxes and the recipients of subsidised services. Why should all taxpayers subsidise rail users? Is the implied income redistribution equitable?[44]

On the basis of "public interest" rule, the public sector should invest and expand output when the marginal social benefit of expanding output exceeds the marginal social cost, and should contract production when the marginal social cost exceeds the marginal social benefit. But such pursuit of the "public interest" through public utility pricing depends upon the government correctly assessing the public interest and pursuing it relentlessly. In practice, politicians have tended to interfere with the prices set by nationalised industries to hold down inflation, boost budget receipts and preserve jobs even when it has been difficult to perceive a public interest objective. To critics the result has been higher inefficiency in the public sector and lowered managerial moral. A key argument for privatisation of state industries has been the removal of damaging political control and the restoration of commercial pricing.

Therefore, the fact that prices are as likely to reflect political considerations as true marginal social costs is a major weakness of state intervention in pricing. This is likely to be an even more acute problem for government services such as social security, education, health and defence. In such service, usually no price is charged, or it is a nominal charge and all or most funding comes from taxation.[45]

---

[43] *Ibid.*, p. 141
[44] *Ibid.*, p. 142
[45] *Ibid.*, p. 143

Externalities and Public Goods

MNCs can have substantial impact on the externalities and public goods. They can intensify both the negative and positive externalities. Due to their immense economic power (and political influence, too) they have bigger opportunity to carry out economic activities having intensive negative externalities, especially in the case of environment impacts (air, water pollution), particularly in the underdeveloped countries where state control and regulation is weak and less developed. That is, in this case the society as a whole should bear the negative external costs.

At the same time these companies can create widespread positive externalities through their intensive research activities aiming to meet the high requirements of the international competition. These companies have become the main sources of the technological innovation, patents, licences, know-hows, new brands. A lot of inventions made by them in fact has public good character. That MNCs play more and more role in the basic research the result of which is almost pure public goods. Basic research is a kind of fundamental inquiry that may produce a wide range of application. It was, for instance, basic research in physics that led to the ideas behind so many of the things we take for granted today – the laser, the transistor, atom energy. For example, the transistor, which revolutionised electronics, was invented at AT&T's Bell Laboratories.

Yet, when transistors spawned better radios, television sets, and other products, AT&T received little return from these benefits. The company's major return was only the capacity to develop better and less expensive telephone equipment. There are some marked advantages to having the fruits of basic research easily accessible; there may be large social gains when many researchers attempt to apply new basic ideas. However, sealing up the basic ideas in a patent could slow the progress of others engaged in related lines of research. The same result can be achieved by internalisation, that is using the results and advantages of the research inside the boarder of the companies and that is what the MNCs do very often, for example, they establish a new production factory as part of the company to exploit the positive externalities of their scientific discovery. In fact, this is one of the main incentives for the MNCs to engage into this kind of research.

Schumpeterian Interpretation of Monopolistic Competition

There seems to be a contradiction between the growing monopolistic power of MNCs, which by its nature should create a lot of inefficiency and the ever expanding material wealth, improving efficiency in the globalising world economy as a whole and in the vast majority of national economies. This seemingly paradox situation can be explained rather convincingly by using Schumpeter's theory about the monopolistic competition.

According to the neo-classical analysis of the monopoly, it is associated with higher price, higher profits and lover output than under perfect competition; there is a loss of consumer welfare (the consumer has no choice in the market place, part of the competitive consumer surplus has been transferred to the monopolist as additional profit, that is, the monopoly leads to a net loss of welfare, while a further part of the benefits received by consumers in the competitive market is transferred to the monopoly suppliers in the form of supernormal profit); higher costs (the lack of competition may lead to waste or x-inefficiency, which means higher costs of production at all output).

Despite these arguments, monopolies can have some advantages. One of these is the economic of scale. This might arise in production, investment, R & D, marketing, distribution or management. The monopoly may be able to achieve substantial economic of scale due to larger plan, centralised administration and avoid unnecessary duplication (e.g. a monopoly gas company would eliminate the need for several sets of rival gas pipes under each street). If significant economic of scale exists, the monopolist's cost can be lower at the profit-maximising output than the competitive firm's costs. In which case, it is possible for both the monopolists to earn higher profits and the consumer to benefit from lower prices. This could result in more consumer surplus than if production had occurred in a competitive industry. Also, the profits earned by the monopolist might be ploughed back into more investment and R & D spending to the ultimate benefits of consumer. Another one is the possibility of lower cost curve due to more R & D and more investment. Although the monopolist's sheer survival does not depend on its finding ever more efficient methods of production, it can use part of its supernormal profit for R & D and investment. It thus has a greater ability to become efficient than the small firm with limited funds. There is competition for corporate control.

Although a monopoly faces no competition in the goods market, it may face an alternative form of competition in the financial markets. A monopoly, with potentially low costs, which is currently run inefficiently, is likely to be subject to a takeover bid from another company. This competition for corporate control may thus force the monopoly to be efficient in order to avoid being taken over. Very important advantage is the special incentive for innovation and introduction of new products. The potential of supernormal profits, protected perhaps by patents, may encourage the development of new industries producing new products.

These monopoly advantages can outweigh the inefficiencies accompanied by the monopoly position, especially if we take dynamic approach, which is overlooked by the traditional economic theory taking usually a static approach. This cannot be said about the theory of Schumpeter, his concept of "creative destruction" is a strong and interesting dissent from the prevailing neo-classic view.[46]

---

[46] Joseph A. Schumpeter, *Capitalism, Socialism anf Democracy* (Harper and Row, New York, 1942)

Schumpeter posits competition as an exciting process of dynamic disequilibrium, rather than a set of equilibrium conditions reached at one time. Competition and progress occur tighter, he said, but in a series of temporary and ill-fated monopolies. In each time period, each market may be dominated by one firm that raises prices and earn monopoly profits. These profits attract other firms, one of which soon innovates a better product and pushes aside the first dominant firm. The new dominant firm then has its chance to set monopoly prices, causing the usual distortions and monopoly burdens. But soon it, too, is ousted by the next newcomer, and so on.

This cycle of creative destruction continues – innovation creates dominance, which gains monopoly profits, which stimulate new innovation, which creates new dominance, and so on. As time passes, the average degree of monopoly profits in each period may be very high. Indeed the profits, disequilibrium, distortion, and market dominance may all be large at each point of time. Yet the process of innovation is rapid, and it is the main feature. As an engine of process, it soon generates benefits of technical progress far exceeding any costs of static misallocation caused as market power is created and destroyed. So in Schumpeter's view, the disadvantages of monopoly were more than offset by advantages of rapid innovation the monopoly profit funded.

The growing role of the MNCs together with the very fact of the economic development have strengthened the rationality of the argument of Schumpeter. MNCs devise global strategies for the production and marketing of products heavily reliant on created assets proprietary to individual firms or, where technical alliances exist, groups of firms. Products of this kind may be described as dynamic or "Schumpeterian" goods and/or services: firms producing these goods are in a constant state of flux as changes take place within an industry, especially the distribution of stock of proprietary technological assets among the competitors, affect their ability to compete and, therefore, their viability. Speed-to-market of new products and of new generations of existing products can affect the return on investment in proprietary technology. It is vital that firms maintain a rate of product innovation and development necessary to keep with their competitors. Firms engaged in global competition in Schumpeterian goods and services generate quasi-rents from exports and from the use of proprietary assets abroad and are, therefore, important contributors to the economic welfare of a home country.

Global competition is a field where prices and competitive forces across country markets are strongly linked together, and the term international and global market has a true meaning. In the global competitive industry, a firm's competitive position in one country both affects and is affected by its competitive standing in other countries. Rival companies compete against each other in many different countries, but especially in countries where sales volumes are large and where having a competitive presence is strategically important to building a strong global position in the industry. In global competition, a firm's overall competitive advantage grows out of its entire world-wide operations; the competitive advantage it has created at its home base is supplemented by advantages growing out of its operations in other countries (having plans in low-wage countries, a capacity to serve customers with multinational operations of their own, and brand reputation that is transferable from country to country). A global competitor's market strength is directly proportional to its portfolio of country-based competitive advantages. Global competition exists in automobiles, tires, telecommunications equipment, copiers, watches, and commercial aircraft.

In some Schumpeterian industries, the rate of investment in competitiveness-enhancing assets can be used as a strategic weapon by firms with ample cash flow and easily available external finance. An industry can be described as "explosive" if the loss of competitiveness by a firm in one year, with an attendant diminution of free cash flow, could generate a vicious circle as a diminishing cash flow impedes the ability to spend on competitiveness-enhancing activities and causes a firm to fall further behind. In the absence of some favourable external events, established firms could fail.[47]

And if we take into consideration that in real life there is no perfect monopoly, the oligopolistic competition is the major characteristic feature of the market in which there is tough competition between the firms, especially in global scale, the advantages of powerful MNCs oligopolistic companies are even far greater than their disadvantages coming from their oligopolistic market power. Of course, if they move toward the perfect monopoly position this relatively favourable picture can change. The danger of this cannot be excluded if we look at the rapid process of the mergers taking place among the MNCs all over the world. Mergers have become commonplace.

Various motives have been suggested for mergers including growth, economic of scale, market and monopoly power, increasing share value, reduction in uncertainty, and plain taking advantage of opportunities. Among them one of the strongest motive is to reduce competition and thereby gain greater market power and larger profit. Merger activity tends to be undertaken in waves: several years of low merger activity are followed by periods of feverish activity. These periods tend to correspond to periods when the stock market is buoyant with rising share prices, therefore, the finance of merger is easier. These periods in turn tend to correspond to periods of rapid growth in the economy, and where, therefore, business confidence is high.

The first of these booms began in the mid-1960s and reached a peak in 1972. Then during the mid-1970s and early 1980s there were relatively few mergers. This period of low merger activity continued until 1983, when first the value of mergers

---

[47] *Transitional Corporations*, Vol. 4. No. 3 (December, 1995) p. 52

and then the number began to increase dramatically. By the late 1980s mergers were occurring at four times the rate of a decade earlier. Then after 1989 merger activity began to slow down along with slowdown in growth of economy (see Table 14). We can experience a new boom in the second half of the 1990s. For example, global merger activity surges to new record in 1998 (see Tables 15 and 16). The merger of Exxon Corp. and Mobil Corp. is the largest corporate combination in history.

TABLE 14. Acquisition and mergers by UK industrial and commercial companies

Year	1970	1971	1972	1973	1974	1975	1976	1977	1978	1979	
Number of companies acquired	793	884	1,210	1,205	504	315	353	481	567	534	
Expenditure (£m)	1,122	911	2,532	1,304	508	291	448	824	1,140	1,656	

Year	1980	1981	1982	1983	1984	1985	1986	1987	1988	1989	1990
Number of companies acquired	469	452	463	447	568	474	842	1,527	1,499	1,337	779
Expenditure (£m)	1,475	1,144	2,206	2,344	5,475	7,090	15,363	16,486	22,740	27,250	8,329

Source: Financial Statistics (CSO).

TABLE 15. Oil, financial services, top list of biggest deals in 1998 (announced U.S. deals involving change in majority ownership)

Buyer	Acquisition	Transaction TYPE	VALUE (billions of USD)
Exxon	Mobil	Stock Swap	78.9
Travelers Group	Citicorp	Stock Swap	72.6
SBC Communication	Ameritech	Stock Swap	62.6
NationsBank	BankAmerica	Stock Swap	61.6
AT&T	Tele-Communications Inc.	Stock Swap	53.6
Bell Atlantic	GTE	Stock Swap	53.4
British Petroleum	Amoco	Stock Swap	48.2
Daimler-Benz	Chrysler	Stock Swap	40.5
Norwest	Wells Fargo	Reverse Takeover	34.4
Banc One	First Chicago NBD	Stock Swap	29.6
Berkshire Hathaway	General Re	Stock Swap	22.3
American International Group	SunAmerica	Stock Swap	18.1
Washington Mutual	HF Ahmanson	Stock Swap	14.7
McKesson	HB0	Stock Swap	14.3
USA Waste Services	Waste Management	Reverse Takeover	13.3

Value at announcement, excluding assumed debt
Source: Securities Data Co.

TABLE 16. Top ten deals with European partners. Deals pending or completed where one or both partners are European companies

Acquiring company	Target company	Deal value (in billions of USD)
British Petroleum	Amoco	2.1
Daimler-Benz	Chrysler	5.1
Fortis	Generale de Banque	12.3
Commercial Union	General Accident	11.2
Sanofi	Synthelabo	11.1
Credito Italiano	Unicredito	11.0
Texas Utilities	Energy Group	10.9
Universal Studios	Polygram	10.2
Istituto Bancario San Paolo	Istituto Mobiliare Italiano	9.5
Deutsche Bank	Bankers Trust	9.1

Source: IFR Securities Data.

IMPACT ON MACROECONOMICS

Rational for Macroeconomics and its Main Content

Economists have always recognised that it is the unique and critical task of governments to engage in responsible and efficient macroeconomic management, even though there has been much controversy over how this task can be done. "Sovereign states have legitimate goals toward which they try direct the resources under their command."[48] Government may sometimes be justified in extending their macroeconomic boundaries to embrace issues of competition, education and science, and industry.[49] The theoretical basis for this is provided by macroeconomics, the macroeconomic theory. As J. M. Keynes, who has the seminal contribution to macroeconomic theory and policy-making, believed that, unaided market forces could not always ensure the full and efficient employment of resources, and that government intervention might be necessary to achieve this goal. Macroeconomics focuses mainly on the more direct economic facets of a firm's wider environment, that is the macroeconomy. In contrast to microeconomy (the immediate environment of a firm involving prices, revenues, costs, employment levels and so on), this refers to the factors which are external to the immediate environment of the firm: it

---

[48] Raymond Vernon, *Sovereignty at Bay* (Longman, London, 1971) p. 247

[49] *Governments, Globalisation, and International Business.* John H. Dunning, ed. (Oxford Univesity Press, New York, 1997) p. 44

involves changes in general inflation and employment, for example, rather than changes in the firm's own production prices and workforce.

Macroeconomics, therefore, refers to the aggregate national and, increasingly, international economy of which the firm is sub-unit. Macroeconomics tries to identify the forces that determine the level of aggregate output, employment, and inflation. It does this by studying what causes changes in the demand and supply curves in the labour, product, and capital markets, and through these by explaining the behaviour of those macroeconomic variables which are of the greatest importance to business decision-making. Such macroeconomic variables are: economic growth, inflation, interest rates, availability of credit and monetary growth, total investment, public expenditures, taxation (personal and corporate), total savings, wages and earnings at the economy level, employment trends, imports, exports, balance of payments. The list could be extended considerably but the message is that firms operate within an environment that is extremely complex and dynamic. In addition, all of these economic variable are interrelated to some extent. For example, changes in monetary growth affect interest rates; changes in taxation have implications for the level of public expenditure as well as for consumer spending and investment. Furthermore, all of these variables are either directly controlled by the government or indirectly affected by government economic policies.[50]

The Main Elements of Government Economic Policy

Economic policies may be summarised under the general headings of:

Fiscal policy. It is concerned with the composition of and changes in the levels of public expenditure and taxation.

Monetary policy. It is defined as government measures to influence the cost (i.e. the rate of interest) and availability of credit in the economy thereby affecting the overall supply of money.

Exchange rate policy. It refers to government intervention on the foreign exchange markets to influence the level and direction of the external value of the country's currency. The degree of intervention depends upon the government's specific exchange rate objective: whether to have a fixed, freely floating or managed rate and, where the exchange rate is fixed or managed, at what level to "peg" the rate. Exchange rate policy has important implications for trade and capital flows in and out of the country, i.e. for the balance of payments. It has an impact upon domestic policy since interest rate levels may be set to protect the exchange rate by influencing international capital flows.

---

[50] Joseph G. Nellis and David Parker, *The Essence of Economy* (Prentice Hall, New York, 1990) p. 3

International trade policy. Trade policy involves measures taken by government, in addition to exchange rate policy, to influence the magnitude and direction of foreign trade. There may be many reasons for these measures, notably correction of balance of payments problems, preserving domestic employment, encouraging economic growth and promoting foreign co-operation. The measure may take the form of subsidies for exports, tariffs (duties) on imports and other protectionist measures such as implicit quota.

Supply-side policy. It refers to government policies that are directed at tackling problems involving the aggregate supply (i.e. production) of goods and services in the economy. Supply-side policy, therefore, is in contrast with the policies described above, especially fiscal and monetary policies, which are concerned with affecting the level of total or aggregate demand for goods and services. Measures used are directed specially at influencing productivity and output costs. These may involve the introduction of new technology, the encouragement of competition and enterprise, privatisation of state assets, efforts to increase labour efficiency and other measures to improve the operation of the market economy.

Price and income policy. Price and income policies are examples of direct intervention by government in the working of a market economy. They involve government intervention in setting prices for goods and services and in influencing wage settlements. These policies have two fundamental aims: control over general inflation and the protection of jobs in the domestic economy. In addition, prices and income policies can have a significant impact upon the distribution of income. There is a general view among economists, however, that prices and income policies should be regarded only temporary or emergency measures: they distort the operation of markets by undermining wage and price levels, which reflect the demand for and supply of goods, services and labour.

Employment policy. It is concerned with government efforts to create jobs and thereby reduce unemployment. The policy may be implemented either indirectly, via stimulation of aggregate demand in the economy, or directly through job creation schemes and traning programmes.

Industrial policy. The rational for industrial policy is to strengthen national firms. From the adaptation of an import-substitution model to the provisions of support for "national champions", the objective of industrial policy – irrespective of a country's level of development – is to help firms in the public or private sectors to compete against imported products or acquire the size that will enable them to enter – or to stay in – the selective "club" of the world leaders in some industries.

Clearly, there is a large degree of overlap between these various policies and their impact upon the macroeconomic variables listed earlier.[51]

---

[51] *Ibid.,* p. 6

Economic Objectives of Governments

Governments have a number of economic objectives, although the importance of each and the trade-offs between them vary from time to time. Among them the following are the most important for the economy:
- A high and sustainable level of economic growth;
- full employment of economic resources, including labour;
- low or zero inflation;
- a sound balance of payments coupled with a strong currency value in the foreign exchange markets.

From time to time other objectives may be emphasised such as a reduction in regional imbalances, a redistribution of income and wealth, more and less state ownership, and promotion of competition and private enterprise. The pursuance of these objectives is made all the more difficult by the existence of policy conflicts or what are often called policy trade-offs. Trade-offs may arise, such as between a lower rate of inflation and a higher rate of employment, in the policy measures adopted by government.[52]

The implementation of these objectives is expected to follow the logic of the macroeconomic theory. For example, Keynes identified a three-step process by which an expansive monetary policy increases aggregate demand (Figure 12):

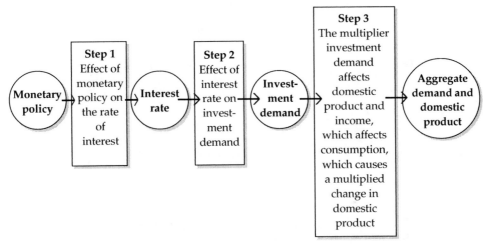

Keynesian economists trace the effect of monetary policy through three steps:
1. Monetary policy can affect the rate of interest
2. Changes in the rate of interest can affect investment demand
3. Changes in investment demand have a multiplied effect on aggregate demand and domestic product.

FIGURE 12. How monetary policy affects aggregate demand and domestic product: the Keynesian approach

---

[52] *Ibid.*, p. 14

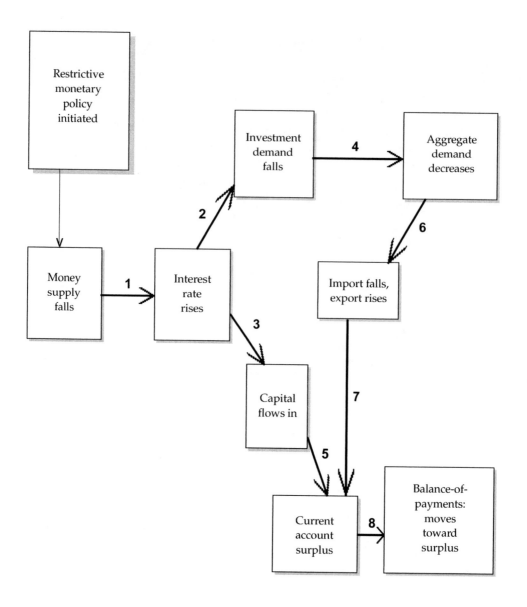

A restrictive monetary policy raises domestic interest rates (arrow 1). This affects the balance-of-payments accounts in two ways:

a) Because investment and aggregate demand decrease (arrow 2 and 4), there is a tendency for imports to decrease and exports to increase (arrow 6). Thus, the current account moves toward a surplus (arrow 7).

b) A higher domestic interest rate causes a capital inflow (arrow 3) and the capital account moves toward a surplus (arrow 5). Thus, the overall balance-of-payment moves toward a surplus (arrow 8).

FIGURE 13. Effects of restrictive monetary policy on the balance-of-payments

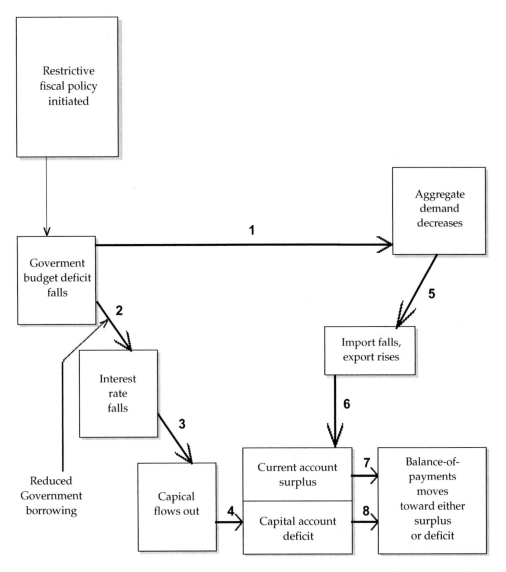

A restrictive fiscal policy decreases domestic aggregate demand (arrow 1). Furthermore, it reduces the government's need to borrow and therefore tends to lower domestic interest rates (arrow 2). There are two kinds of effect on the balance-of-payments:

a) The reduced aggregate demand causes imports to decrease and export to increase (arrow 5), moving the current accounts toward a surplus (arrow 6).

b) The lower interest rate causes a capital outflow (arrow 3), moving the capital account toward a deficit (arrow 4).

Because the current and capital account move in opposite directions, we cannot tell whether the overall effect (arrows 7 and 8) will be to move balance-of-payments towards a surplus or a deficit.

Figure 14. Effects of restrictive fiscal policy on the balance-of-payments

183

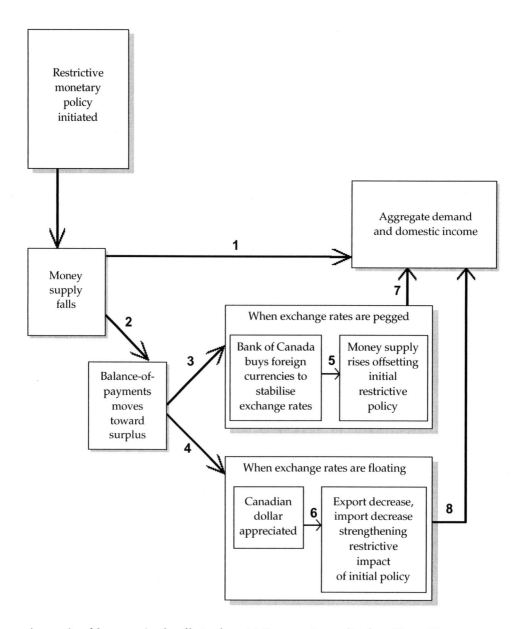

Arrows 1 and 2 summarise the effects of a restrictive monetary policy from Figure 14.

With the fixed exchange rates (arrow 3), Bank of Canada purchases of foreign currencies tend to increase the Canadian money supply (arrow 5); this increase in the money supply tends to offset the initial restrictive policy (arrow 7).

With floating exchange rates (arrow 4), the balance-of-payments surplus causes an appreciation of the Canadian dollar. As a result (arrow 6), Canadian net export tends to decrease, which further reduces aggregate demand (arrow 8).

FIGURE 15. Monetary policy is more effective with floating exchange rates than with fixed rates

1. An open market purchase generally causes a lower interest rate.

2. A lower interest rate encourages business to invest more. It is cheaper for them to borrow money to finance the purchase of new machines or building of new factories.

3. Higher investment demand will have a multiplied effect on aggregate expenditure and domestic product.[53]

The other examples can be the effects of monetary and fiscal policy on the balance of payments with fixed exchange rate and with a floating exchange rate.

To see what happens to the capital flows under a restrictive monetary policy, note that policy will make interest rates in Country A, let say Canada, rise relative to Country B, let say USA rates. This encourages both Canadian and American investors to sell USA assets in order to buy the Canadian assets that are now yielding a higher return. Thus, the result of this tight monetary policy is a capital inflow into Canada – that is, a movement in the capital account toward a surplus. Similarly, an easy money policy will result in lower Canadian interest rates moving the capital account toward a deficit.

Fiscal policy also has an impact on the capital account. The reason is that fiscal policy affects interest rates. For example, if the government moves toward a tighter fiscal policy by decreasing expenditure or raising taxes, the result is a smaller government budget deficit (or even a budget surplus). Hence, there is reduction in the amount that the government has to borrow in the bond market. But decreasing government borrowing will tend to push down Canadian interest rates and this will cause a capital outflow from Canada. That is: whereas tight monetary policy and tight fiscal policy have the same effect on the current account (they move it a surplus), they have different effect on the capital account. A tight monetary policy raises interest rates and therefore results in a capital inflow, whereas a tight fiscal policy lowers interest rates and results in a capital outflow. (Figures 13 and 14 illustrate these effects.)

How does the relative effectiveness of monetary and fiscal policy depend on whether Canada has a fixed exchange rate or a flexible exchange rate?

Figure 13 showed a restrictive monetary policy having a favourable effect on both the current account (arrow 7) and on the capital account (arrow 5). Resulting move toward a surplus in the balance of payments is shown as arrow 2 in Figure 15. Under a fixed exchange rate, the Bank of Canada must buy foreign currencies in order to prevent the Canadian dollar from rising (arrow 3). But, this expands chartered bank reserves and therefore the money supply (arrow 5). This tends to offset the original restrictive monetary policy. In other words, Figure 15 confirms one of the major criticisms against a fixed exchange rate system. With fixed exchange

[53] Ake Blomqvist, Paul Blomqvist and Ronald Wonnacott, *Economics* (McGraw-Hill Ryerson Limited, Toronto, 1990) p. 242

rates, international complications make it difficult for the authorities to use monetary policy effectively, as shown by the "inner loop" of arrows 3, 5, and 7 in Figure 15.[54]

With a floating exchange rate –, again assuming a restrictive monetary policy with a resulting balance-of-payments surplus – the Bank of Canada simply lets the Canadian dollar rise in value (arrow 4 in Figure 15), because the Bank makes no attempt to hold the Canadian dollar down by buying foreign exchange, there is no complication in the form of an expansion of the money supply. But a rise in the Canadian dollar does effect Canadian exports and imports: the higher-priced Canadian dollar makes Canadian goods more expensive relative to foreign goods, and thus reduces Canadian exports and decreases Canadian imports (arrow 6). The resulting reductions in Canadian output – in both Canadian export and import-competing industries – augment the restrictive effects of the initial tight money policy. Thus, the "outher loop" of Figure 15 (arrows 4, 6, and 8) shows how a floating exchange rate strengthens the traditional domestic impact of a tight monetary policy. That is: the system of fixed exchange rates makes it difficult for a country to use monetary policy effectively. Flexible exchange rates reinforce the effectiveness of monetary policy.[55]

Impacts of the Globalisation on the Economic Policies

All of these logics of macroeconomics presuppose that sovereign national states and their governments implement these policies under great autonomy and scale of freedom of decisions. However, this is not the case due to the globalisation of the world economy and to the influence of the MNCs on the economy. They have major impact on the macroeconomics. It poses the question: Does it make sense to keep the same macroeconomic paradigm for economic policy decision at the national and multinational levels despite the changing behavioural patterns of firms and States?[56] Today, most governments are facing several economic policy dilemmas. To a large extent, the current confusion reflects the inadequacy of the traditional paradigm as a framework for economic policy at the macroeconomic and (as we could see in the earlier part of our discussion) microeconomic levels. Monetary and fiscal policy, trade policy, labour policy and industrial policy are deeply affected by the new rules of the game in today's world economy.

The world economy today is a multidimensional system within which factors of production move according to decisions that are made by transnational agents op-

---

[54] *Ibid.*, p. 270

[55] *Ibid.*, p. 272

[56] Charles-Albert Michalet, Transitional Corporations and the Changing International System. *Transitional Corporations*, Vol. 3, No. 1 (February, 1994) p. 9

erating in oligopolistic markets. To understand the dynamics of the new world economy, it is necessary to consider together trade flows, capital movement, inward and outward FDI, technology flows and labour movements. Such an approach implies not only that exports and imports of goods and services are no longer the exclusive forms of economic transactions among nation-states, but also that the various dimensions of the world economy are tightly interconnected. Therefore, it is no longer feasible to develop separate analytical frameworks for trade, financial markets, international monetary movements and migration as if these belonged to distinct fields that are subject the separate theories. Neither can the working pieces of world economy be made understood by simply adding up distinct pieces of knowledge. The very nature of the world economy is the existence of close interactions between FDI, trade, technological transfer, financial and labour movements. Exports that flow from country A to country B induce new opportunities and constrains for FDI.

These investments are finances from local and international sources. Technology transfer and the presence of expatriates with experiences in a company's activities can improve an affiliate's performance. Foreign affiliates generate import and export flows that can benefit country A and country B. In the new world economy, trade has become a part of a package that includes also capital, technology and human resources. Competitive performance is more and more dependent on the country's and firm's ability to combine various fields of expertise. World-wide economic integration is no longer built solely on more intense trade flows among countries; it is now the result of a multidimensional and complex set of interrelations. A new way of comparing the level of economic development among countries is by observing the predominant forms of their integration into the world economy. The most developed countries are connected through both inward and outward flows of trade, FDI, technology and capital. Less-developed countries are connected mainly only through trade. For those countries, FDI, technology and capital flows play only a minor role – especially outward FDI, technology transfer and capital lending – when compared with exports of raw materials.[57]

Factors of production are increasingly crossing national borders. In most cases, FDI implies an outflow of capital from home to host countries. As far as labour movement is concerned, managers, engineers and technicians often become expatriate workers in foreign affiliates. Technology, a component of all FDI projects, also flows to host countries. Finally, the process of delocation, that is, the closing of productive facilities in the home countries and the establishing of new productive units abroad, may be thought of as moving a piece of land from one country to the other. Therefore, with factor endowments continuously changing, it is no longer possible to define a national-State's comparative advantage. In fact – and depending on the

---

[57] *Ibid.*, p. 13

level of development of a host country – FDI is becoming a crucial determinant of a country's pattern of specialisation.

Furthermore, and in the contradiction with the old paradigms, national-states are no longer the only players in the world economy. Decisions regarding the location of new factories, or the relocation of existing ones, are taken by MNCs. Increasingly, the funding of economic activities in developed, as well as in developing, countries is made by transnational banks operating from off-shore financial centres that are outside the jurisdiction of central banks.

A significant share of the international trade – about one third – consists of intra-firm flows. Price of goods and services that are channelled from one foreign affiliate to the other are not determined by the market as in the traditional paradigm. Ex-post specialisation in production is the result of MNC decisions to locate some of their activities abroad. Such decisions are made after comparing the benefits offered by alternative locations. Finally, MNCs themselves select the location best suited to enhancing their own competitiveness. In the new world economy, gains from competitiveness benefit MNCs; and this is a substitute for the old paradigm's welfare gains generated by free trade and assumed to benefit equally national-states. The world market does not resemble the perfect market laid down in the textbooks of international trade. Oligopolistic competition is the rule of the game and economists are aware that an oligopolistic market does not produce the conditions for an optimal allocation of resources.

Finally, because of the strategies and structures of the new world economy's main actors, the MNCs, the borders of national economies have become blurred. The historical coincidence between a state and a nation is put into question and with that the traditional basis for political sovereignty, too. This is why economic policy is becoming more complex and the outcome of a government's economic measures is often uncertain. *This situation is one of the major implications resulting from the nature of the emerging world economy.*[58]

In today's world economy, there are many instances in which domestic economic policies appear to be working badly. The impact of monetary policy and fiscal policy on growth, investment, employment, trade and capital movements is often uncertain. Industrial policy has lost a good deal of its *raison d'être,* following the growing difficulty in answering the question "who is us". The bottom line of economic policy dilemma is found in the widening dichotomy that exists between the globalisation process and national interest.

Macroeconomic theory, which is used as a framework for government intervention, refers to national aggregates based on national accounting techniques that ignore the role of the game of the new world economy. Industry-policy objectives are determined by a nationalistic approach that no longer corresponds to the strategy and structures of MNCs, whatever their country of origin. The old paradigm im-

---

[58] *Ibid.,* p. 14

pedes governments from realising: the political frontiers of a country no longer coincide with the economic borders. The widening dichotomy between a nation and a state is not only the result of a greater openness of the economy – with openness defined in terms of trade flows – but also, and above all, the result of the multidimensional nature of its integration into the world economy. This has an important implication: MNCs – as we have seen it earlier – are the most significant economic players in the world economy, although this is not yet recognised by the existing official economic data, national administrations and international institutions.[59]

Moreover, MNCs' strategies and structure have been evolving in the past four decades, with significant implications for host and home countries. Since the 1980s, an increasing number of MNCs has followed global strategies and adopted global structures. Gradually, more and more MNCs are moving away from multinational strategies and structures. A global approach means, first of all, that investment decision-making is less local market oriented than in case of a multinational strategy; MNCs' main target is expanding world market share. Second, foreign affiliation located in different countries tends to be specialised, and flows among them are internalised to reduce transaction costs. The implication of global strategies and structures of the MNCs explain most of the paradoxical results that presently confront those host and home country governments that uphold the traditional policies. Illustration of these results may be found in monetary, fiscal, trade and industrial policies.

Monetary and fiscal policies, the two traditional main instruments of economic policy, have become less effective under the rules of the game that characterise the new world economy. With capital mobility, the targets of monetary and fiscal policies can no longer be reached with certainty. In certain cases, changes in interest rates or taxation may trigger unexpected and counter-productive effects. Governments are no longer in a position to use monetary and fiscal measures without considering their domestic impact from a world-wide perspective. The power of transnational banks, when confronted with policies of central banks, does need to be proved. The effect of changes in interest rates on firms' investments are dubious. By borrowing abroad (e.g., in the Euromarket), MNCs are able to avoid paying higher interest rates for financing domestic investments. Although lower interest rates may have a positive impact on a firm's domestic investments, the money borrowed may be used to finance FDI as well. Similar uncertainties regarding the effectiveness of government policy may be observed in fiscal policy. With capital mobility, the taxation of profits from financial investments cannot be significantly different among countries; national tax rates have to be adjusted to lower existing rate if capital flight is to avoided.[60] The following examples can illustrate these:

---

[59] *Ibid.*, p. 17
[60] *Ibid.*, p. 15

189

- Referring to Figure 13, a restrictive monetary policy raises interest rates to decrease aggregate demand and to create surplus in the balance of payments, but if the MNCs borrow money from abroad with lover interest rates and invest it in the given country, the result can be just the opposite: increase of the aggregate demand due to the intensifying investment activities with expanding import resulting less than expected surplus (or deficit) in the balance-of-payments.
- An expansionary monetary policy decreases the interest rates to bust investment and through this increases aggregate output and the level of employment, but if this money borrowed at low interest rates is used by the MNCs for financing FDI, the expected improvement in the economic growth and the employment situation does not occur.
- Referring to Figure 14, a restrictive fiscal policy intends to decrease domestic demand by decreasing government expenditures, the result is smaller government budget deficit (or even a surplus), hence, there is a reduction in the amount that the government has to borrow in the bond market, and the decreasing government borrowing tends to push down interest rates, however, if MNCs borrow money with this low interest rates in the given country and invest it for expending productive capacity, the result can be the opposite: increasing domestic demand.
- An expansionary fiscal policy intends to increase the aggregate demand by increasing government expenditures to accelerate the economic growth and to create new jobs for unemployed workers, but if the MNCs through "downsizing" and/or decreasing the real wages offset this increase in the demands the final result can be a falling aggregate demand.
- MNCs can eliminate the crowding-out effect too, that is, reduction in demand that results when a fiscal expansion raises the interest rate, if they borrow money at lower interest rate abroad and invest it for expanding production capacity of the given country.
- The fiscal policy intends to accelerate economic growth by decreasing taxes influencing the MNCs to expand their production (using the logic of the so called supply-side economics), but if in the interest of the budget position the government expenditures are decreased (for example, cutting back the expenditures for health, education, research), this shrinking the government expenditures can offset the positive impact of adding production of the MNCs to the economic growth.
- Referring to Figure 13, the restrictive monetary policy results a surplus in the balance-of-payments and under a fixed exchange rate regime to prevent the Canadian dollar from rising the Bank of Canada should buy foreign currency (selling Canadian dollar). But doing this Bank of Canada has to face the risk of piling up irrationally large exchange reserves (or lets the Canadian dollar appreciate), which risk is intensified by unavoidable speculation lead by the MNCs

(including multinational banks, financial institutions) against the Canadian dollar, and also it should offset the initial restrictive monetary policy by raising money supply, and in addition to these the exports decrease; if there is an expanding monetary policy resulting in deficit in the balance of payments under the fixed exchange rates regime, the Bank of Canada should buy Canadian dollar to prevent it from decreasing, but in this case the Bank's addition to the currency speculation should face the risk of running out of the exchange reserves (or let the Canadian dollar fall instead, creating another risk, the risk of inflation).

All of these constrain the freedom of the Bank of Canada, its monetary policy and its exchange rate policy and sooner or later it should act according to the roles of the globalised financial markets. Globalisation, or more particularly the mobility of capital, has made it harder for most governments to ensure the national currency so as to provide firms with stable money. Money, that is, which keeps its value in terms of goods and services within the national economy, and which keeps its value in terms of exchange rates with other currencies. (For example, in France, the price of shadowing the mark by keeping the franc within the limits set by the EU has caused high and rising unemployment).

- It is a fact that by the 1990s the governments of most rich countries were resorting to debt to supplement taxes as a means of financing their spending. From an international political economy perspective, it can be argued that they were tempted to do so by the readiness of financial markets, domestic and foreign, to accommodate them; and that they were obliged to do so by the immunity from tax confronted by globalisation on many large enterprises. If corporate taxes could not be raised for fear of losing national competitiveness as a host country, and personal taxes, direct and indirect, were felt to be already up against a political ceiling of electoral resistance, borrowing was an easier option for most states than cutting spending. (Even for states that were spending much less than the USA on defence, the costs of maintaining the kind of welfare system expected by the voters were rather rising than falling.)

The multinationals protest that they do not evade paying taxes, but their protests are often less than convincing. Not only are holding companies often located in the tax havens where tax demands are minimal, but when it comes to calculating tax liability to the various governments where their main productive operations take place, there is nothing as clear international tax regime. Negotiation between each corporate treasury and the two or more tax authorities concerned take place in private. The two hosts share an interest in exacting as much as possible, but at the same time are rivals, inhibited by rivalry from making demands so heavy that the company is frightened away.

The trade and industry policy are also confronted with dilemmas of the widening dichotomy that exist between the globalisation process and the national interest.

Notwithstanding the rules of the World Trade Organisation (WTO) countries cannot use tariff and non-tariff barriers against foreign imports to improve their current account without taking into consideration the fact that protectionist measures could also hurt their exports-oriented activities so as to become more competitive in the world market. On the other hand, the growing liberalisation of trade favours outside sourcing and, as a consequence, the subsequent import of components by national firms from their affiliates abroad. Exchange-rate intervention may also have counterproductive results. An undervaluation of the national currency does not guarantee an automatic improvement of the current account, at least in short term. Once again, the import content of the goods reduces the positive impact of a depreciation on exports. At the same time, a depreciated domestic currency may deter local firms from investing abroad and, as a result of missing an acquisition opportunity, or because they have failed to be a first mover, national firms can lose world market shares.[61]

In addition to these, with MNCs following global strategies and structure, any effort to assess a country's competitiveness on the basis of its current account is misleading. Following a global approach, MNCs are locating their activities according to the comparative advantages of potential host countries. These companies manufacture and market their products in a number of countries. As a consequence, imports of home countries consist, in part, of inputs produced abroad by the affiliates of the home country's MNCs. At the same time, an increasing share of the turnover of those MNCs is generated by its foreign affiliate selling in the markets of host countries, or expanding to third countries, including the home country. Finally, to evaluate the competitiveness of a nation's economy on the basis of the performance of its trade balance is becoming irrelevant. In today's world economy, the competitiveness of a country has to be measured by the world market share of the companies located in its territory. According to that approach, market shares include exports from a country and sales abroad of the foreign affiliate of MNCs based in the country.

If country X has a negative current-account balance in the automotive industry or in chemical, for instance, this does not mean that the competitiveness of that country in these industries is weak, because, at the same time, companies originating from country X and operating in those industries may have increased their world market shares and improved their cash flows. Under these circumstances, is it still relevant to refer to the national origin of a company? The promotion of FDI is a good case for pointing out the ambiguities of the question raised by Robert Reich: "who is us?"[62]

MNCs following a multinational strategy – as opposed to a global strategy – adopted to the restrictions imposed by host countries so long as access to local mar-

---

[61] *Ibid.*, p. 16
[62] *Ibid.*, p. 18

kets was guaranteed and protected from external competition. For MNCs adopting a multinational strategy, the international competitiveness of their foreign affiliates was of secondary importance as long as their output was sold in the protected local market. Any additional costs included by trade-related investment measures would be passed on the local consumers. With a global strategy, the logic is totally different: outward FDI, the delocation of manufacturing or services, mergers and acquisitions are all aimed at strengthening a firm's competitiveness in their world market. Therefore, local constraints, such as "red tape", complex regulation etc., are no longer acceptable to MNCs, because they increase transaction costs and, thus, affect their international competitiveness. A global firm is not ready to spend a lot of time negotiating with a host-country government; instead, it looks for another more convenient location. Today, countries are no longer in a position to screen and control potential investors, as was the case in the past decades; on the contrary, companies select countries on the basis of their local-specific comparative advantages. But those comparative advantages are not to be confused with those in the Ricardian paradigm. Comparative advantages are evaluated by MNCs according to their likely contribution to the strengthening of their own international competitiveness.

In a multi-dimensional world economy, not only are the *ex-ante* static comparative advantages of the old paradigm irrelevant, but also the comparative advantages that make a territory attractive are no longer the result of natural endowments. Increasingly, comparative advantages are created. Comparative advantages are built up first, by the activities of foreign affiliates and their linkages with local firms and, secondly, by the governmental measure aimed at improving a country's investment climate. To use Michel Porter's "diamond",[63] a country with a large diamond will be at the same time attractive to both foreign and national investments, notwithstanding the fact that foreign and local firms are not necessarily investing in that country for the same reasons. From the point of view of employment and value added, the best situation can be reached when the delocating operations of the home-based MNCs are compensated by new activities developed by foreign-base MNCs. As a result, the traditional foundation of industrial policy – to support national companies – is no longer relevant: what is good for General Motors in France is as good for the French economy as what is good for Renault.

Participation in an international economy presents states with a trade-off between efficiency and loss of autonomy, and in many instances governments have chosen to preserve the latter. Without judging the merit, in opting for import substitution policies such as, for example, forcing local production of automobiles, policy-makers were willing to trade off higher local costs for automobiles (reduced efficiency) for the promise of a more developed industrial capacity and increased future autonomy.

---

[63] *Ibid.*, p. 19

That option is not available in industries such as telecommunication, pharmaceuticals, semiconductors, and aerospace, where even the largest national markets are too small to support the R & D efforts needed to remain competitive. If transnational markets are an absolute requisite of continued technological innovation, governments face a discrete zero-one decision rather than a continuous, marginal trade-off. Accepting higher costs (e.g. lower efficiency) for some degree of autonomy is not a realistic possibility; mutual dependence is inevitable and breaking its bond implies a degree of withdrawal that few state could tolerate. The choice is to compete trans-nationally or forgo the next generation of microprocessors, pharmaceutical, or telecommunications technology entirely.[64]

At minimum, states must allow their firms to participate in global markets. While in theory governments could participate in the global economy while closing their borders to participants by others, that option is not viable in practice. At least in those strategic industries, independence or autonomy is a very limited option. In an electronically networked global economy the borders of national markets, thus the distinction between the domestic and international economy, or domestic and international policy, become even more problematic. Bits are transmitted electronically, typically by satellite rendering the borders of nation markets virtually meaningless. If software is imported in the form of disks and manuals, it is subject to border control, tariff, and the like. However, it is transmitted digitally – downloaded from the Internet, for example, any sort of control becomes problematic and autonomy is directly constrained.

State autonomy or independent decision-making power is clearly compromised by the fusion of markets and emergence of an electronically networked global economy. Indeed, in the strategic industries of concern here national markets have lost meaning as economic constructs. They are too small to support competitive technological development efforts and territorial borders are no longer clear lines of separation between the domestic and international economics.[65]

Managing labour relations has some new characteristics as well. Wherever political change over the past century has introduced some of democratic control over government, the result was that the state has intervened in the labour market to protect the interest of labour from the demands of management. First, unions were made legal. Then the right to strike was secured in law. And in some countries – post-war Germany is the obvious example – the law guaranteed the representation of employees in corporate policy-making processes. In others, neo-corporatist mechanisms gave unions equal representation with management in collective responsibility for national economic decisions. All that has changed – or is being changed – by globalisation. The political responsibility for maintaining good labour relations and avoiding industrial strife has largely shifted out of the hand of government into

---

[64] *Governments, Globalisation, and International Business.* Jonh H. Dunning, ed., p. 156
[65] *Ibid.*, p. 157

corporate boardrooms. It is the managers who now have the delicate diplomatic tasks of reconciling the essentially opposed interest of their high-wage workers at home with their low-wage workers in developing or ex-socialist countries. This is a classical illustration of the point that politics is no longer be seen as a domain exclusive to the politicians.[66]

More than half century ago, most economists were convinced that government has the power to correct the tendency of market economies to oscillate between boom and slum. By contravailing power, as J. K. Galbraith called it, and following Keynesian analysis and doctrine, demand in the economy could be checked when the economy became overheated, and stimulated when investment and consumption showed signs of flagging. Now, the governments, especially the U.S. government as the only remaining superpower, although they have still some means to counteract the slowdown or heating up of the economy, but in fact they have lost the power to manage the national economy. (For example, Mitterand tried it in the early 1980s but had to abandon the attempt in face of capital flight and the loss of confidence in franc in financial markets). *Globalisation and the integration of national economies in one world economy means that Keynesian counter-cyclical intervention has to be global and systematic, collectively agreed, co-ordinated, and financed.*[67] That is what has been tried to do by the G7 or 8 countries using the International Monetary Fund and World Banks as institutional means.

The success of their efforts is far from what would be needed for the efficient development of world economy. One of the main reasons of that is: they could not overcome the problems arising from the basic contradiction between the market as a global identity and the government as a body of a sovereign national state. To do this would require a global government – international governance – that could cope with special interests of the MNCs in such a way that their interests would be subordinated to and co-ordinated with the interest of the efficient, balanced, sustainable growth of the world economy. However, this leads our discussion to the topic of public choice theory.

IMPACT ON PUBLIC CHOICE THEORY

As we know, something of a cross between economics and political sciences, public choice theory applies the principles and methodology of economics to collective choice. Public choice theory maintains that politicians and bureaucrats are guided by essentially the same motives as consumers and business decisions-makers. There-

---

[66] *Ibid.*, p. 140
[67] *Ibid.*, p. 137

fore, unless we set up rules that bring the self-interest of the political players into harmony with the wise use of resources, the process will go awry. Waste and stagnation will result. This theory has proved: there are two basic methods of making economic decisions:

- the market mechanism and
- the public-sector (collective-government) decision-making.

> Of course, it is a rather simplified categorisation because on the one hand in the market there is the firm as economic unit inside which there are economic decisions elaborated mainly in a hierarchic way and on the other hand, in the public sector, in addition to the government, there are non-government organisations (NGOs) which have public functions and special decision-making systems as well. The two kinds of decision-making systems in some cases can overlap each other, too. However, our selected subject allows us to make this simplification.

These decisions give the answers to the fundamental questions of the economics: what will be produced? How will it be produced? For whom will goods be produced?

Market decision-making: methods of organisation that allow unregulated prices and decentralised decisions of private property owners to resolve the basic economic problems of consumption, production and distribution. (Who, how, to whom is to produce?)

Collective decision-making: method of organisation that relies on public sector decision-making (voting, political bargaining, parliament, government, lobbies, bureaucracy). It can also be used to resolve the basic problems of an economy, that is the problems of production and income distribution, for example, using state ownership or providing social service.

In every economy including that of capitalist and socialist countries a large number of decisions are made both through the decentralised pricing system and through public-sector decision-making. Many economic activities are undertaken by private firms, others are undertaken by the government. In addition, the government alters the behaviour of the private sector through a variety of regulations, taxes, subsidies. That is why we call the capitalist economy a mixed-economy. For example, in the developed western market economy 30–60 percent of the GDP is distributed by the government, mainly through the budget of government; government employs at least 10–15 percent of the workforce; government provides social security, unemployment benefit, pension system, health care, housing, education service; government regulates the market (export-import activities, prices, banking and many other fields). Even in the former socialist, communist countries (or in China, Vietnam, Cuba today), which have a fundamental ideological commitment to resolving the economic problems, the production and allocation issues by government planning rather than by market and prices there has been experimentation and practice with combination of government allocation and market allocation; in this combination, even where the economy is very centralised there is price and wage, or there was and there is so called "underground or grey, or second economy" where market transactions were or are taking place.

It is very important to know: both the market and public, government sectors have an *important role* in the economy and at the same time there are *market* short-comings or *failures, as well as public* shortcomings or *failures,* too.

Market Failures

Market is the most powerful force for promoting efficiency; to produce cheaper, with less cost to meet the demand of consumer, to innovate, to improve the quality. Those who cannot do these fail and lose everything. Efficiency is a basic precondi-tion of a prosperous economy and of a prosperous society, because through this the society achieves the maximum production possibility and consumer satisfaction, the society and the economy operates on the frontier of its maximal production and utility possibility schedule, that is, Pareto-optimum has been reached: no one can be made better of without making someone worse off.

However, the market can fulfil this role if it works, operates freely, without re-striction under the condition of perfect competition: there is free entry into market; producer and consumer are so-called price takers and not price makers, everybody has perfect information about the quality of the commodities and their real interest, for example. In the real world, however, perfect competition may be looked on as a limited case and the market cannot solve the problem of making economic stability and the problem of income distribution either.

The market failures are present where *monopoly* exists. Those producers and con-sumers who are in a monopolistic position are not forced to produce at the lowest cost and the best quantity or to pay the price that covers the cost. Market fails if there are *externalities* and the case of the *public goods.*

Information problem can create market failure as well, especially to uninformed consumers. (For example, sick people who do not have proper information about drugs, medicines, can be cheated easily and it could be fatal on them.) There can be *incomplete markets.* Markets are incomplete whenever they fail to provide a good service even though the cost would be less than what individuals are willing to pay.

There is the problem of macroeconomic stability. The market also fails to meet effi-ciency standards if the aggregate economy is characterised by instability and uncer-tainty: when there are high inflation and unemployment, economic depression, cri-ses, unbalanced budget or foreign trade, very low growth rate. Perhaps the most widely recognised symptoms of market failures are the periodic episodes of high unemployment and recessions, depressions.

Market is also blind to the equitable distribution of income. The free market does not do a satisfactory job of distribution income. The virtue, merit of the free, perfectly competitive market have to do with its efficiency, not with its equity. Competitive market may give rise to very unequal distribution of income, which may provide some individuals with insufficient resources on which to live. It may include luxury for rich and few necessities for poor. Moreover, in many cases the poor – in particular the disabled, sick, unemployed – may become destitute through no fault of their own. They can sell nothing in the market, therefore they cannot earn any income to live on; in spite of the fact that they have to live, have to get food, shelter, home, medical care, education, etc.

Actions of Reducing Market Failures

To correct these market shortcomings or failures it is necessary that, besides the market decision-making mechanism, another decision-making mechanism should operate as well: this mechanism cannot be other than the collective, public sector: government decision-making mechanism.

> Here, again, we do not deal with decision-making carried out inside the firm which is mostly hierarchic and by internalising some market transactions eliminates the market failures and we do not deal with NGOs either which can also correct or eliminate government failures.

When market failures are present, there is no optimal efficiency, the society, and the economy are working inside their production possibility curve, schedule and utility possibility schedule as well. The government corrective actions can increase the efficiency, the size of the economic pie, so government can generate benefits for the players – consumers and producers – of the market. *This is the merit of government*. Government

- regulating monopoly reduces inefficiency;
- regulating firms which create air pollution decreases the negative externalities;
- providing education service creates positive externalities;
- providing different public goods meets the basic need of the society;
- implementing fiscal and monetary policy exerts a powerful influence on economic stability;
- redistributing income from rich to poor makes a more just income distribution and providing health care, unemployment benefit and other social services corrects the market failures relating to the income distribution.

These positive effects create the rationale for government actions, for public decision-making. Through these the government makes economy more efficient and makes the income distribution more just for the society; by doing these it strengthens the social peace as well. Therefore *the government – public decision-making – has the following important roles to play in the economy:*

- regulation;
- allocation of resources;
- distributing of income;
- stabilising of macroeconomy.

However, *public-decision-making is merely, only an alternative form of economic organisation, not an automatic corrective device, governments cannot work perfectly either, there are government failures, as well as market failures.*

Government Failures

What is a government failure? It is present when the political process (government decision) leads to economic inefficiency and waste of scarce resources. When the economy operates inside its production possibility and utility possibility frontiers, curves follow due to government actions. The factors that may cause government failures can be summarised in the following way.

1. Government income distribution can weaken the incentive for hard work and for improving efficiency

Excess burden of taxation (for example, tax financing social welfare) decreases incentive to work, to employ workers, to extent production.

When the poor getting job earn more, there is reduction in subsidies, social aid, benefits they receive, which reduces their incentive to work.

2. Failures of political systems

In the totalitarian political systems there are insufficient regulations (the weakening or direct absence of feedback in these systems causes the systems to be unable to adequately identify changes in external conditions and budding internal problems; for this reason they react to them inadequately and belatedly, if at all; which is related to the absence of feedback in the political system), *and suppression of creative potential* is institutionalized (people are not able to sufficiently exercise their disposition and skills, which undermine the overall functioning and effectiveness of these systems, and results in a frustrated population.)

In direct democracy there is problem with referendums (the very form of the question can influence of the vote – for example, if the question is posed in the negative, as a result, or in positive, as an acceptance of the issue –; it is difficult to formulate a question which is clear, yet includes all the important issues pertaining to the decisions; the implementation of a decision arrived at through a referendum can significantly differ from the true wishes of the majority of voters); and *unspecified majority defeats a clearly defined minority* (when a small group takes a principled and specific stance on a certain issue, yet the majority of citizens take the opposite stance, although it may be half-hearted and not representative of their specific interests, the choice of the majority prevails).

In representative democracy there is the so called *paradox of voting* (those who set the conditions under which election are to be held, have an opportunity to influence the results of the election and the success of individual candidates; those who would not have had a chance to make their opinions heard are able to continually suggest new agendas to be decided upon; this causes an election cycle, which leads to the defeat of political coalitions that find themselves in a state of imbalance); and there are *preference intensity and bundling* (several political issues exist, which influence the decisions of voters and during an election, a candidate can win even if he did not gain the majority on a single issue, as long as he succeeded in satisfying individual groups of voters in those issues that concern them most); there is *estrangement of elected* representatives from their electorate (the principle-agent theory describes the relationship between the principle, or supreme holder of power – in this case the vote – and the agent, or the actor who is delegated to authority to wield this power – in this case the elected representative –; the theory points out that elected representatives may display opportunistic behaviour, or behaviour that does not necessarily reflect – and can sometimes be in direct opposition to – the wishes of the electorate; the electorate cannot easily control the behaviour of the representative; this needs time and money and can never be completely successful).

The influence of organised interests (lobbying), so called rent-seeking behaviour. That is the political action of individuals and groups seeking personal advantage at the expense of others. This also wastes social resources. For example: for politicians the best way to get elected or re-elected is to gain the backing of special interest groups (farmers, industrialists, trade unions), because support of special interest lobbies will generate vocal supporters, campaign workers and company contributions, money. In the age of media politics there is strong pressure on politicians to support special interest, who pay campaign fund using to project a positive image on TV. After the election the politicians have to pay "the bill" as well. The election campaign costs a lot of money. The resources used for lobbying and other means of rent-seeking will not be available to increase the efficiency, the national production, "the size of the economic pie".

3. The influence of mass media

The format and content of repeated information have an influence on the public's perception of public affairs. This does not have to involve purposeful manipulation; the choice of genres, agendas, and events, as well as targeting certain types of viewers, listeners or readers is sufficient. This is one of the reasons for stating that the political system, generally does not allow public policy to learn against responsible consideration of social costs and benefits.

4. In the public, government sector there is little incentive for operational efficiency

There is no force analogous to the threat of bankruptcy in the private sector that will bring inefficient behaviour to halt. Government offices, agencies are less likely to go bankrupt. There is no profit motivation to improve efficiency. Since public sector resources are communally owned their users are less likely to be conscious than private resource owners. As public officers spend other peoples' money, they are less likely to be conscious of cost than they would be with their own resources.

5. In the government decision-making there is a so called short-sightedness effect

In government, where decision-makers do not hold private property rights to the resources they control, both politicians and voters tend to support projects, decisions that promise substantial current benefits at the expense of difficulty to identify future cost. Politicians and very often voters, too, put off tough, long term decisions. For example, high taxes would bring political pain, but most of the benefits would lie in the future, or borrowing to finance short term programs that benefit the voting population is attractive even though the long-run results will be higher future taxes and real interest rate, or the housing rent control later results deterioration in the quality of house stocks.

6. Collective decision-making places authority power in the hand of some to exercise over other

Such redistribution of power provides opportunities for inequity and abuse corrupt practices. (For example: bribery to obtain contracts with foreign government for weapon sales abroad or to get import licenses.)

7. Public-sector action is "crisis-oriented"

There are two reasons for that:
- the crisis tends to loosen up budgetary purse strings, budget discipline; special interest groups, politicians and agencies use a crisis to justify larger budget request, for example, increase of crime rate can justify the increase of police budget;
- other crises, however, occur simply because an important action was postponed. (For example, the reform of the ex-socialist countries, or to postpone needed maintenance of city housing may be very costly, but most of the cost lies in the future.) By the time the problem reaches crisis proportions, other politicians will be likely to have to deal with it.

The Public Choice Theory also indicates that the political actions and other measures can reduce economic inefficiency due to government failures, as proper government actions can reduce loss caused by market failure.

Actions of Reducing Government Failures

Usually the following actions are taken to reduce government failures.

1. Improving the constitutional rules

What does it mean? It means:
- introducing or strengthening the democratic decision-making process;
  a) democracy can prevent that special interest groups achieve permanent monopoly and
  b) it also can prevent concealing mistakes of government over a long period of time, because the voters in the regular elections vote out this government and its interest groups from their power position; after a relatively short time the mistakes of democratic government become known for the public and usually after the election corrections can take place; in over-centralised and non-pluralistic market decision-making systems, where the political power is extremely concentrated there is no such a remedy; in its absence a system – as Eastern-European Countries have shown it – may become prone to stagnation, or to explosive social change, on the other hand, because of their structure inhibit, they cannot make possible proper experimentation and gradual reforms;
- *constitution and parliament can bar the government to spend too much money* having no proper resources produced by the economy;
- *decentralisation in government* can permit states and localities to adopt different and flexible governmental environment; for example, in Hungary, local governments have got more freedom to collect taxes and spend their revenues, but at the same time they have to take on more responsibilities as well, they can become rich, or they become poor, they can go bankrupt as well;
- *improve "the role of the game" for the players of the market;* providing proper regulation of property ownership and the contacts in economic transactions are of crucial importance; without the ability to protect property individuals would have little incentive to accumulate assets, without laws defending property rights, only the exercise of force would stop one individual from stealing from other (it would create good ground for Mafia activities), the legal system should enforce contracts between individuals, too.

2. Deregulation

As we have already mentioned, on one of the major territories of public decision-making, government is the regulatory activity. The regulatory process is one of the most powerful ways in which government can influence activities in the private sector of the economy. As an alternative to taxing and spending to achieve national objectives, governments have come to rely increasingly on mechanisms that operate through directly controlling the actions of institutions and people in the private sector of the society.

There are two types of government regulation:

- traditional *economic regulation* (for example, price, banking tariffs regulation) and
- *social regulation* (for example, providing cleaner, healthier environment, it is designed to improve health and safety and environment conditions).

We have to note that in the recent years while the economic regulation has been relaxed, the social regulatory activity has been expanding rapidly. This is due to the importance of protecting the quality of life. It is getting more and more valuable, therefore it is given more and more protection, although it is getting more and more costly, as well.

We also have to refer to

- the demand for regulation often stems from special interest and redistribution of income consideration (tariff to protect home production for example) rather from the pursuit of economic efficiency;
- regulation often fails to adjust to changing market condition and with the passage of time.

Therefore steps towards deregulation that relax entry barriers and price fixing policy, as well as allow new entrance and intensify competition can substantially increase the efficiency of some industry.

3. Privatisation

In some cases when private firms are compared to government activities providing the same goods or services, the private firms have been shown to provide them more economically; when the original reason for establishing a public owned enterprises may disappear (for example, an unprofitable firm that has been taken over by government in order to preserve jobs may become profitable again, or a new technology developed by a state-owned firm may become ready for commercial application, as in case of nuclear energy plants).

In such cases the privatisation – transfer of the public property to private use – can increase the efficiency because the private owner of the assets can make better use of it than the public owner.

4. The reform of the income redistribution of the government

The failure of government's income redistribution should be corrected and it has to be taken into consideration, too that social expenditure could not rise forever at a faster rate than GDP. A check is to be administered. The various objectives of public expenditure should be critically scrutinised, their respective merits assessed and the different means of attaining them investigated – with cost clearly seen, in every case, not as a mere book-keeping entry, but as the sacrifice of some other benefits, whether public or private, that must then be foregone. Scrutinizing public expenditure is nothing new. It goes on all the time. But recession gives it a new edge and, by virtue of its severity, makes it feasible to assess with more objectivity some items of expenditure that were formerly regarded as sacred cows. From the point of view of public welfare, this can be a gain.

The Proper Balance Between Market and Government

Public choice theory also teaches us that markets only become truly efficient when they are embedded into systems developed by the state and private co-operation that then play the role of government. In addition to this, history has proved as well that state-dominated development has failed, but so will stateless development; development without an effective state is impossible. As it was used to be said: "The market resembles fire: it is a good servant, but a cruel master" – it cannot work in a vacuum, it should properly be controlled by government. In this respect it is not so much a question of whether or not government should intervene in the markets, but rather what kind of intervention would be needed and for what purpose. The philosophy of Public Choice Theory is that decisions on what is to be produced and how it is produced is best left mostly to the collective will of thousands of firms and millions of consumers.

At the same time, this philosophy also presumes that underpinning an educated labour force, an adequate transportation and telecommunications network, a strong anti-monopoly policy, a sound macroeconomic policy and a wealth-creating culture, the market cannot do the job as expected of it. Besides its various social and strategic responsibilities, it is the government's task to cultivate and support – though not necessarily undertake – all of these market-enabling actions. If markets gain overbalance influence against the government, the market failure will increase and the power of government for correcting market failure weakens, and if the government gains overbalance influence against the markets, government failures will increase and the power of markets for correcting government failures weakens. However, it is very hard to find the proper balance between market and government.

The Impact of Globalisation and Multinational Corporations on Government and Market Failures

Globalisation and the MNCs have a major and substantial impact on both the market and government failures and also on the way and direction of government policies and measures aimed to correct and/or eliminate market and government failures.

204

THE MARKET IS GAINING INFLUENCE AGAINST THE GOVERNMENT

One of the most noticeable developments is that *the market has been gaining influence over/against the government mainly stemming from the fact that the MNCs have became the major and the most influential actors of the globalised market*. It can be witnessed during the last three decades.

If we investigate the reasons of the post-Second World War stability in the world we can find that it was not based on the extension of unfettered markets; it was made possible by institutional reforms that constrained the ill effects of markets on society. On the one hand, final and intermediate product markets were organised according to oligopolic competition, cartel formation at the national and international levels as well as in accordance with sophisticated public regulations. Consequently, price wars were replaced by gentlemen's agreements between large firms, which adopted mark-up price formation and cosmetic product differentiation.

On the other hand, two fictious commodities were protected from competition coming from market pressures. First, money and credit had a too important role in macroeconomic equilibrium to be left to the influence of myopic expectations and the free banking principle. The Keynesian revolution taught us that a stable monetary regime was a public good to be provided by central banks and financial institutions. Second, wage formation was too serious an issue to be left to the vagaries of pure market forces. Implicit in the post-Second World War order was a genuine capital-labour compromise that codified the respective benefits drawn from the implementation of the Fordism, efficient mass production.

Managers were free to organise production and labour processes, whereas workers benefited from an implicit (or explicit) indexation of nominal wages with respect to consumer prices along with productivity sharing schemes.[68] In addition to these, a rather well developed public welfare system has been implemented contributing to a great extent for the social peace by providing a high degree of equity in the income distribution.

This entire set of co-ordinating mechanisms has severely been challenged during the last tree decades. In sum, virtually all the organisational forms, which formed the basis of the unprecedented growth of the 1950s, 1960s and 1970s, involved by this have been challenged (see Table 17).[69]

Price competition has become a convential method for solving competitive struggles between large multinational firms, as well as between small and medium-sized companies. Due to recurring excess capacities, most businesses have tried to sell abroad all the production that could not be absorbed by the home market due to austerity policies in public spending and wage moderation. Given the huge fixed

---

[68] *States against Markets*. S. Robert Boyer and Daniel Drache, ed., p. 83
[69] *Ibid*., p. 88

costs associated with most process and hi-tech industries, some sectors (e.g. electronic components, air transportation, telecommunications) have experienced the equivalent of the price wars of the 1930s. At a more theoretical level, modern analyses of contested markets tend to suggest that pure competition should and will prevail as soon as free entry is possible without experiencing too high sunk costs. The ideal of pure and perfect competition has replaced that of a gentle and organised system.

The labour flexibility debate has put a strong emphasis upon the need for more competition in the labour market, especially concerning wage formation. Unions, managers and policy-makers have been urged to design much more flexible pay systems and labour contracts with variable hours or easy termination. According to this interpretation, if labour markets are not self-equilibrating – and this was clearly the case in the mid-1980s since unemployment had been rising permanently in highly ununionised European countries – then complex public regulations and high unemployment benefits were clearly responsible for what was perceived as the inefficient state. Were the labour market is truly competitive, this line of reasoning goes, full employment would be obtained at each moment in time. Even if these diagnoses have been challenged, they have been very influential in the design of deregulation policies, not only within conservatives strategies, but for some social democratic government as well. The ideal of many firms is now to grant only short-run labour contracts, with flexible wages and easily varied hours worked, in order to make labour markets function as conventional commodity markets do.[70]

Numerous financial innovations have similarly transferred national and international regimes. The banking system inherited from the New Deal and post-Second World War legislation used to apply highly administered interest rates and credit rationing in such a manner that the money market was a more convenient metaphor for presenting the IS-LM model, elaborated by John Hicks to interpret *The General Theory*, than an actual market co-ordinating money supply and demand. The major imbalances generated by the surge of inflation during the 1960s and early 1970s, the financial shocks associated with the rise of oil prices and the emerging competition between banks to capture deposits and grant credits, have promoted the invention of genuine and sophisticated financial instruments. Consequently, the competition over money and financial markets has become more effective and structured than the strategies of the firms and even the households searching for the best returns for their liquidates. Central Bankers have been losing a large part of their control over credit which manifests itself via the rapid obsolescence of most of the monetary aggregates designed to monitor monetary supply. Again, competition on the financial market is back and recalls some of the episodes of the interwar periods, even if most of the New Deal regulations have not been removed. (This

---

[70] *Ibid.*, p. 70

Table 17. The pervasiveness of market forces in most of the basic Fordist institutional forms during the 1980s

Institutional forms	Interwar period	The Golden Age 1945–1967	Uncertain restructuring of the 1970s and 1984s
1 *Wage labour nexus*			
– Industrial relations	– Low institutionalisation, weak unions' bargaining power	– Rather large institutionalised unions and collective bargaining	– Decentralisation of bargaining, decline of most unions
– Wage formation	– Highly decentralised and rather competitive	– More administered than market determined	– More competitive pressures and market-driven wages
– Welfare payment	– Embryonic	– A significant part of indirect wage is institutionalised	– Rationalisation or scaling down; some trends towards private insurance
2 *Competition among firms*			
– On product market	– Strong, price wars during the Great Depression	– Rather weak, competition by the perceived quality	– Fiercer due to international competition and technical change
– On financial market	– Large concentration, but prices are still rather competitive	– Large concentration at the national level, prices are oligopolistic	– Large restructuring at the world level, price wars are back again
3 *Monetary regime*			
– Credit versus securities	– Incomplete pure credit system, major role of stock market and speculation	– Institutionalisation of pure credit systems, little speculation	– Globalisation of finance speculation
– Financial regulations	– Emerging but very partial	– Highly regulated and protected banks	– Significant financial deregulations
4 *State interventions*			
– Public services	– Except for defence, quite limited	– Developed for health, education, transportation	– Austerity and rationalisation policies
– State-owned firms	– Very few, except after the crisis of 1929	– Rather significant in some European countries	– Important privatisation in some countries
– Welfare	– Emerging but generally not institutionalised	– Institutionalised to varying degrees across countries	– Some reorganisation and slimming down, more insurance, less welfare
5 *International regime*			
– Trade	– Rather open and then protectionism and currency wars	– Progressive liberalisation of trade	– In spite of projectionist temptations, ongoing internationalisation
– Finance	– Highly active financial flows	– Rather limited *private* financial flows	– Explosion of short-run private capital flows, financial globalisation
– Capital	– Limited extent of foreign direct investment	– Significant, mainly American, direct investment	– Important surge of foreign investment

Source: Synthetic table derived from a series of historical studies in terms of 'regulation'.

explains, for example, why the December 1997 Wall Street crash did not trigger any commutative depression.) Nevertheless, the ideal of financial authorities is still to debalkanise the previously fragmented credit institutions and organise a global market implementing more competition if not a pure and perfect one.

Governments have pursued significant deregulation policies just to curb or interrupt the apparent adverse trends associated with larger and larger income transfers by the state. A major conservative counter-revolution has taken place during the last three decades. Whereas the post-Second World War state was allowed to be interventionist in order to promote the emergence of Fordist industrialisation, to enhance the implementation of welfare systems and to control the level of economic activity by fine tuning, rising difficulties have resulted in a drastic shift towards more *laissez-faire* strategies.

According to this approach, nationalised firms in the productive sector should be privatised (and actually have been, for example, in the United Kingdom and in France), under the view that, by nature, private managers are more competent than bureaucrat. The public welfare system has been seen by a vocal fraction of businessmen as an incentive to laziness, inefficiency and low saving rates. From a conceptual point of view, the principle of solidarity has been challenged and replaced by the objective private insurance. Let free individuals choose the type of income security they can afford. In addition to these, the argument goes that the state should remove most of the regulations which prevent firms, workers and bankers from concluding mutually beneficial arrangements.

Finally, according to the neo-Austrian school and the rational expectation theorists, individual economic agents are assumed to be better informed than distant and probably not-so-competent bureaucrats. Any attempt to influence the level of macroeconomic activity will be circumvented by clever agents who know that in the future the government will have to raise taxes in order to pay for present public deficit spending or that any excess in money supply results in inflation, without any long-term impact upon unemployment. As far as ideology and theory are concerned, Keynes is dead and Doctor Pangloss has been revived! Let the market guide and co-ordinate the difficult choices that nobody is able to outline, let alone explain![71]

The current international regime is a strange mix of a decaying Bretton Woods system with more and more market adjustments upon currency markets. Following the interwar distrust of the ability of markets to make compatible contradictory national monetary and economic policies, the Bretton Woods agreement implemented a largely institutional process of adjustments, with a limited scope for market logic. The exchange rates were fixed and set by national authorities in accordance with principle shared by the international community. The progressive demise

---

[71] *Ibid.*, p. 91

of this international regime has brought back competitive mechanisms in the interest rate and exchange rate formation. Consequently, the floating rates which were supposed to deliver smooth adjustments and high predictability have generated totally opposite outcome; large swings in the relative position of the dollar, the yen and the Deutschmark have repeatedly surprised even the most sophisticated analysts. Since speculation is now the leading motive for buying or selling a currency, financial markets have lost their previous built-in stability. Nevertheless, in the absence of alternative and more coherent international financial regime, the market mechanism is still assumed to be the only co-ordinating device available to make various and contrasted national policies more or less congruent.

Surprisingly, the poor macroeconomic and financial outcomes observed since 1971 have not seriously affected the optimism of most advocates of pure market mechanism. Clearly, the invisible hand of Adam Smith is affecting all the institutional forms generating during the post Second World War period.[72]

As a consequence of the increasing market power and the decreasing government power, some of the market and government failures have become more visible and in their negative impacts greater. It can especially be seen from the markets side in the cases of growing oligopolistic power of the MNCs, increasing income inequality resulting in less equity in the income distribution, the hardening control of the activities of MNCs causing negative externalities, more frequent problems of unbalances of national and international economies, and from the government side, especially in the cases of the extending and more and more efficient rent-seeking activities of the MNCs, their growing lobby power and the growing estrangement of the elected representative, including the parliament and government as key institutions of democracy. Among them the last two, the lobbying and the estrangement deserve special attention, especially because others have already been discussed or will be discussed to a certain extent.

THE GROWING LOBBY POWER OF MULTINATIONAL CORPORATIONS

The MNCs have a very influential lobby power, there is no question about that, due to the huge wealth they own and control. As R. Vernon wrote: "General Motors's $25 billion in annual sales is, it noted with concern, larger than the gross national product of about 130 countries. Size, it is presumed, means power. And power lies somewhere near the heart of the problem."[73]

From that time on when Vernon put down these lines, the sizes of the MNCs have become even bigger. In many important fields they have technological mo-

---

[72] *Ibid.*, p. 99
[73] Raymond Vernon, *Sovereignty at Bay*, p. 7

nopoly (including weapon technology) due to the fact that modern technology requires huge expenditure that only a large and wealthy company can envisage. They control the world-wide financial markets. They have monopolistic access to many key elements of the planet's natural resources. In the field of media and communication monopolies – which cannot only lead to uniformity of culture but can also open up new means of political manipulation – their position is the strongest. And as we know: *wealth can easily translate into power, and power into privilege*. Those who have power are recognisable, because they are able to affect the range of options within which others can choose what to do. It might seem that others choose freely, but the risks and penalties of going outside that range of options are so punitive that they are not seriously considered. Power and privilege can gain position in politics as well.

Politics may be defined as the activities by which an individual or a group of individuals seeks to win the support of other wills for some objective that they wish to achieve. In case of MNCs it can be to get lower trade barriers, less regulation of capital movement, to effect the take-over of another enterprise, replacing a management with another one. The means may be persuasion or by coercion, or by an astute combination of the two. It is not essentially different from the activities in which politicians engage when they build coalitions or marshal votes behind a bill.[74]

MNCs are moving from one country to another looking to compete on labour costs, they seek national jurisdictions where employment standards are lowest. For example, under NAFTA, corporations have greater latitude to invest, divest, and locate in new production side in Mexico, Canada or the USA. Thus, the modern multinational corporation is in a good position to benefit from the Agreement's inability to define common social standards. Moreover, transnational corporate and business interests now successfully lobby for sectoral agreements in Brussels and are able to win new trade concessions directly from Washington. The other example is, that the highly technical and seemingly complex nature of international financial issues together with the huge capital power provides the MNCs with a high degree of autonomy to influence the financial and monetary policy. This has created a proliferation of private interest governance mechanism at the international level. MNCs alone have the resources to be global players.

It seems that there is a shift in bargaining power toward the MNCs from the national governments. As Figure 16 implies that the relative bargaining power of the MNCs and the host countries are a function of three related elements:

a) the relative demand by each of the participants for resources which the other control;

b) the constrains on each which affect the translation of potential bargaining power into over outcome;

c) the negotiating status of the participants.

---

[74] *Governments, Globalisation, and International Business.* Jonh H. Dunning, ed., p. 136

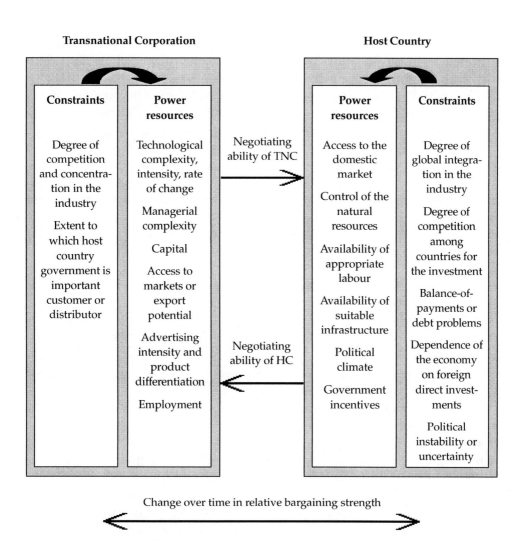

FIGURE 16. Components of the bargaining relationship between TNCs and host countries
(Source: based on material in Kobrin, 1987)

Figure 16 intends to suggest that host countries are subject to greater variety of constraints than are MNCs, a reflection of the latter's greater potential flexibility. Nevertheless, the extent to which MNCs can implement a globally integrated strategy is constrained by national state behaviour. Where a company particularly needs access to a given location and where the host country does have leverage, then the bargain, which is eventually stuck, may involve the MNCs in making concessions.

It is in this kind of context that the host country's ability to impose performance requirements on foreign firms is greater. At the extreme, of course, both institutions – MNCs and governments – possess sanctions that one may exercise over the other. The MNCs ultimate sancion is not to invest in a particular location or to pull out of an existing investment. A national state's ultimate sanction against the MNCs is to exclude a particular foreign investment or to appropriate an existing investment.

In much of the manufacturing industries – particularly in those sectors in which technological change is frequent and where global integration of operations is common – the bargain will become obsolete slowly, if at all, and the relative power of MNCs may even increase over time. In so far as such industries are becoming increasingly important in the world economy, the associated shift in bargaining power towards the MNCs will pose a major problem for host countries.[75]

THE GROWING ESTRANGEMENT OF THE ELECTED REPRESENTATIVE

Due to the globalisation *a special form of estrangement of elected representatives from their electorate* has developed, it can be called *"democracy illusion"*. As we know: democracy is based upon the sovereign national state whose parliament and government are democratically elected by the voters and this state being at minimum responsible to the voters for any number of critical functions: for the welfare of their citizens, for basic social and physical infrastructure, and for ensuring economic viability.

It used to be taken for granted that nations should be considered as communities of people that share responsibility for mutual well-being. Yet, this is becoming less and less so. What defines the so-called post-national nation state are two characteristics: first, weak national economy since the country's well-being is externally determined by its export and trade bloc performance; second, a substantial reduction in the ability of the state to engage in day-to-day internal economic management.[76]

Due to globalisation, countries have less democratic control over the formation of their economic policies. Decisions that used to be determined by democratically elected legislature will now be forced by non-elected commissions set up under the terms of some kinds of free-trade agreements. As well, the power of central banks to operate independently of elected popular bodies effectively places the control of money, credit and interest rates outside of democratic accountability. The mobility of financial capital limits viable difference among national interest rates and thus severely restricts the ability of central banks and governments to pursue monetary

---

[75] *The Rules of the Game in the Global Economy Policy Regimes for International Business.* Lee E. Preston and Duane Windsor, ed. (Kluwer Academic Publishers, Boston, 1991) pp. 411–412

[76] *States against Markets.* S. Robert Boyer and Daniel Drache, ed., p. 51

and fiscal policies appropriate to their internal economies. This loss of macroeconomic policy autonomy has been particularly worrisome to many during a period of high unemployment when they would have preferred governments to have pursued more expansionary policies than international financial markets sometimes permitted.

In addition to concerns about macroeconomic autonomy, there are concerns about the autonomy of the fiscal policy: the new liberal international financial environment has imposed new constraints on certain government's tax and regulatory policy by increasing the opportunities for powerful market actors to "exit" the domestic financial system when they disapproved of such policies. In broader political terms, there have also been concerns that states are being forced to become increasingly "internationalised", responding to the judgement of those who move internationally mobile funds rather than to the opinions of their domestic citizenry.[77]

Nation-states have lost more and more of their internal sovereignty over economies. For example, most European countries have long effectively lost sovereignty over their monetary policies as they have for almost two decades now following the lead of the Deutsche Bundesbank. Moreover, the Bundesbank has become the *de facto* European central bank, not just because of the size of German government and as its insulation from political pressure made it uniquely capable of behaving in conformity with the pressures of internationalised capital markets. It is on the model that the European Central Bank (ECB) or the "Eurofed" will be built. And also, in agreeing to monetary union, European states will formally give up something that they effectively no longer have. This holds also for Germany which, among other things precisely because of the special status of its central bank, has been aptly characterised by some authors as a "semi-severing state".

Moreover, under monetary union European monetary policy will be handed over to an institution that is carefully crafted, in the image of the Bundesbank, not to require or encourage the growth of a state at a supranational level. Indeed, the ECB will operate like an independent regulatory agency, reflecting and responding to objective market forces rather than a political will to "correct" or, for that matter, "distort" market; protecting common currency from being put at the service of political purposes like full employment; and accommodating, not to political pressure, but to an international capital market that has long outgrown national borders and national control.[78]

National political systems embedded in a competitive international market and exposed to supernationally ungoverned external effects of competing systems are tempted to protect their formal sovereignty by developing responsibility for the economy to the market – using what has remained of their public power of inter-

[77] *Ibid.*, p. 195
[78] *Ibid.*, p. 307

vention to limit, as it were constitutionally, the claims politics can make on the economy, and citizens on the polity. In many countries today, disengagement of politics from the economy is defended with reference to constraints of economic internalisation that would frustrate any other economic strategy. If citizens can be persuaded that economic outcomes are, and better be, the result of market forces, and the national governments are, therefore, no longer to be held responsible for the economy, national sovereignty and political legitimacy can be maintained even in conditions of tight economic interdependence: with the nation-state having off-loaded its responsibility for its economy to the world market, its own insufficiency and obsolescence in relation to the latter ceases to be visible.

Deploying internal sovereignty to liberate and accommodate market forces instead of trying to domesticate them – so as to end once and for all the use of public power for market-correcting purposes – may have become the only national political programme that can still be imposed on internationalised national economies without jeopardising the integrity of the national state.[79]

Although the market has grown far beyond the scope of democratically organised political and cultural identities, an electorate still regard national democratic politics as their principle source of protection, not least from economic dislocations caused by market forces, and perceive supranational governance as an undemocratic imposition of external control. As nation-states factually lose and formally relinquish control over their economies, electorates become liable to fall victim to a "democracy illusion": comparable to Keynes's "money illusion": that by exercising their political rights of citizenship they can purchase their political fate. As the gap between formal and effective sovereignty widens and the purchasing power of national citizenship deteriorates, and unless voters can be persuaded that markets must always be given free rein come what may, popular beliefs in the lasting efficacy of national democracy are bound to give rise to distorted expressions of collective preferences, perverse political alliances and self-defeating definitions of interest, opening up extensive opportunities for political opportunism and populist demagoguery.

In democracy under fragmented sovereignty, both voters and politicians are inevitably torn between refusing to recognise the externalities that increasingly govern national polities and blaming everything on them – at one time calling for national solutions where these are no longer possible, and at another, demanding, for example, "European solutions" while in the name of national sovereignty and diversity refusing integrated Europe the means to deliver them, defending national democracy against meddling by "bureaucrats in Brussels" in its internal affairs. An example of the twisted populist politics of independence under factual interdependence is offered by the first Danish referendum on the Maastricht Treaty, when the

---

[79] *Ibid.,* p. 308

electorate rejected European Monetary Union to defend the nation's economic-self-determination against what was perceived as a German-dominated supranational institution – in a country whose monetary policy had by the time of the referendum for more than a decade been directed by the Bundesbank in Frankfurt. By voting against Monetary Union, Danish voters thus effectively endorsed a situation in which their elected representatives had no influence at all on their country's monetary policy, and refused to endorse an arrangement under which at least one in twelve governors of the new Eurofed would have been from Denmark.[80]

More of this is likely to come in future years, and not just in Denmark. Nationally confined democracy is increasingly disfigured, not so much by nationalism or "xenophobia", but by the fact that, it is losing the tools to realise the popular will to which it is supposed to give expression, and in particular the capacity to give citizens a modicum of protection from economic uncertainties. As democracy is pre-empted, the space for popular participation becomes available for symbolic and ritual performances of all kinds. Politicians have strong incentives to pretend to their voters that they are in control, or in any case could and should be, and voters have incentives to believe them. As the British example shows, the rhetoric of domestic sovereignty tends to be fiercest where its object is most energetically abandoned to the forces of the market.

One day such a rhetoric may come home to roosts, and democratic politics, having cultivated illusions of political capacity and raised expectations of political protection, may be asked to deliver. The politicians may find themselves in urgent need of scapegoats on which to blame their impotence, a role for which, for example, in Europe the "bureaucrats in Brussels" seem to be the privileged candidates. Political regression has many faces; in coming years national democracy under international interdependence is likely to offer ample opportunity to explore them.[81]

IMPACT ON POLICY IMPLEMENTATION AIMED TO CORRECT GOVERNMENT FAILURES

The globalisation and the MNCs have a determining impact on the government policies aimed to correct government failure. It can especially be seen in the cases of social policy, deregulation, liberalisation and privatisation where in many instances while these policies intend to correct the government failures they go so far that the final results are increasing market failures, decreasing efficiency of the government policies in terms of growing income inequality and occurring waste of economic resources. Let us review these policies in this respect.

---

[80] *Ibid.*, p. 312
[81] *Ibid.*, p. 313

For decades, no political party on the right, nor the left dared to question the need for market-correcting social programmes to protect their citizens against unregulated markets. Today, that is no longer the case. Social democratic, liberal reform and centre governments all intend to cut benefits despite their electoral promises not to do so. Now even the strongest economies have succumbed to slow-growth monetarist practices. Governments want to cut their spending to the bone. Taxes on business have to be reduced in order to make the private sector more apt to invest in restructuring industries. Consumers are promised cheaper goods while the unemployed are guaranteed new jobs once a recovery begins. So far, the promises have remained just that – only promises. In a world where the roles of the global economy are being redefined the state policy in this respect has changed as well.[82]

The old policy commitment to full employment inspired by Keynes and Beveridge has been abandoned and a totally new concept of "high employment" is now the accepted norm of the political élite throughout advanced industrial economies. What the concept means, in effect, is that people will have to work longer and harder without the protection of social security nets, pension and retirement.

The push to dismantle existing social programmes comes from business which believes that it must change its cost structure to compete internationally. The public welfare system has been seen by a vocal fraction of businessmen an a incentive to laziness, inefficiency and low saving rates. The message of the manageress of Philips International labour relations in a seminar put the case with brutal frankness, arguing that Europeans "have lived above our means too long. High wage and no-wage costs ... drive European industries to relocate in areas such as eastern Europe and China where costs were around a tenth or lower." What business wants, she said, was "a very high amount of flexibility on jobs, employer contributions, social security premiums and the like." The bottom line is that business can no longer afford to pay its current share of social programmes.[83] Universal social programmes are increasingly stigmatised as being outdated and obsolete in the fast-changing world of the 1990s. From a conceptual point of view, the principle of solidarity has been challenged and replaced by the objective of private insurance. Let free individuals choose the type of income security they can afford.

In this Thatcherist world, the wealthy will be given the choice of opting out of welfare benefits. By relinquishing their entitlements to certain publicly provided services, they will receive a tax rebate. The state will benefit because the public costs of providing pensions, education and health benefits will fall as many middle-class professionals choose to opt-out. It is unlikely that many states will accept such a

---

[82] *Ibid.*, p. 314
[83] *Financial Times*, 10 September, 1993

radical dismantling of welfare programmes. But the driving principle behind this proposal is one that many governments now openly entertain. Wherever possible, social benefits will become increasingly individually secured rather than universally guaranteed.

Welfare reform is now a priority for most governments. The goals behind the reform are not in doubt. People who are on welfare have to get off it. If benefits are not to be paid indefinitely, the argument goes, the individual will be forced to free him or herself from the vicious cycle of welfare dependency. By removing the social net, individuals will be forced to take responsibility for themselves. Many find this kind of social policy thrust unacceptable. Instead, much more stress is put on the idea of making people "employable". People who can work will have to. The alternative to the outright ending of social welfare is to require those on welfare to take jobs at the minimum wage or just below it. The welfare states will be replaced by the "work ethic state". The Clinton Administration has already set targets for the gradual introduction of workfare. States receive only federal assistance if at least 20 percent of the "employable" welfare case load is working.

The working premise of these and other reform-minded proposals is that all individuals will have to look after their own welfare as much as possible. For those with regular employment prospects, access to education, medical services, job training, unemployment benefits, all of which were once protected with the status of an entitlement, will no longer have that standing that put them beyond the reach of the market and greedy employer. Now business wants to provide a vast array of those services to the public at a profit. Homecare, healthcare, day care, care for the disabled, skill-training, reskilling, technical training are perceived not only as a business opportunity for the burgeoning service economy, but something very different indeed. More and more governments now accept the idea that the delivery of these services is a business right and entitlement.[84]

In this dramatic sea of change, what is being lost is any viable notion of social responsibility – the institutional capacity for the achievement of a more equitable society. Those who want training have to pay for it. Those who want a better education will have to finance it. Those who want day-care will have to ante up. Those who receive welfare will have to accept workfare. What else is different is that society will no longer pay for these entitlements through taxes. On both sides of the Atlantic, organised labour on the public sector is required to enter into social contract with the express aim of reducing pension, retirement, vacation and other pay related benefits. As governments tax the corporation loss, governments have less money to spend overall and on social policy. Should this trend continue, it is the end of social welfare programmes as we have known them.[85]

---

[84] *States against Markets*. S. Robert Boyer and Daniel Drache, ed., p. 44
[85] *Ibid.*, p. 45

Globalisation provides a far more powerful justification than neo-conservative ideology for retrenching the welfare state. For neo-conservatism at least appears to be a matter of political choice, albeit one which to best promotes competitiveness and economic growth. Globalisation appears as an external constraint – not a matter of political choice at all – but rather of economic necessity – so that nation states can do little besides follow the dictate of footloose capital in a downward spiral of deregulation, lower social spending and lower taxes (especially corporate). The logic of this approach seems to be privatising social welfare altogether, reducing the role of the government to that of a provider of last resort (residual welfare). If that trend continues, it would return us to pre-Second World War forms of insecurity and inequality.[86]

The idea that a strong system of social welfare incompatible with the conditions and need of the global economy and therefore obsolete is voiced mostly by business interests and political parties of the right. But it comes increasingly from the left, too. It is argued, that post-Second World War capitalist state was based on the strength of its mass production industries, job security in the workplace and social stability, thanks to an extensive network of social policy programmes. The largely male workforce, the power of unions to bargain collectively as well as the pump-priming macroeconomic policies of governments to protect the economy from the business cycle, reflected the needs of this method of production. Markets had to be stabilised and social conflict minimised. With the shift towards lean production and flexible workplace, many existing programmes are seen a fetter on capitalist accumulation. Increasingly, they are regarded as being dysfunctional economically and unsustainable politically by the élite everywhere.

For example, unemployment benefits are seen as hampering worker mobility and the downward adjustment of worker expectation about wages. Universal income-support programs are being seen as unaffordable and wasteful in that they need high levels of taxation, yet, they do not provide adequate benefits to the needy. Current level of taxation and government expenditures are now considered as a disincentive to enterprise and investment and are unpopular electorally. Governments often talk about reform or the need to reform social policy. In fact, what they really want to do is replace Keynesian welfare-inspired measures with what has been called post-Fordist forms of welfare. Whilst the exact nature of this new form of welfare remains somewhat unclear, something akin to a pro-market and production-oriented approach is suggested. Basically, it means shrinking the state welfare sector in order to lighten the tax burden and lower social benefits; abundant universality and making benefits and services targeted to a needy population; encouraging privately provided or employer-provided benefits; and introducing more competition in the supply of social welfare through privatisation and profit-seeking

---

[86] *Ibid.*, p. 317

activity. This reorientation in social policy is seen as driven by economic imperatives.[87]

Looking at development since the mid-1970s, a common thread can be discerned. Irrespective of their political complexion most welfare states have abandoned full employment as a national objective, reducing levels of taxation, especially on corporations and high-income earners, trimming social expenditure and privatised some parts of the welfare state. Universality as a principle of social provision has been compromised. In this sense, welfare states have been constrained to follow a particular direction.[88]

A distinctive feature of the welfare state has been its success in meeting both the accumulation needs and the legitimation deficits of post-Second World War capitalism. What is different about the 1990s and, as far as one can see, beyond, is not only the change in the accumulation needs of a globalised, post-national capitalist economy, but also a profound change in its legitimisation needs.

A major reason why business interest and the political right came to accept the modern system of welfare entitlements was that it helped to legitimise market capitalism. From its earliest beginning in Bismarck's Germany, the social welfare state was conceived primarily as a political response to the growing means of worker discontent and socialism. This particular function of the welfare state has, of course, been closely associated with the rise of labour movement and the growth of political parties. The possibility that a socialist society, superior in economic and social organisation to capitalism, might one day supersede the capitalist system has formed the essential context for the development of the welfare state. The post-Depression era made the threat to the capitalist order far more real. The 1930s saw the rise of fascism. The post-Second World War era saw the spread of communism to nearly half of the world. There was a growing acceptance of collectivist and socialist ideas, which went hand in hand with the development and consolidation of left parties.

The bipartisan acceptance of full employment and the welfare state, it can be argued, had a lot to do with the legitimisation problems of *laissez-faire* capitalism seen in the context of worker militancy and the socialist alternative. Politically and ideologically, capitalism was very much on the defensive. The anarchy and waste endemic in a market system, with its booms and slumps, was tragically evident in the 1930s. The economic crises and its cost in human suffering highlighted the supremacy – moral and material – of a system of planned production and distribution integral to socialism. However flawed, Soviet socialism model with its full employment, collective consumption and egalitarian orientation represented the translation of this ideal into reality. The Soviet model, followed in broad outlines by the many countries that formed a part of the growing socialist world, was both a challenge and a reproach to unregulated capitalism.

---

[87] *Ibid.,* p. 319
[88] *Ibid.,* p. 323

Moreover, there was a strong current of evolutionism and historicism in Western social thought represented most forcefully by Marxism but also by social democracy. These ideologies saw capitalism as a transitory social system destined to be superseded by some form of socialism. This evolutionary perspective also served to de-legitimise capitalism in that it appeared not only a system inefficient economically and unjust socially, but also as one that was doomed historically. *The post-Second World War welfare state was, in no small measure, capitalism's answer to these legitimisation problems.*[89]

Today, capitalism no longer faces the challenge of a socialist alternative. The collapse of communism as a social system, after having failed as the exemplar of the future society for the best part of this century, has conferred a new legitimacy on capitalism. With no competitor in sight it has acquired a new lease of life, becoming, so to speak, a monopolistic social system! No wonder some see in the situation the "end of history" itself.[90] The virtual demise of Marxism as a creditable social theory and especially as a philosophy of history has also rebounded to the favour of free market capitalism.

Income inequality, a prominent feature of market capitalism, is on the rise everywhere. For example, in the United States the growth in the incomes of the richest one percent of America has been so large that just the increase between 1980 and 1990 in the after-tax income of this group equals the total income of the poorest 20 percent of the population. Inequality of income and wealth has acquired a new aura of legitimacy. It now appears as a necessity and inevitable, if not also a highly desirable, phenomenon – a small price to pay for many blessings of capitalism. Lastly, the working class and the trade union movement find themselves much weakened as a result of globalisation, the resurgence of a free economy, and other changes which have fragmented the solidarity of the workers' movement. As a result of these developments, the rule of capital has few challengers compared with the past. Not only the socialist alternative but also the social democratic alternative to neoconservative political economy have both been marginalised.

The decline of the workers' movement, and of the left more generally, as a moral and political force means that one of the major functions of the welfare state – namely legitimisation – is no longer a pressing one. Indeed, one might say that the democratic consumer capitalism has become self-legitimating. In the absence of credible alternative to market capitalism the inequality and insecurity inherent in the system have become far more acceptable. *The absence of a credible alternative and the acceptance of inequality indicate a new situation unprecedented since the birth of industrial capitalism.* At the very least it suggests that welfare programmes and arrangements can expect a period of decline, albeit gradually, given electoral competition, vested

---

[89] *Ibid.,* p. 326

[90] Francis Fukuyama, The End of History? *The National Interest,* No. 16 (Summer 1989)

interests and democratic procedures. Chronicle unemployment – through loss of revenue and payment of benefits – will exert a steady pressure on the budget. Fiscal constraints plus the need for a "flexible" labour market will ensure that unemployment benefits are whitted down. Those of working age, whether on welfare or unemployment benefit will be under increasing pressure to get into "workfare", i.e. they will be obliged to undergo some sort of training or perform some labour in return for their welfare cheque, weakening the notion of entitlement further. Universality of social programmes will be eroded through such devices as the taxback of benefits from high-income earners, the reduction of service (e.g. delisting of medical procedures), and the underfunding of services which make middle- and upper-income earners look for private solutions.

These developments, combined with the increasing polarisation of work incomes, will inevitably result in greater poverty and inequality. There might be seen an increasing "Americanisation", or dualisation of industrial societies. This would mean a division into a contented majority with regular jobs, work-related benefits and other forms of private protection and a marginalised and impoverished minority in low-paying jobs or lacking regular employment and dependent on state welfare benefits alone.[91]

No doubt countervailing influences are at work, too, and how far they might be effective in checking the trend toward privatisation and dualisation remains to be seen. The economy is being freed from public control everywhere. At the same time we are also witnessing a strengthening of democratic values. Demand for greater political participation, more popular, say, in the decision-making process (e.g. through referenda and call for greater accountability of politicians to their constituents), is also being heard increasingly. The formation of new interests and social movements continues apace. Women's movement, environment groups, the aged, etno-cultural groups are among the new and revitalised groups seeking to influence public policy. However, the relationship of these groups to the hegemonic forces of market capitalism remains problematic.

The contradiction between the declining sovereignty of the nation-state over the economy and rising democratic and participatory values are likely to intensify, especially if globalisation results in substantial dislocation of the economic life of nations. A sharp decline in the living standards of large sectors of the population could provoke a reaction. Increasing incidence of crime, violence and other forms of deviance could create a strong sense of insecurity among citizens forcing élites to compromise. *However, so long as creditable alternatives are lacking, it is unlikely that the system will have any difficulty in dealing with manifestations of protest and unrest,* such as increasing crime, violence and urban riots through repressive measures. In any case,

---

[91] *States against Markets.* S. Robert Boyer and Daniel Drache, ed., p. 327

given the deficit on the left, it is right-wing populism and extremists that are likely to benefit from economic and social dislocations. Discontent and insecurity may therefore be channelled into racism, economic protectionism and other forms of national chauvinism.[92]

Liberalisation and Privatisation

Another important current trend related directly and indirectly by the MNCs is the growing effort of governments *to liberalise the foreign trade, the financial markets, the currency exchange, to deregulate and to privatise major economic sectors*. The impact of them on MNCs is mainly indirect, yet potentially significant, both because of the political trends underlying those developments and because of the effects on the structures of sectors concerned. A clear consequence of the underlying political trends has been the slowing down of a number of earlier efforts to bring MNC activities under domestic scrutiny and control. The structural impact of deregulation measures may be discerned in the spreading effects of the break-up of AT&T in the United States on the world telecommunication industry and of the deregulation of United States airlines on the world air transportation.

An emerging trend in policies of the developed market economies is clearly apparent in the case of the United States, but barely visible in the case of other countries, is the increased integration of policies and measures relating to foreign economic sectors and issues. Policies concerning foreign trade in goods and service, foreign investments, and other financial transactions and the international flow of factors of production, in general, are now perceived as an integrated, cross-cutting package. The fundamental novelty lies not so much in the comprehensiveness of coverage and the close linkage of treatment of relevant issues. Contemporary technological development, especially in micro-electronics, has made such integration a necessity as well possible. Problems and policies come to be viewed as a unified whole, the central aim being to avoid exacerbating stresses in some directions through measures designed to serve strategies in other areas and to enhance, to the extent possible, the mutually beneficial effects of policies. The linkage of diverse sectors and issues (trade, investment, intellectual property etc.) is thus matched by the integration of policies being complemented by a set of internationally-oriented actions and measures.[93]

The last decade has especially been marked by a considerable strengthening of the movement towards deregulation of important economic sectors, which had started in the late 1970s. The focus has been primarily on service sectors, such as

---

[92] *Ibid.*, p. 328
[93] *Transitional Corporations in World Development. Trends and Prospects*, p. 241

transportation, by air or over land, telecommunications and insurance. Its major and most widespread impact has been on the financial services, where combined with technological developments has brought about major changes in the functioning of financial institutions and markets all over the world. Taking everything into account, it seems clear that, considering the financial services sector's (and also the transportation's, the telecommunication's, the insurance's) internalisation and their importance for MNCs, their continuing deregulation is bound to have a significant impact.

An important facet of deregulation policies is the movement towards *privatisation*, which has acquired considerable impetus in most of the developed market economies. To a degree, privatisation is a response to the perceived inefficiency of public corporations and to an assessment that the sector has grown too large. According to this approach, nationalised firms in the productive sector should be privatised (and actually have been privatised, for example, in the United Kingdom), under the view that, by nature, private managers are more competent than any bureaucrat. If, however, it is seen in the context of the other economic policies subsumed under the general heading of deregulation, it becomes clear that privatisation involves an effort to bring into the realm of competition sectors and industries, whether or not involving natural monopolies, which have until now been under political control. To the extent that now private enterprises are fully exposed to the market, the clear possibility arises that they will be of interest to MNCs, as possible targets for take-overs or with a view to co-operating with them through minority participation.

There are a number of policy considerations that need to be taken into account about the extent of linkage between the distinct privatisation drives of the developed market economies and the activities of MNCs. First, legal or administrative procedures have been introduced to explicitly limit the extent to which foreign participation is possible in specific or across-the-board privatisation processes (for example, France has established by law a 20 percent upper limit). In other cases, both foreign registry as well as antitrust authorities can and have used their power to limit the extent of foreign participation. Finally, choices can be made that give a preference to national enterprises or national investors as, for example, happened in Italy in the acquisition case of Alfa-Romeo by Fiat against Ford's parallel bid. On the whole, and since in most developed market economies the public sector has a major role in strategic or "natural monopoly" situations, political sensitivity and legal or regulatory provisions are likely to be brought into the picture against take-overs by foreign enterprises in the pursuit of diverse privatisation efforts.[94]

Liberalisation has a long history. Even before the beginning of Second World War, there was widespread international opinion, particularly in the United States

---

[94] *Ibid.*, p. 255

and in the United Kingdom, that a totally new system of monetary and trade relationships should be developed. It was generally believed that international trade conflicts and exchange disequilibrium were principle causes of the world-wide instability during the interwar period and, ultimately, of the war itself. Establishment of a trade regime based on unrestricted international competition, with the elimination of country preferences and exchange control, became a particular objective of United States policy.

Reliance on competition and freedom of contract was not, however, adopted as the guiding principle with respect to international investment and capital flows. The policy arrangements adopted during the immediate post-war period did not take into account the possibility that a world-wide foreign investment boom, accompanied by explosive growth in the number and size of MNCs, would follow. Only half a century later are some elements of a comprehensive international investment regime beginning to emerge. There are contests both among nations and among regions within nations to attract mobile wealth-creating capital. Therefore, there has been a general liberalisation of investment policy in many, especially developing countries. And the pace of liberalisation has accelerated. Of 82 policy changes adopted by 35 countries during 1991, for example, 80 reduced restriction on foreign investment.

Furthermore, 64 bilateral investment treaties for the promotion and protection of FDI were signed during the first 18 months of the 1990s, compared with 199 such treaties signed during the 1980s. By the early 1990s, an almost fully liberal regime of international financial movements had emerged within the OECD region, granting financial operators more freedom to act internationally than they had experienced since before the First World War. And of course, privatisation and deregulation of communication, as well as of financial markets, have helped extend the sense of greater mobility of critical resources.[95]

The financial liberalisation trend across the advanced industrial world in the last three decades has been partly propelled by two developments. One of these has been the increased political prominence of supporters of market-oriented or "neo-liberal" thoughts. Neo-liberal advocates have favoured the elimination of capital controls partly on efficiency grounds; capital would be able to move across borders to find its most productive employment. They have also argued that financial liberalisation would allow private international financial markets to discipline government policy effectively. In addition, the abolition of capital controls has also been seen as desirable in that it gives individuals the freedom to diversify their financial portfolios and thus reduce their risks and vulnerability to financial upheavals.

A second development encouraging financial liberalisation has been the growing demand for it from large financial firms and multinational business. In almost

---

[95] *Transitional Corporations*, Vol. 3, No. 1 (February, 1994) p. 59

every one of the episodes in which advanced industrial states have abolished their capital controls over the last two decades, these business groups have been key domestic constituents pressing for the move. With rapid internalisation of corporate activities in Europe, North America and Japan in the 1970s and 1980s, capital controls have increasingly come to be seen as a cumbersome interference by these firms.[96]

The post war commitment to trade liberalisation initially embodied in the GATT and expended in the WTO involves two key concepts: 1. the reduction of trade barriers; and 2. the elimination of discrimination and preferences among trading partners. These two ideas are quite distinct, since it is possible (indeed, historically typical) to reduce barriers or grant preferences for some trading partners while maintaining, or even increasing them for others (thus maintaining or increasing discrimination). GATT-WTO claim to defend "fair competition", however, these organisations in many cases serve the interest of MNCs. Deregulation recommended by GATT-WTO benefits MNCs by reducing the space in which states and particularly developing countries' states can exercise management.

The evolution of the post-war trade and exchange regime has been particularly associated with the growth of MNCs in both number and scale. On the one hand, trade liberalisation and ease of currency exchange created a favourable setting for the expansion of international business activity in all forms, and particularly for FDI. Since the theory of the MNC involves the optimisation of investment, facilities, production, and marketing among various locations, it follows that ease of movement for both capital and output, reduction in exchange control and tariffs, etc., tend to facilitate MNC expansion.[97]

On the other hand, the growth of MNCs takes a large amount of international economic activity out of the market arena and into the internal control of individual firms. Once MNC structures are established, local revenues become available for expenditure in various jurisdictions and local capital sources become accessible as well; the need for international financial transfers is correspondingly reduced. In a sense, the growth of the MNCs, nurtured within the framework of convertible currencies and liberalised trade, has created a situation that makes the framework itself less important. The apparent "weakening" of the monetary regime, in particular, may be in fact a reflection of the "strengthening" of the forces that have grown up within it, both the increasing volume of foreign investment of all types and the vast amount of foreign currency trading taking place within the "floating rates" environment.[98]

[96] *States against Markets*. S. Robert Boyer and Daniel Drache, ed., p. 194
[97] *The Rules of the Game in the Global Economy Policy Regimes for International Business*, p. 141
[98] *Ibid.*, p. 142

Need for Global Governance – Global Polity

ARGUMENTS AND RATIONALES FOR GLOBAL GOVERNANCE, GLOBAL POLITY

There is no doubt that the globalisation has created tasks and problems that require some kind of *global governance, global polity*. Many arguments supporting this requirement can be found in the literature dealing with this subject. Among them the most explicit ones are given by Held.[99] His arguments are as follows.

International economic and cultural connections reduce the power and effectiveness of governments at the national-state level – they can no longer control the flow of ideas and economic items at their borders and thus their internal policy instruments become ineffective. The increasing difficulty that governments face in dictating what their citizens will see and hear curtail the efficiency of information-restriction policies exercised in the interest of many varied purposes, from supporting a repressive dictatorship at one extreme to encouraging local cultural industries at the other. Access to the Internet, for example, provides a massive hole in the information-restricting barriers. The globalisation has reduced government power in some traditional areas. Sophisticated communication, and vast amounts of short-term capital in the hands of MNCs, make it impossible for governments to control international capital movement in the ways that they routinely did in the area of fixed exchange rates from 1945 to 1970. (Indeed, the globalisation of capital markets had a lot to do with the breakdown of the Bretton Woods systems of fixed exchange rates.)[100]

State power is further reduced because transitional process grows in scale as well as in number – especially important is in this respect that MNCs are often larger and more powerful than many governments.

In many of the industries now regarded as strategic, the minimum market size needed to support a competitive R & D effort is larger than even the largest national markets. Perhaps of more fundamental importance, politics is still organised in terms of geography – territory and borders – while economic activity is increasingly organised in term of globality. The result is a developing asymmetry of scope and mode of organisation between a territorially based and geographically organised international political system comprised of nation-states and an emerging world economy where national markets, and indeed the very concepts of territoriality and geography, are becoming less relevant. There is a growing need to decrease or to eliminate this asymmetry.[101]

---

[99] Malcolm Waters, *Globalisation* (Routledge, London, 1995) p. 97

[100] *Governments, Globalisation, and International Business.* John H. Dunning, ed., p. 92

[101] János Hoós, *The Unfolding New World and Economics*, p. 22

Globalisation is requiring supervision at the international level of many issues involving trade and investment. The importance to most countries of a relatively free flow of international trade has led them to transfer power over super-national bodies. System frictions provide another powerful reason for the reallocation of power to supranational authorities. These arise when, owing to globalisation of trade and investment, policies with respect to such matters as labour practices, industrial competition, R&D support, subsidies, and intellectual property protection, which were formerly thought to be of purely domestic interest, arouse international concern because they affect international flow of trade, FDI, and factors of production. Trade liberalising arrangements are now working towards "deep integration" in which the sources of system frictions are subject to agreed international control, which implies major transfer of power from national to super-national levels of government. More generally, super-national organisations are needed to prohibit certain activities and to regulate others. Prohibition is needed in two types of situation.

The first is where the policy game played by individual governments is of the prisoner's-dilemma variety (non-co-operative behaviour starts by helping individuals but ends up hurting everyone), as with tariffs. Here, international organisations are already well developed. The WTO and various regional free trade agreements, such as the EU, NAFTA allow countries to tie their hands in advance, preventing them from taking individual actions in prisoner's-dilemma situations.

The second is where the policy game is zero-sum (one person's gain is another's loss), as when countries compete to attract some given set of footloose industries. The new policies for "deep integration" allow governments to tie their hands against using "domestic" policies for international purposes and thus to avoid playing such zero-sum games. Regulation, rather than prohibition, is called for where the policy game is positive sum so that everyone gains, as with the creation and transfer of new technologies. In these cases, good policies are needed, not to stop the game from being played, but to help in playing it better.[102] States have thus been obliged to surrender sovereignty within larger political units (e.g. EU, ASEAN), multinational treaties (e.g. NATO, OPEC), or international organisations (e.g. UN, WTO, IMF, World Bank). The core of the world's economy is managed on an international scale – financial markets are managed through IMF and World Bank, trade is managed through WTO and economic policy co-ordination is done through G7.

A system of "global governance" is therefore emerging with its own policy development and administrative systems which further curtail state power.

This provides the basis for the emergence of a supranational state with dominant coercive and legislative power.

---

[102] *Governments, Globalisation, and International Business*. John H. Dunning, ed., p. 94

According to Held, the sovereignty of state is already in decline and "world government" and globalised polity, although not taking the same form as contemporary nation-state governments and polity, is a real possibility.[103] In fact we can see a lot of signs of the development to this direction.

To speak of global polity can invoke the image of a world government, a single unitary and centralised state similar to contemporary nation-states, or even a world empire. This need not be the case. Globalised polity can have the characteristics of a network of power centres, including nation-states, co-ordinated by means other than command. In principle such power centres might be co-ordinated because their controllers have shared common norms and common interests and sought to move towards consensus on such issues. Such a view is not romantically optimistic as it my appear. Regional grouping of states, such as the EU, and a wide range of specialised interests associated already co-ordinate their activities on just such a basis. However, such an outcome is less likely than a polity organised as a market, or more precisely as multiple markets. Here processes of allocation (e.g., of welfare, economic development, peace and security, pollution, cultural performances) would be governed by competition between power centres much in the way that global flows of finance or of information are the consequences of multiple and complex decisions.

The vehicles within which these parallel processes of consensus building and competition can occur are *international organisations*. Political scientists normally make a distinction between two types of international organisation: inter-governmental organisations (IGOs) and international non-governmental organisations (INGOs). Individually such organisations are not necessarily global in scope and indeed may cover as few as two national societies. However, taken together they constitute a web-like network through which goal setting and allocative decisions can flow. IGOs include not only the obvious organisations of whole states, such as the UN, but also links between the parts of governmental systems, between parliaments, central banks or environmental departments. Such links are greatest in the areas defined as common global problems. INGOs might be regarded as more important in globalisation terms than IGOs because they outflank nation-states and threaten borders. They are unruly because their complexity defies command and their capacity to link diverse people in relation to common causes and interests undermines the saliency of the state.

Many data refer to the initial development of international organisations at around 1920. Prior to that data international relations had been conducted largely by means of the state-based systems of trade, diplomacy, colonialism, military alliances and war. Only in the areas of postal communications and health regulation were there serious previous IGO activities. A critical turning point was the Versailles peace conference that sought to impose an international order in the aftermath of the First

---

[103] Malcolm Waters, *Globalisation*, p. 97

World War. It took two critical measures: it gave states to the nationalities of dismembered Austro-Hungarian, Ottoman, Prussian and Russian empires; and it set up a League of Nations to serve as a forum for consensus building on issues of peace and security. However, the League was to fail because the USA turned isolationist and, having originally promoted the idea, refused to join, because the Fascist and Communist states were not members, and because the organisation had no power of enforcement at its disposal. It collapsed with the outbreak of the Second World War in 1939.

The close of that war in 1945 marked the emergence of a far more effective IGO system. The key developments were the establishment of UN and its subordinate agencies FAO, UNCTAD, UNESCO, UNICEF, UNDRA, WHO, the IMF, World Bank, and GATT and the military alliance systems, CENTO, NATO and the Warsaw Treaty Organisation. More recent developments include IGOs for regional economic co-operation and trade and for monitoring environmental degradation and population control. There has therefore been a marked upswing in the number of IGOs since 1945 and in 1992 they numbered over 3,000.[104]

The burgeoning growth of INGOs has been even more remarkable. Some examples can illustrate their importance and the breadth of their activities. They include environmental and health groups (e.g. Friends of the Earth, Greenpeace, WWF); professional and academic associations (e.g. International Sociological Association; religious forums (e.g. World Council of Churches, World Moslem Congress); sports organisations (International Olympic Committee); and welfare organisations (e.g. International Federation of Red Cross and Red Crescent Societies, Caritas). By 1992 there were nearly 15,000 such organisations. Together they constitute a complex and ungovernable web of relationships that reach beyond the nation-states.

The international system was, until the First World War, numerically dominated by states and their mainly bilateral relations. IGOs were very few in number and INGOs almost non-existent. An expansion of the global system began in the first quarter of the twentieth century when all three types of organisations grew rapidly in number and importance. However, the second half of the twentieth century the world was dominated by IGOs in which states surrendered a considerable measure of their sovereignty. A key feature of the accelerated phase of globalisation since about 1960 has been the rapid growth of INGOs, which lends support to the claim that the main thrust of this phase is cultural, rather than material or political in character. The question of how much power the INGOs actually have will obviously be a major point of debate but their existence and expansion should at least convince us that their value and effectiveness is in little doubt for those individuals who construct them. It is clear that national governments are obliged to take IGOs and INGOs seriously and treat with them.[105]

---

[104] *Ibid.*, p. 112
[105] *Ibid.*, p. 113

A critical and striking feature of political globalisation is that it does not in any area exhibit the extreme level of globalisation found, for example, in financial markets. Political globalisation is most advanced in the areas of international relations and political culture. However, the state remains highly resistant, largely sovereign and a critical arena for problem solving. A possible explanation is that politics is a highly territorial activity and that the organised nation-state is the most effective means for establishing sovereignty over territory than human beings have yet devised. Globalisation is a process with spatial reference but paradoxically threatens territorial sovereignty. The state might therefore be just the final bastion of resistance to globalising trend and the indicator of their ultimate effectivity.[106]

In economic field globalisation has eroded the power of national states, and therefore demand a globalised management of economic, financial and monetary systems. However, no economy exists without politics and without a state. Therefore, economic globalisation logically requires the construction of a world political system able to respond to the challenge, a power system capable of managing social compromise at world-wide level, just as national states manage them at their level. However, sufficient maturity does not exist in the area, not even among the group of dominant capitalist countries – OECD or within the Europe of the EU, and *a fortiori* not on a large scale. It is therefore, for example, not possible, objectively, to have a universal currency and thus a world central bank. The currency and the bank imply that the political problem has been solved, which is not the case. The proposal for a world central bank reiterates the arguments advanced by Keynes in 1945. Keynes wanted the IMF be a world central bank having independence from the national states, but countries, especially the United States, preferred a weaker institution, that is why the recourses of IMF have always been limited, despite its borrowing. The IMF may be able to act as a catalyst, by defining the rules of conditions, for instance, but it cannot go much further, not mentioning that it is under the heavy influence of the G7, particularly, the USA and due to this in may cases it is unable to defend and to represent global interest of the world

The same reasons that made the project utopian at the time are still valid today, despite the progress of economic globalisation. It seems that capitalism is unable to overcome the growing contradiction between its economic management in an increasingly globalised space, and its political and social management which remains fragmented among national spaces.[107] *The asymmetry between territorially based and geographically organised international political system comprised of national states and an emerging world economy where national markets are becoming less relevant still exists.* The world is still far from the existence of global governance, global polity. At the same time there are many serious *problems*, *concerns* and *tasks* transcending national bor-

---

[106] *Ibid.*, p. 122

[107] Samir Amin, *Capitalism in the Age of Globalisation* (Zed Books, London, 1997) p. 22

ders, which would need or at least they *need strong and effective international co-operation*. Among them the following deserve distinctive attention:

Managing regional crisis. The threat of a nuclear war between the superpowers has given way to a mushrooming of smaller conflicts, entailing costly problems of refugee relief and rehabilitation. No solid international framework exists for managing these conflicts or helping avoid them. A more integrated assessment of how state polities and international assistance help manage nascent conflict would be needed in designing economic and social policy.

Promoting global economic stability. Concern has been growing about the potentially destabilising effects of large and rapid flows of portfolio capital, particularly when a crisis in one country spills over into other markets. A variety of international mechanisms have been suggested to guard against such problems but still prudent and responsive economic policies at home countries are considered as the best protection of the countries. Growing international labour mobility is also raising a host of issues requiring international collective action.

Protecting the environment. There are urgent global environment issues including climate change, loss of biodiversity, and protection of international waters. International collective action can help through better co-ordination, greater public awareness, more effective technological transfer, and better national and local practice.

Fostering basic research and production knowledge. Technology should be developed and disseminated by international collective action to meet the challenges in domains of food production, environment protection and health.

Making international development assistance more effective. To become more effective, foreign aid needs to be tied more closely to the policies of the recipient countries. A high priority for aid agencies is to systematically channel resources to poor countries with good policies and strong commitment to institutional reinvigoration.[108]

It is much easier to list these concerns and tasks than to manage them efficiently in practice. The progress has been slow, however, enhancing the worry that it will take many crises to get and to force the respective international organisations and countries into concerted action. In this respect the G7, the IMF and the World Bank have great responsibility in selecting and pursuing proper economic policies dealing with the world economy as a whole and with the economy of each country relating to the IMF and the World Bank. *It seems that it is time to make a paradigmatic change in their economic policies*. In fact the IMF and the World Bank are the executives for strategies defined by the G7 – strategies that are based on the least common denominator among the positions of the United States, Japan and the EU.

The IMF's original mandate was to ensure monetary stability in an open world economy, as a substitute for the gold standard, which had fulfilled this function

---

[108] *World Development Report. 1997. The State in a Changing World* (Oxford University Press, Oxford, The World Bank, Washington, D.C., 1997) p. 12

successfully until the First World War. This implied that the IMF's interventions were to impose adjustments on all parties, whatever their payment balances were, surplus or deficit. During the first period of its existence, the IMF gave the impression of certain efficiency as it helped to re-establish the convertibility of European currencies (1947–1957), then it helped European economies to adjust (1958–1966). From 1947 on, however, the Fund has failed to maintain stability despite the creation of SDRs. The adaptation of the general system of floating currencies in 1973 may be considered to mark the end of the Bretton Wood mandate. At that point the continued existence of the IMF was called into question. The institution survived by taking on new functions: management of unilateral structural adjustments in developing countries and, from the end of the 1980s, interventions in Eastern-European countries to ensure their reincorporation into the international economic, especially, monetary system.[109] The World Bank devotes a great part of its resources to what are known as sectoral adjustment programmes, a necessary complement to the strategies instituted by IMF under the wing of G7.

The IMF and the World Bank are the leading advocates of the neo-classic economic theory and the neo-liberal economic policies having been implemented during the last three decades all over the world. Both institutions serve as powerful representatives of global capital – enforcing debt collection, supervising the financial accounts of poor nations, promoting wage suppression if it is needed for structural adjustment policies, preparing the countries for eventual acceptance of the global trading system. The two agencies give instructions on the principles of neo-classic economics. If a nation learns well, it may become eligible for loans and projects. If it refuses to conform, it has to face negative economic discriminations making it hard or even impossible to carry out successful national economic policies. However, due to the growing political and economic problems, crisis contradicting the principles of these institutions, more and more critics and challenges of these policies can be heard around the world.

As a result of these, some changes can already be experienced in their policies and philosophy, especially in the evaluation and judgement of the role of the state. The World Bank, for example, put intense focus on the state's role in the economic development. As it can be read in its World Development Report, 1997: "An effective state is vital for the provision of the goods and service – and the rules and institutions – that allow markets to flourish and people to lead healthier, happier lives. Without it, sustainable development, both economic and social, is impossible. ... (that is) ... markets and governments are complementary. ... Good government is not a luxury – it is a vital necessity for development."[110] But in spite of that the policies that IMF and World Bank have been pursuing in practice do not mirror this

[109] Samir Amin, *Capitalism in the Age of Globalisation*, p. 18
[110] *World Development Report. 1997*, p. 15

view put down in the Report. Their practical policies are still based upon the so-called *Washington consensus* elaborated in the World Bank's annual development reports in 1991.[111]

The Washington consensus formed by U.S. economic officials, the IMF and the World Bank is focusing on trade liberalisation, deregulation and privatisation as the main requirements to make an effective market economy and its prime goal is macroeconomic stability using the following policy prescription: managing the budget deficit and current account deficit – that is reducing the size of government, the budget deficit, and the current account deficit –, getting prices right, controlling inflation. Once a government deals with these issues – essentially, once the government "gets out of the way" – private markets would allocate resources efficiently and generate robust growth. As such the Washington consensus policies were based on a rejection of the state's active role and the promotion of a minimalist, non-interventionist state. The unspoken premise is that governments are worse than markets. Therefore the smaller the state the better it is.[112]

THE NEED TO RE-EXAMINE AND CHANGE THE WASHINGTON CONSENSUS

It seems now is a good time to re-examine and change the Washington consensus. The uncertainty of its success, especially in the big-bang format, and the substantial social costs incurred in the process have drawn attention to alternative policies. As Mexico, Russia and most of sub-Saharan Africa, for example, have been hewing to liberalisation now for a long time with meager success, the theoretical arguments in favour of this policy inclination are losing their force. The current crisis in East Asian, Latin-American countries and Russia are just underlining the doubts about this policies.

> We can be witnessing more and more signs of attempts to elaborate concepts and policies which are different from the Washington consensus. For example: Gordon Brown, the British chancellor of the exchequer, writes about a need of a "New Global Financial Architecture" and U.S. Treasury Secretary Robert Rubin elaborated the Clinton administration's plan for improving the "architecture" of international finance (*The Wall Street Journal Europe*, October 6, 1998, pp. 10–11). George Soros wants to replace the global capitalist system having serious deficiencies, – like "the uneven distribution of benefits, the instability of the financial system and the question of values and social cohesion" – with an "open society" which is open to improvement (*The Atlantic Monthly*, the February 1997). However both "new architecture" and "open society" are terms whose meaning may be hard to pin down. Joseph E. Stiglitz has a more specified vision for modification

---

[111] *Word Development Report. 1991* (Oxford University Press, Oxford, The World Bank, Washington, D.C., 1991)

[112] Joseph E. Stiglitz, *1998 WIDER Annual Lecture on More Instruments and Broader Goals: Moving Toward the Post-Washington Consensus* (Helsinki, 7 January 1998) p. 18

of the Washington consensus. He advocates to use "more instruments" and to broaden "the objective of development to include other goals, such as sustainable development, egalitarian development and democratic development" (J. E. Stiglitz: *More instruments and Broader Goals: Moving Toward the Post-Washington Consensus*. WIDER Annual Lecture 2. Helsinki, on January 1998).

The assumptions underlying neo-classical economic theorems about benefits of liberalisation are revealing themselves as a peculiar that they do not work out in practice.[113]

The direction of the change of these policies could be the broadening of the goals and instruments (means) of the policies intending to promote economic development, and in addition to these, there is a need for a better timing, sequencing during the policy implementation.

As regards the goals, they should include not just short term economic growth, but long-run, sustainable economic growth accompanied by increases in living standards – including equitable income distribution, improved health and education – and by preserved natural resources, and protected healthy environment.

As regards the policy instruments, it means on the one hand, they should include building up of efficient financial systems, promotion of the competition, appropriate regulation and more effective and efficient state not only in dealing with macroeconomic stability, inflation, appropriate deregulation, liberalisation and privatisation but in the field of social protection, welfare, building of human capital, technological development and transfer, and on the other hand, better use of the main instruments of the Washington consensus (that is, of the macroeconomic stabilisation policies, fiscal- and monetary policies, anti-inflation policies, deregulation, liberalisation and privatisation).

It would be important to provide an increase in living standards which ensures that all groups in society, not just at the top, enjoy the fruits of development. *In that case it would be possible to reach two important goals at the same time: to enlarge the aggregate demand and to strengthen social peace*, as it was the case after the Second World War due to the creation of the welfare state, establishing a certain kind of social safety net. The recent development of globalisation has increased the inequality of income and wealth distribution and has not provided favourable conditions for the growth of aggregate demand. The economic policies did not follow that line that was based on Keynesian economics after the Second World War and that had those governing doctrine, that focused on maintaining full employment and aggregate demand for mass consumption. These policies of the globalisation discards old political commitments to social equity and reduce benefit systems for pensions, health care, income support and various forms of ameliorative aid.

---

[113] William Greider, *One World, Ready or Not* (Simon and Shuster, New York, 1998) p. 278

The greatest beneficiaries of the economic growth were the wealthy. For example, the real profit on owning U.S. bonds was 8.2 percent in the 1990s, compared to 6.7 percent in the 1980s and across the twentieth century, the average return on holding long-term bonds has been only 1.6 percent. In other words, creditors were at present receiving returns on their wealth five times the average, while real economies functioned at a relatively low level of growth, labour wages declined and governments sank in debt.[114] In the USA the rise in unit labour costs for 1993 was among the lowest annual increases in three decades and the pay raises were running even lower in 1994. Clinton's presidency was distinctive for that fact: throughout his first term, despite economic recovery, wages were flat or falling for all but the top 20 percent of the wage earners' ladder.[115] *Some kind of so called rentier's regime has been developed, a governing system by and for the rentiers, wealthy share-holders who drive their incomes from returns on capital.*[116] One of the best examples of that is the following fact: a number of nations, including the United States, had already put their operating budgets in balance and were actually running surpluses – except for the annual interest payments due to their bondholdings.

Though many Americans were perhaps unaware of the achievement, the federal government had moderated spending sufficiently so that the so called primary budget was in surplus – a surplus of $68 billion in 1995 and about $100 billion in 1996. That is, the spending on all the government's actual programs was less than its tax revenues. It was the debt costs that wholly accounted for the annual deficits. Germany, Italy, the Netherlands, Britain and Belgium – even Hungary – have achieved a similar fiscal condition, though at much difference in their levels of indebtedness. Despite this budget discipline the debt costs continued to escalate. In reality, the U.S. government had to borrow more money every year – $200 billion or more – simply to pay the interests due on its old debt. The arithmetic was compounding: paying the rentiers has become a major function of national governments. In the U.S, interest costs had swollen from $52.5 billion in 1980 to $184 billion in 1990. By 1996, debt payments reached about $260 billion despite the deficit-reduction campaigns by Clinton and his predecessor, George Bush. U.S. spending devoted to debt was roughly equal to national defence or Medicare and Medicaid combined.[117]

Political imperative to revise this condition not only grew stronger each year, but also became more difficult to accomplish since it posed stark implications for social division: governments were expected to withdraw more and more benefits from dependent classes of citizens – the poor and elderly and unemployed – but as in various ways from the broad middle class, in order to honour their obligations to

[114] *Ibid.*, p. 300
[115] *Ibid.*, p. 302
[116] *Ibid.*, p. 285
[117] *Ibid.*, p. 308

the creditor class., the people and institutions with accumulations of wealth. There was no precedent in the history of modern industrial democracies to suggest this transfer could be achieved – not without dramatic electoral repudiations or social upheaval.

The rentiers, to be sure, were a more diverse social class than the wealthy alone, but still a much narrower group than liberal rhetoric pretended. Millions of middle-class families have acquired modest shares in the government's pool of bonds through mutual funds (which held about 6 percent of all U.S. long-term debt) or a presumed interest in pension funds (which held another 6 percent of the total). But, in reality, most families did not have a mutual-fund nest egg or even net saving of any kind. The majority of families, aside from any equity they had accumulated in their homes, were net debtors. The ownership of financial wealth, like incomes, has shifted dramatically to the top rungs of the society, further aggravating the gross inequalities of wealth that had always existed. Edward N. Wolff, an economist at New York University, found, for example, that the share of total financial wealth held by the bottom 80 percent of American families had declined during the 1980s, from 9 percent of total to 6 percent. The top 1 percent meanwhile, increased its share of financial assets from 43 to 48 percent.[118]

There is another unfavourable impact on the living standards and on the aggregate demand, it is the pressure for the wages to keep them low or/and their increase less than the increase of productivity. The unhinging of wages from productivity was driven by a fundamental structural change: the mass production system that for many years had guaranteed a happy convergence of interests between workers and owners was itself being dismantled – smashed by the technological revolutions and by the global dispersal of production. In the post-war decades, a "vicious circle" had operated in the core manufacturing sectors, a self-reinforcing prosperity that, in effect, shared the gains of rising productivity among owners, workers and consumers, distributed the form of profits, wages and prices.

The old system resembled a splendidly harmonious wheel: economies of scale in mass production fostered rapidly rising productivity (that is, per unit labour costs were reduced as the volume of production grew). These cost savings permitted steady wage increase for workers (and low unemployment) as well as cheaper prices for consumers. The rising incomes for workers made the robust growth in consumer spending possible, which, in turn, fed back into supporting the more profitable economies of scale.

The "vicious circle" did not vanish entirely, but it was gravely destabilised by the industrial revolution and globalisation. New producers from the poorer nations flooded into the marketplace, offering cost advantages based on an opposite premise: lower wages. Simultaneously, the new technologies undermine the simplicities and

---

[118] *Ibid.*, p. 309

standardisation of the mass-production assembly lines. Rapid change, a stream of newly differentiated products and constant competition to elaborate their quality, undercut the costs savings that companies expected to derive automatically from repetitive mass production.[119]

The emerging system produced less surplus to share, as profits were squeezed the owners of capital stopped sharing with the workers. The erosion of middle-class incomes in affluent nations like America was directly connected to this breakdown of the "vicious circle". The capital owners stopped sharing gains with labour because they found they had the power to do so. Starting in the 1970s, U.S. companies gravitated toward a different strategy in which global price pressure were offset by extracting more from labour. Corporations discarded their long post-war truce with unions and began moving jobs, first to the low-wage South and then offshore. They closed factories and demanded wage contracts that depressed wages. They mobilised both political and economic power to weaken labour's bargaining position.

The "virtuous circle" of the 1950s and 1960s had also been sustained by the existence of industrial oligopolies – a few big companies that dominated major sectors like autos, steel and aircraft and were powerful enough to set prices and wages in a clubby, arbitrary fashion. The rise of foreign producers, especially from Japan, broke up that comfortable arrangement forever. As firms shifted production to low-wage workers, organised labour lost members and became steadily less able to discipline management. The decline in wages was not confined to union members, however, but was more general.[120]

In the globalised economy the wage arbitrage moves the production and jobs from a high-wage labour market to another where labour is much cheaper. The producers thus reduce their costs and enhance profits by arbitrating these wage differences, usually selling their finished products back into high-wage markets. The classical example of the wage divergence is shirts: American garment workers could make a shirt with 14 minutes of human labour, while it took 25 in Bangladesh. But the average U.S. wage was $7.53 an hour, while in Bangladesh it was 25 cents, an edge that would not be erased even if the Bangladeshi wages were doubled or quadrupled. Or steel: U.S. industry required 3.4 hour of human labour to produce a ton of steel, while Brazil took 5.8 hours. But the wage difference was 1: $13 an hour versus $1.28.[121]

The cost of transporting things between distant markets has always been the practical obstacle to successful arbitration, but modern technologies have greatly reduced these labour costs, even for moving entire factories. Transportation is a trivial factor alongside the potential gains of exploring the waste disparities that

---

[119] *Ibid.*, p. 76
[120] *Ibid.*, p. 77
[121] *Ibid.*, p. 75

exist among wage levels in different parts of the world. A crude equilibrium system for wages is thus gradually emerging in global commerce: a discrete form of price discipline that links the best-paid, most prosperous industrial workers in the world with the cheapest and poorest.[122]

These two factors – the restriction of social expenditures of budget and the pressure on the wages – are pushing downward the aggregate demand even further damaging the "vicious circle" of self-reinforcing prosperity. From this, however, we can learn another lesson as well: there is a need for cautiousness about the so-called budget discipline. Reducing the size of budget deficit (and the current account deficit) as an important component of macroeconomic stability of the Washington consensus. Cutting of the budget deficit does not always promise a genuine solution to a larger economic problem. If the deficit is only due to annual interest payment paid for the bondholders, its reduction by other expenditures of the budget can harm the sustainable economic growth. For example, the cut of the expenditure supporting education can reduce both short- and long-term economic growth rate. And, also, if the deficit can be financed by foreign direct investment which is used for profitable, efficient aims, for example, for financing the profit earning production capacities of export, and it tends to be very stable a relatively large deficit, even in the percentage of GDP, can be rational. And it goes for current account deficit as well. In addition to these, the case for maintaining or achieving budget surpluses in countries in the face of an economic downturn, where the rate of private savings is high and public debt-GDP ratios are relatively low, is far less compelling.[123]

There is also a need for a more balanced evaluation of the inflation, which is different from the judgement of the Washington consensus. In this respect the view of J. E. Stiglitz can be accepted, that is controlling high and medium-rate inflation should be fundamental policy priority, but pushing low inflation even lower is not likely to significantly improve the functioning of the markets and the economy.[124] What is more, the so-called rentiers, the finance capital, have a major interest to push down inflation as low as possible. The rentier's core goal is stable money – zero inflation, if possible – and the entire intellectual framework for managing economic life is reconstructed around that premise. Everything else – sales, employment, social relations, government obligations – is considered secondary to the objective of protecting stable money, though the doctrine assumes that everyone in the society would benefit on the long run if stability was maintained. Wealth holders, of course, benefited immediately from this regime, since it both defended the value of money of their stored savings and produced the higher real interest rates paid to the creditors.[125] That is why the neo-liberal policies support the finance capital's

---

[122] *Ibid.*, p. 57

[123] Joseph E. Stiglitz, *1998 WIDER Annual Lecture*, p. 8

[124] *Ibid.*, p. 7

[125] William Greider, *One World, Ready or Not*, p. 287

demand for balancing budgets and stern monetary policies to harden money values and protect against inflation. The central promise of these policies is a conviction that the domestic economies must be restrained – limited to modest or even tepid levels of growth – in order to restore stability. Even they are sensitive for the suspected latent inflation. For instance, when the Fed chairman initiated his campaign to slow down the U.S. economy, his concerned critics were correct that no tangible evidence of accelerating inflation was present, but said this was irrelevant. Markets were already alarmed by the quickening economic activity – a robust but unspectacular growth of 4 percent during 1994 – that, he said, required a preemtive strike. Given the central bank's intervention, it would be forever impossible to know whether his fear had been valid since the tighter monetary policy forced the economy to subside rapidly to a growth level around 2 percent and actual inflation declined still further. In the rentier logic, vigilance became its own self-fulfilling proof.[126]

A nation would not necessarily be rewarded for reducing inflation. The study of global interest rates commissioned by finance ministers from the Group of Ten nations discovered that in the 1990s in general the countries with highest measured real interest rates experienced the largest declines in average inflation between the 1980s and 1990s. What happened to them was that while their nominal interest rates on long-term debt rose along with other nations' economies while their inflation rate subsided, the actual cost of borrowing for their economies – the real interest rate determined by subtracting inflation from the nominal rate – rose higher than the others.

The politicians, with rare exceptions, did not challenge the operating rationale of the rentier regime. The U.S. central bank, for example, promoted a conclusion that the economy could not expand on average faster than 2 to 2.5 percent without endangering the hard-won gains in price stability. Alan Greenspan explained his simplistic formula for determining these limits: the labour force expended by about 1.1 percent a year and overall productivity grew by about 1.4 percent. Added together, this meant that a 2.5-percent growth was the economy's potential – "the maximal growth of a nation's well-being", Greenspan put it.[127]

The globalisation resulted in a relatively high real interest rate expressing the strong bargaining power of the rentiers, the capital owners. As national financial markets gradually converge in globalised trading, the price demanded by capital has risen to a high plateau – in effect, claiming a larger share for lenders or investors from the overall returns of economic enterprise. Starting in the 1980s, this shift has been reflected in historically high levels of real interest rates (nominal interest rate discounted by inflation). It means that in most places both debtor governments and private enterprise must devote an increasing share of their revenues or profits to the

---

[126] *Ibid.*, p. 301
[127] *Ibid.*, p. 303

capital owners. In the United States, for instance, the real interest rate on long-term borrowing runs consistently between 4 and 5 percent – twice the average rate of U.S economic growth and nearly twice the historical average for interest rates. A recent study of the ten largest economies found that the real interest rates were at 4 percent, having crept up a full percentage point in recent decades.

The effect of such high interest rates is like a vise, slowly squeezing more out of the economic system, requiring it to run faster just to keep up with its old obligations. The condition can become pathological when the interest-rate cost persistently grows faster than economic activity expands a malignant relationship present in nearly all of the spectacular collapses of debt. The arithmetic is straightforward: a family or nation taking on new debt at 4 percent interest while its income is flat or growing more slowly has to make up that gap somehow, either by discontinuing other kinds of spending or borrowing more to pay the mounting interest. As the debt principal accumulates, the impact compounds.[128]

Why did capital become more expensive? Three factors can help to explain this: the heightened risk present in the global system, the upward pull of competing returns available to investors, and governments' abolition of interest-rate ceilings.

The first and perhaps most important factor is risk: investors may look wildly optimistic as they bid up stock prices, but they can also read ominous portents in the debtors' increasingly precarious positions, including the risk that governments may someday try to inflate their way out of their growing debt burdens. So financial investors demand "risk premiums" on their lending, especially from the sovereign governments traditionally regarded as the safest borrowers. Second, free-roaming capital now enjoys a much wider range of choices – so that staid old investments like U.S. Treasuries or the financing of a new American factory must compete with high-flying possibilities overseas. The stock market until the recently outbroken Asian crises in Hong Kong has generated a twenty-year average annual return of 21 percent; India's yield was 18 percent. Argentina's 28 percent, compared to 11 percent in the U.S. stock market of Germany's. The risk and price volatility are much greater in the emerging markets, but their higher yields exert an upward pull on returns offered by other, more traditional forms of investment. Finally, when the United States and some other nations deregulated their domestic financial systems and abolished the ceilings on bank-deposit interest rates, huge volumes of savings were, in effect, freed to chase the higher market returns. This might be regarded as a just outcome for the virtuous small savers, but it effectively abolished the credit subsidy implicit in the old controls that benefited borrowers, large and small. Taken together, these three factors all flow the free-market reforms of financial systems and give capital more leeway and leverage to bid up the price.[129]

---

[128] *Ibid.*, p. 234
[129] *Ibid.*, p. 235

The high level of interest rates can have other negative effects on the economy as well. To be sure, if an economy is initially facing high levels of inflation caused by high level of excess aggregate demand, increases in the interest rate will be seen to strengthen the economic fundamentals by restoring macro-stability. For an economy where there is little initial evidence of macro-imbalances but a predicted large exogenous fall in aggregate demand, high interest rates will lead to an economic slump and the slump will combine with interest rates themselves to undermine the financial system. Advocates of high-interest rate policies have asserted that such a policy is necessary to restore confidence, especially the confidence of wealth holders who provide credit for the country, in economy and thus the erosion of the currency's value. Halting the erosion of the currency, in turn, is important to both restore the underlying strength of the economy and prevent a burst of inflation from the rise of the price of imported goods. This prescription is based on assumptions about market reactions – i.e., what will restore confidence – and economic fundamentals. However, where currency turmoil is the consequence of a failing financial sector, the conventional policy respond to rising interest rates may be counterproductive. The maturity and structure of the bank and corporate assets and liabilities are frequently very different, in part because of strong incentives for banks to use short-term debt to monitor and influence the firms they lend to, and for depositors to use short-term deposits to monitor and influence banks. As a result, interest rate increases can lead to substantial reductions in bank net worth, further exacerbating the banking crisis. Empirical studies by IMF and World Bank economists have confirmed that interest rate rises tend to increase the probability of banking crises.[130]

The basic idea of the Washington consensus is to correct financial imbalances first and deal with real economy later, restoring reliable national currency so that foreign capital may safely return to lend and invest. In focusing on trade liberalisation, deregulation, and privatisation, policymakers have ignored other important ingredients, especially improvement in human capital, R & D, transferring technology, regulation together with the competition, that are required, to make an effective market economy with sustainable, long-term economic growth.

The long-term economic growth needs building human capital and efficient R & D.

The role of human capital in economic growth has long been appreciated. The return to an additional year of education in the United States, for instance, have been estimated at 5–15 percent. The rate of return is even higher in developing countries: 24 percent for primary education in Sub-Sahara Africa, for example, and an average of 23 percent for primary education in all low-income countries. Growth accounting also attributes a substantial portion of growth in developing countries to human capital accumulation. The East Asian economies, for instance, emphasised the role of government in providing universal education, which was a neces-

---

[130] Joseph E. Stiglitz, *1998 WIDER Annual Lecture*, p. 13

sary part of their transformation from agrarian to rapidly industrialising economies. Left to itself, the market will tend to under-provide human capital. It is very difficult to borrow against the prospects of future earning since human capital cannot be collateralised. These difficulties are especially severe for poorer families. Governments thus play an important role in providing public education, making education more affordable, and enhancing access to funding.

Studies of the returns to R & D in industrial countries have consistently found individual returns of 20–30 percent and social returns of 50 percent – far exceeding the return to education. Like investment in education, investment in technology cannot be used as collateral. Investments in R & D are also considerably riskier than other types of investment; technology also has enormous positive externality; in some respect, knowledge is like public goods. Therefore, without government action there will be too little investment in the production and adaptation of new technology.[131]

Competition is an essential ingredient in a successful market economy. But competition is not viable in some sectors – so-called natural monopolies. Even there, however, the extent and form of actual and potential competition are constantly changing. New technologies have expanded the scope for competition in many sectors that historically have been highly regulated, such as telecommunication and electric power. Traditional regulatory perspective, with their rigid categories of regulation versus deregulation and competition versus monopoly have not been helpful guides to policy in these areas. These new technologies do not call for wholesale deregulation, because not all parts of these industries are adequately competitive. Instead, they call for appropriate changes in regulatory structure to meet the new challenges. Such change must recognise the existence of hybrid areas of the economy, parts of which are well suited to competition, while other parts are more vulnerable to domination by a few producers. Allowing a firm with market power in one part of a regulated industry to gain a stranglehold over other parts of the industry will severely compromise economic efficiency.[132]

Better regulation is especially important in the financial sector. Let to themselves financial systems will not provide efficient outcome. Problem of incomplete information, incomplete markets, and incomplete contracts are all particularly severe in the financial sector, resulting in an equilibrium that is not even constrained by Pareto efficiency.[133]

The emphasis on transparency in recent discussion of East Asia demonstrates growing recognition of the importance of good information for the effective functioning of markets. Capital markets, financial markets, in particular, require audit-

---

[131] *Ibid.*, p. 19
[132] *Ibid.*, p. 17
[133] *Ibid.*, p. 11

242

ing standards accompanied by effective legal systems to discourage fraud, provide investors with adequate information about the firm's assets and liabilities, and to protect minority shareholders. But a legal framework combined with regulation and oversight is necessary to mitigate these information problems and foster the conditions for efficient financial markets.

Regulation serves four purposes in successful financial markets: maintaining safety and soundness (prudent regulation), promoting competition, protecting consumers, and ensuring that underserved groups have some access to capital.

The Washington consensus developed in the context of highly regulated financial systems, in which the regulations were designed to limit competition rather than promote any of the four legitimate objectives of regulation. But all too often the dogma of liberalisation became an end in itself, not a means of achieving a better financial system. *The key issue should not be liberalisation or deregulation but construction of the regulatory framework that ensures an effective financial sector.* In many countries this will require proper changing the regulatory framework by eliminating regulations that serve only to restrict competition, but accompanying these changes with increased regulations to ensure competition and prudential behaviour and to ensure that banks have appropriate incentives. Even once the design of the desired financial system is in place, care will have to be exercised in the transition. Attempts to initiate overnight deregulation – sometimes known as the "big bang" – ignore the very sensitive issues of sequencing. Thailand, for example, used to have restrictions on bank lending to real estate. In the process of liberalisation it got rid of these restrictions without establishing a more sophisticated risk-based regulatory regime. The result, together with other factors, was the large-scale misallocation of capital to fuel a real estate bubble, an important factor in the financial crisis.[134] And this leads us to *the question of timing, speed, scope and sequencing of the government measures and reforms.*

It is easier to set requirements for these than to implement these requirements, for example, economic and political crises can provide opportunities for radical change. By nature, some reforms take longer than others: price reforms can be done quickly, but institutions take time to develop; many gradual reforms can be implemented successfully; trade liberalisation can fail in economies with distorted factor markets, macroeconomic instability, and inappropriate exchange rate policies; assets market adjusts faster than goods markets, so the premature deregulation of capital flows can lead to speculation and financial instability; the sequencing of privatisation and regulation is also very important – privatising a monopoly can create a powerful entrenched interest that undermines the possibility of regulation or competition in the future.

---

[134] *Ibid.,* p. 11

The experiences have shown that a lot of countries following the Washington consensus have not achieved the expected result, even some of them had serious failure during the reform process. The magnitude and success of China's economy over the past two decades and the crisis of Russian economy represent good examples in this respect. Chinese policymakers not only eschewed a strategy of outright privatisation, they also failed to incorporate numerous other elements of the Washington consensus. Yet China's recent experience is one of the greatest economic success stories in history. If China's 30 provinces were treated as separate economies – and many of them have populations exceeding those of most other low-income countries – the 20 fastest-growing economies between 1978 and 1995 would all have been Chinese provinces. Although China's GDP in 1978 represented only about one-quarter of the aggregate GDP of low-income countries and its population represented only 40 percent of the total, almost two-third of aggregate growth in low-income countries between 1978 and 1995 was accounted for by increase in China's GDP. While measurement problems make it difficult to make comparisons between Russia and China with any precision, the board picture remains persuasive: real income and consumption have fallen in the former Soviet Union, and real income and consumption have risen rapidly in China.

China extended the scope of competition without privatising state-owned enterprise. Russia has privatised a large fraction of its economy without doing much to promote competition. China has a closed capital account and non-convertibility. This makes the country less vulnerable to balance-of-payment crises compared to more open economies like Russian economy. Its financial markets remain relatively closed, limited the risk of severe shock arising from a loss of confidence. In contrast, Russia has a convertible currency and relatively open financial market, open capital account; because of that it is more vulnerable as it is relatively easy to speculate against its currency (and at the stock market). The contrast in performance could not be greater, with Russian output below the level attained almost a decade ago, while China has managed to sustain double-digit growth for almost two decades. Though the differences in performance may not be explained by the policies they have pursued, both the Chinese and Russian experiences pose quandaries for the Washington consensus.[135] And one lesson can be drawn from the experiences of the two countries: *regarding to the timing, speed, scope and sequencing every country should act – and should be allowed to act – according to its special conditions and situation and the general requirements should be met in the framework of them.*

As we have seen there is a need to change the Washington consensus and for creating a new one, a new doctrine which is better suited to meet the requirements of the globalised world today. The new doctrine should rely less on financial accounting and more upon economic reality and social equity. The globalised world,

---

[135] *Ibid.*, p. 16

its globalised policy making and globalised economy lack the institutions and mechanisms necessary for this change, but there is no political will to bring them into existence. It does not mean that it is totally out of reality to start such a process and development which can result in a new doctrine with institution and mechanism capable to manage and to govern efficiently – or better than it is done present – the globalised world, at least its globalised economy. The possibility of this development will be increased by economic and political crises especially if they occur with more frequency and damaging effects creating intensive social and political pressure of the citizens toward the policy makers for change. *History has taught us that the major, paradigmatic changes could never happen without such a pressure. But such a change would definitely be needed by the new reality of today's globalised world.*

CHAPTER V

THE IMPACT OF GLOBALISATION AND MULTINATIONAL CORPORATION ON THE ECONOMIES OF THE FORMER SOCIALIST COUNTRIES

(Including Eastern and Central European Countries and Asian Socialist Countries, Especially China)

THE POSSIBILITY OF THE EMERGENCE OF A FULLY INTEGRATED, GLOBAL CAPITALIST ECONOMY

The end of the Cold War in Europe marked the beginning of a period in history in which the emergence of a fully integrated, global capitalist economy has become a potentially achievable goal. The rapid spread across much of Eastern and Central Europe of political regimes committed to the establishment of market economies, together with the economic liberalisation in China means that the two major geopolitical blocs to have remained largely outside the sphere of international business, economic globalisation during the post-war period – and indeed throughout most of the twentieth century – have now become areas of fresh opportunity for international investment and economic activities.[1] We can no longer identify three worlds or two superpowers, but rather a singular system in which the critical basis for international relations is no longer the ownership of military hardware but both economic muscle and the ability to influence ideas and commitments.

The soviet system proved unable to provide its citizens with a standard of living similar to that found in the West while simultaneously maintaining a command economy and globally active military forces. In 1989 the USSR gave up its attempt to control Eastern Europe where market democracy emerged. Russia itself started to marketise and democratise and the country can no longer be regarded unambiguously as a superpower. Many ex-satellites and ex-Soviet republics are now seeking NATO and EU membership.

This development can be judged as a result of globalisation, or more precisely it is a consequence, outcome of the fact that the Soviet economy could not utilise the possibilities, advantages of globalisation. The Soviet-type planned economy basically moved away from the world market, from the very medium where the eco-

---

[1] *The Growth of Global Business.* Horward Cox, Jeremy Clegg and Gracia Ietta-Gillies, ed. (Routledge, New York, 1993) p. 1

nomic dynamic which creates the standards of modernisation actually unfold. This negative direction was due partly to political and economic discrimination made by the developed western capitalist countries against the Soviet Union and its alliances and partly due to the very nature of the Soviet economic mechanism. International trade was restricted by quotas and targets set by planners, and the exchange rate was artificial, for it was not the result of market forces, but was fixed by planning authority. The rubel was not convertible; therefore the economy could not utilise the possible gains based mainly on greater competition, economic of scale and comparative advantage. The artificial exchange rate did not permit consumers and producers to translate the price of foreign goods into units of their own currency in such a way that real costs could have been calculated. Foreign competition did not encourage the setting of price and quality standards as to which firms had too much to sell at home and or abroad, nor did it restrain the exercise of monopoly power. Therefore, under this exchange rate domestic production could not compare its efficiency with its foreign counterparts and this prevented it from reaching (let alone surpassing) standards of international efficiency.

In a shrinking world where economic efficiency requires international specialisation, such an isolation has created one of the major obstacles for economic and social development.[2] In addition to these, the economies of the Soviet Union and its alliances had not had access to the sufficient amount of FDI accompanied with high and constantly improving technological, production, financial, marketing managerial skills and knowledge needed for sustainable economic growth. The Soviet Union did not develope MNCs equivalent to counterparts of the developed market economies and the foreign MNCs had also very restricted possibilities to make business activities in the country; therefore, its economy could not benefit from all of the positive impacts that MNCs could have made and that were the main contributors of the economic successes of the rapidly globalising market economies.

THE ROLE OF MULTINATIONAL CORPORATIONS IN THE INTEGRATION OF THE EX-SOCIALIST COUNTRIES AND CHINA INTO THE WORLD ECONOMY

The attempt of these countries to join the globalisation process, however, started already in the 1960s. Since the mid-1960s, there was an increasing awareness of the economic necessity of improving the efficiency of participation by the socialist countries in the international division of labour, which came into conflict with some of the earlier perceptions with the role of foreign ownership and control. That contra-

---

[2] János Hoós, *The Unfolding New World and Economics* (Akadémiai Kiadó, Budapest, 1997) p. 101

diction explains to a large extent the slow pace and complexity of the evaluation of the economic, legal and institutional framework regulating equity investment in the 1960s and 1970s. Developments in the 1980s necessitated a fresh look at joint ventures, especially with MNCs, as a form of economic co-operation. In the 1980s, the weakness of rigid directive planning in socialist countries became obvious. Such planning led to insufficient flexibility, to lack of adequate incentives to promote quality, innovation and efficiency, and to an inclination on the part of enterprises to overspend. The policy measures introduced in the socialist countries in the late 1970s and 1980s were aimed at liberalising the national economic environment. The changing priorities in the domestic economic policies during that period gave preference to qualitative aspects of economic growth (quality improvement, productivity increases, greater efficiency in the use of labour and capital, etc.) instead of the traditional quantitative targets.

As a result, the number of directive indicators were reduced and profitability was accepted as an important criterion of enterprise performance. Socialist countries continued to consider joint ventures as an important source of new technology provided in a form of new products, production process, know-how, marketing and managerial skills. Through joint venture, those countries sought to upgrade the technological level of selected economic sectors and improve domestic supply. The availability of additional external-capital resources served as another strong motivation, particularly for the socialist countries which accumulated relatively high debts during the 1970s and early 1980s. Decision-makers saw in the joint-venture form, based on risk and profit sharing, a way of ensuring a long-term consolidation of the interests of the partners involved to an extent not achievable under other forms of industrial co-operation.

In the 1980s MNC approach to doing business in Eastern Europe and the Soviet Union and China became a good deal more realistic. Following the Helsinki Agreement there appeared to be strong coincidence of interests between Western businesses interested in raw materials and new markets, and Soviet-bloc government interested in importing capital and technology to accelerate growth and restructure industry. These high hopes floundered however, partly with the return to Cold War postures, which followed the Russian invasion of Afghanistan, and partly because it proved extremely difficult to mesh together capitalist MNCs with the state enterprises and other agencies of the centrally-planned economies. Economic stagnation and debt problems in the 1980s made the region in any case less attractive to Western capital. Nonetheless, joint venture and other forms of business co-operation took real if shallow root, particularly in Hungary and Poland where market-oriented economic reform went furthest; in Yugoslavia the same process had been completed a decade earlier.[3]

---

[3] *The Internalisation of the Firm: A Reader.* P. J. Buckly and P. N. Chauri, ed. (Academic Press, London, 1993) p. 141

In the 1980s, there was a significant extension and liberalisation of the conditions attached to foreign participation in all East European countries alongside the development of limited liability and other forms of private ownership, but these attracted mostly smaller Western firms. Large MNCs, dealing with large state-owned enterprises, preferred instead contractual forms of industrial co-operation that limited their direct entanglement with the state control system. Mostly, these centred on technology transfer through licensing, and on contract manufacture by Eastern state enterprises for Western partners.

Over the 1970s and 1890s, thus, formal relations became more familiar and easier to establish in East-West business. But the real content of such relationship was very limited, because of the difficulties of reconciling the two economic systems – even where the path of economic reform had been most consistently followed, in Yugoslavia and Hungary.[4]

In the 1990s the globalisation in this part of the world took a qualitatively new turn. Central and Eastern Europe, the newly independent states of the former Soviet Union, China and Vietnam – countries with about one-third of the world's population – started to transform their centrally planned economies to a market orientation. Most of these economies have rejected all or much of the central planning and have embarked on a passage – transition – toward decentralised market mechanisms underpinned by widespread private ownership. Not all have followed the same path. Despite common features, the mass of centrally planned economies was far from monolithic. It was composed of countries with different histories, cultures and resource endowments. And whereas political change toward multiparty democracy was a prime objective in the post-1989 reforms in Central and Eastern Europe (CEE) and the newly independent states (NIS) of the former Soviet Union, neither China, which initiated economic reforms in 1978, nor Vietnam has experienced a political transformation away from governments dominated by the Communist Party. There is thus a tremendous variety in the departure points, strategies, and outcome of transition across countries. Most of the world's economies at one time or another, have lifted price controls, open trade, freed entry from state control or privatised state enterprises – with varying degrees of success. These countries started to follow this direction, that is, they have been engaged in liberalisation and privatisation. As part of that liberalisation trend, restrictions on transitional activities have generally been removed and often been replaced by incentives for foreign investment.

In this globalisation process the MNCs can play an especially significant role, they can contribute valuable assistance to Eastern European, Russian, Chinese and Vietnamese economic reconstruction in a number of ways. They are the main repositories of the capital, technology, management skills and market access that are necessary for economic regeneration, – foreigner provided capital, technology, management expertise, and access to market:

---

[4] *Ibid.,* p. 142

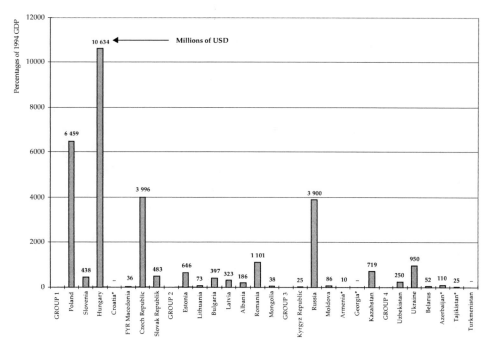

Note: Data are the sum of inflows during 1989–1995: those for Croatia, Georgia and Turkmenistan are unavailable. Data for 1995 are preliminary. Asterisks indicate economies severely affected by regional tension between 1989 and 1995.

Sources: World Bank 1996b; IMF and World Bank staff estimates.

FIGURE 17. Cumulative direct investment inflows

all critical to enterprises restructuring in the transition economies. Foreign owners also can invest in technical and managerial training in such areas as cost accounting, computer, marketing, total quality management, and English-language training. Many MNCs have already had experience of industrial co-operation and joint venture under the old regime on which they can build. And their increased globalisation and wider experience of different forms of international involvement make them better equipped than ever before for integrating the economies of these countries into the world economy.

The presence of the MNCs in these markets can be judged by the FDI, by the amount of what has flown into these countries. (See Figures 17 and 18.) Their success in attracting FDI remains weak by global standards. They have to compete with many other regions and issues for a place on the agenda of the international business and financial community. One might have expected huge imports of capital, both private and official, to participate in financing the costly economic and political transformation required in countries undergoing transition. At the beginning of the transformation in Europe there were concerns that large capital flows to

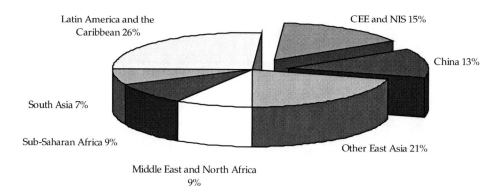

Total flows, 1990–1995: $1,640 billion

Latin America and the
Caribbean 26%

CEE and NIS 15%

China 13%

South Asia 7%

Sub-Saharan Africa 9%

Other East Asia 21%

Middle East and North Africa
9%

Note: Data for 1995 are preliminary.
Source: World Bank 1996b.

FIGURE 18. Transition economies have only a modest share of global flows

CEE and the NIS would raise world interest rates at the expense of developing countries. However, CEE and the NIC have not absorbed a great deal of foreign capital – either private investment flows or official external assistance. Between them the countries of CEE and the NIC observed 15 percent of total flows to developing and transition countries in the period between 1990–1995 (Figure 18). Net resource inflows are much lower and even negative to some countries, once debt service and capital flight are taken into consideration. Capital flight from Russia alone has been estimated at some $50 billion for 1992–1995, although part of this represented capital exported through from other NIS.

Private capital flows to developing countries increased dramatically during the 1990s, with a surge in FDI and portfolio equity investment. CEE and the NIC, however, between them attracted just 13 percent of total private capital flows to developing and transition countries in 1990–1995. In 1994, FDI to CEE and the NIC was only $6.5 billion, equivalent to the total received by Malaysia and Thailand. The distribution of these limited FDI flows among them has also been highly uneven. The Visegrad countries received fully three-quarters of the total, whereas many other in the region are still all but untouched by foreign investment. Capital flows to China more closely followed the trend for developing countries, with private sources accounting for the lion's share. FDI to China was $33.8 billion in 1994, second only to flows to the United States.[5]

---

[5] *World Development Report. 1996. From Plan to Market* (Oxford University Press, Oxford, 1996) p. 136

It can be considered as a relative failure of many CEE countries and NIC to capitalise on the growth of investment in emerging markets. In the countries that could get a relatively substantial amount of FDI positive impact has already been experienced. By increasing competition in local markets, FDI has had a major influence on market structure in several countries of Central and Eastern Europe. Foreign direct investment, particularly in small-size enterprises, has helped to de-monopolise markets and stimulate competitive behaviour. Foreign-investor participation in restructuring and privatisation of large state-owned enterprises has helped to overcome the legacy of monopolisation. Foreign affiliates typically have better marketing capabilities, a superior market performance and also are engaged more actively in exporting than are purely domestic firms. Competition introduced by such firms, either in the form of products and services unavailable previously or of higher quality, is forcing local producers and service providers to try enhance their own performance. This is particularly visible in consumer-related services and manufacturing industries that were neglected under the centrally planned systems. After the market-opening, previously unavailable products and services were introduced through trade and investment. For example, in retailing, hotel, advertising, insurance, banking business the world leading MNCs have taken determining roles and positions.

The rush of MNCs to establish a local presence in these countries has resulted, in many industries, in too many companies fighting for too few customers. That further improved consumer welfare through quality improvements and price decreases and a consumer orientation of goods and services hitherto unknown in the countries of the region. This has further been accentuated by growing competition from local manufacturers who are taking advantage of the new business opportunities and are winning customers back from foreign companies and brands by improving quality and offering less expensive products.[6]

However, competition through FDI also helped to expose goods and services produced by firms in this region, especially in Eastern and Central Europe, to world market prices. This has sometimes led to closures of local companies incapable of competing with foreign affiliates in their own country. As a result, some industries have become almost entirely foreign-owned. In some instances, MNCs have led to reduced competition by, for example, foreclosing market entry, fixing prices and engaging in anti-competition mergers. Eager to attract FDI, several countries in Central and Eastern Europe have made concessions to individual MNCs by, for example, granting exclusive market-supply rights for extended periods.[7]

MNCs can find some advantages and some disadvantages in this region which are taken into account in the decision making process of investing in these coun-

---

[6] *World Investment Report. 1997*, p. 100

[7] *Ibid.*, p. 100

tries. On the one hand, these regions have a good potential to attract foreign investment: many countries are middle-income economies with sizeable domestic markets and pent-up consumer demand for goods and services; some countries are rich in natural resources and have considerable human endowments, relatively highly skilled labour and low labour costs; there are significant industrial capacities, especially in Eastern Europe and Russia, and in many plants there is a great potential for increasing productivity by eliminating sources of waste endemic to the old central planning system; much of the existing industrial technology is Western in origin, and if many products are crude and old-fashioned, processes are often less so, and little investment may be needed to make products acceptable on the Western markets; in some countries and sectors, exports to Western markets have absorbed a significant proportion of output in recent decades; in addition, some firms, especially in Eastern Europe, with experience in the various forms of past East-West industrial co-operation will already be accustomed to Western business practices, and their Western partner firms may be able to develop deeper links quickly and cheaply; what is more, the labour forces of many countries, especially in Poland, Hungary, the former Czechoslovakia, are far more skilled and experienced than labour forces commanding the same dollar wage elsewhere, on any reasonable assumption about effective exchange rates.[8] The proximity of Central and Eastern Europe to the European Union market could entice MNCs to reorganise affiliate networks regionally.

On the other hand, a great deal of the industrial plant and equipment is old and obsolescent: the persistence of extensive growth under the old regimes preserved industrial capacity that would have been scapped long ago in the West. In some sectors, at least, modernisation will therefore be extremely costly. There are the costs of implementing improved environmental standards, and of retraining managers and workers in the principle and practice of capitalism. In many countries there are huge gaps, not only in physical infrastructure, but in the provision of business services of all kinds, which will impose further costs for at least several years. Less developed local capital markets make it difficult to share costs and risks with the local investors, or to assess the future marketability of assets acquired. In most of these countries the lack of developed financial infrastructure makes it hard for local partners, or indeed governments, to mobilise local savings; at the same time, national budgets face many conflicting demands, including the need to establish a social safety-net for the unemployed, and costs of converting unwanted heavy industry and military capacity. Given the uncertainties surrounding such questions, the natural response of MNCs is to place a low value on assets offered for sale, and to avoid significant commitment of funds as long as possible. MNCs have been attracted mainly by the prospects of "cherry-picking" the best Eastern enterprises –

---

[8] *Ibid.*, p. 101

those with a high technological level, or with significant Western market experience, or with dominant national or regional positions in Eastern markets.

At present, foreign investment is welcomed because of desperate immediate need
for investments of any kind, for technological improvements, access to Western
markets and the preservation of jobs. *However, there is a real danger that Eastern Europe may find itself treated as little more than a regional source of cheap labour and cheap
extra capacity for European Union markets, an objective for selective speculative investment, and – as long as government and other trade credits are available – a dumping ground
for excessive production during the recession.*[9]

RUSSIA AND CHINA AS A SPECIAL CATEGORY
IN GLOBALISATION PROCESS
OF THE WORLD ECONOMY AND POLICY

However, Russia and China should have to be considered as a special category in
this respect. Due to their size, huge market, rich natural resources, real and potential military and economic power they have their own substantial impact on the
globalisation process of the world as well; it means that while they have to adjust
their economies (and policies) to the objective requirements of the globalisation,
their economies (and policies) have a well articulated feedback on the world economy
and policy as well. This can especially be experienced in the following territories:

They should be involved – and in fact, they have already been involved – in the
global governance of the world economy and polity. The good examples of that, the
invitation of Russia to the G7 summit, the very important role China has been playing in the recent economic crisis, especially in the Asian financial crises.

These countries have a much stronger bargaining power dealing with the forces
of the globalisation than the smaller countries in transition. For example, they can
demand – and in fact, have got – better and stiffer terms than others to get greater
sharing of production work made in their own countries, that is, higher percentage
of local content of the production established by the MNCs, greater sharing of up-
to-day technology. (In China, in the Volvo's bus venture local content swiftly increased to 50 percent of the body, and by 1997, 90 percent of the bus was made in
China; similar trend can be experienced in Boeing aircraft's venture; AT & T agreed
to manufacture its advanced switching equipment there in order to wire up Chinese cities for modern telephone services. China signed similar deals with Intel and
IBM as the two companies sought entry for their competing microchips.)[10]

---

[9] *The Internalisation of the Firm: A Reader*, p. 149
[10] William Greider, *One World, Ready or Not* (Simon and Shuster, New York, 1998) p. 278

They, especially Russia in the field of energy, already have influential MNCs and in the future they will be able to create such companies, which can compete successfully in the globalised world markets playing the beneficial role in the Russian and Chinese economies what the MNCs have been doing in developed market economies. (For example, the Xian Aircraft Company – XAC – in China has an important role in the globalising industrial system: it is one of the places where the competing multinationals met face-to-face: Boeing, McDonnell Douglas, Airbus are in XAC making aeroplane parts, Volvo was invited to make tour buses and according to one of the directors of Company: "Our strategic target is to become the high-tech and foreign-oriented enterprise, high profit. We want to be the first-class, successful enterprise. All the employees of XAC are marching to this goal.")[11]

All of these mean that though Russia and China do not belong to the most influential forces of the globalisation, they have to be reckoned as major economic and political powers in the globalisation process, the speed and the mode of how they become organic part of the globalised world can determine the actual characteristics and state of world economy and policy as a whole. They can speed up and slow down as well the globalisation depending on the success or failure of their national policies. The outside forces can help them in the adaptation to the requirements of the globalisation, but these forces cannot accomplish this adaptation without them, without their active and innovative participation based upon their basic national interest and special national conditions. Any one-sided or/and short-sighted attempt made by these forces – countries or/and MNCs, international organisations (for example IMF) – to influence from outside these countries could be counter productive for globalisation, or even worse, it could be dangerous for the future development of the world. The successes and failures of Russian and Chinese transformation processes from the centrally planned economy to the market economy has proved that rather convincingly.

---

[11] *Ibid.*, p. 152

SUBJECT INDEX

economic growth
~, long-term 28
electronics 10, 145
electronic media 37
electronic miniaturisation
~, application of 53
emergency world economy 188
employment 24, 127
~ practice 17, 127
English-type sovereign national state 93
environment 26
estrangement of the elected representatives
  10, 25, 212
eurocommercial paper 68
export processing zones (EPZs) 118, 123, 124
externalities 173, 197

FDI 112, 116, 118, 127
financial
~ instruments, innovations 68
~ sector 242
~ ~, effective 243
~ service 66
~ systems 27
financial market 63, 222
~, deregulation of 66
~, internationalisation of 15, 59, 61
firm's
~ acquisition 108
~ objective 10, 18, 147, 156
~ ~, change 147
firms
~, multi-plant 168
~, multi-product 168
~, organisational complexity of 19
floating-rate notes (FRNs) 68
flow of equity capital 125
former Soviet Union 250

globalisation 9, 14, 26, 40, 42, 239
~, characteristics of 31
~ culture 41
~, different developing stages of 44
~, economic 14, 41
~, economy 41

~ impacts of 186
~, main driving forces of 10
~ motives and drivers 49
~, new tendencies of 31
~ of trade 72
~ polity 41
~, prerequisite of 34
~, prime mover of 10
~, speed of 31
globalised
~ management 26
~ world 33, 256
globalising age 33
Golden Age 33, 48
government 181, 198
~, correct 25
~, economic objectives of 181
~ failures 199, 202
~ income distribution 199
~, market's influence against 205
~ measures 243
~, merit of 198

human capital 27, 28, 241
human resource development 127
~, MNCs in 129
Hymer–Kindleberger tradition 83

IMF 26
income
~, equitable distribution of 197
~ inequality 25
~ income redistribution of the government
  203
information
~, processing of 53
~ problem 197
~ technology 15, 54, 55
infrastructure 60
innovations 116
~ of financial instruments 68
~, organisational 15, 51
institutional
~ investors 160
~ sector 161